TRIUMPH CARS
in America

MICHAEL COOK

MBI Publishing Company

First published in 2001 by MBI Publishing Company, Galtier Plaza, Suite 200, 380 Jackson Street, St. Paul, MN 55101-3885, USA.

MBI Publishing Company books are also available at discounts in bulk quantity for industrial or sales-promotional use. For details write to Special Sales Manager at Motorbooks International Wholesalers & Distributors, Galtier Plaza, Suite 200, 380 Jackson Street, St. Paul, MN 55101-3885, USA.

Library of Congress Cataloging-in-Publication Data
Cook, Michael, 1933-
     Triumph cars in America/Michael Cook.
     p.cm.
     Includes index.
     ISBN 0-7603-0165-4 (pbk.:alk. paper)
     1. Triumph automobile--History. I. Title.

TL215.T7 C663 2001
629.222'2--dc21

2001031231

On the front cover: This happy couple posed with their TR3A in the Sutton Place area of Manhattan in 1957. Their car has the optional GT kit which included the hardtop and door handles. *Plain English Archive*

On the back cover: (top) These TR4 Rallyists are waiting for the Dover-Ostend ferry in 1962. European rallies were organized by the Triumph Sports Owners Association. Plain English Archive (bottom) Vickers/Supermarine, maker of the Spitfire aircraft, agreed, on condition, that Standard-Triumph be allowed to use the Spitfire name on its new, low-cost sports car. *Plain English Archive*

Edited by: Steve Hendrickson
Designed by: Bruce Leckie

Printed in the United States of America

Contents

Preface and Acknowledgments

I love to tell stories. Fortunately, my life and my work have been rich with the sort of activities and people that make for full-bodied, meaty tales. I grew up in eight Canadian Provinces and the State of Ohio. I got my first real job in midtown Manhattan. I was a car nut who ended up running the advertising campaign for a British sports car. More than busy, my working life has been an adventure, and the characters I worked with belonged on Broadway. Which, incidentally, was where my office was for nearly four years.

Why write a book about Triumph? Partly to tell *my* story; partly to keep alive the memory of the people who made the Triumph marque a force in America; partly to establish that, while MG may have started the sports car craze, the "other two-letter word," TR, deserves equal credit for keeping the movement alive and growing. Triumph cars have not been made for nearly 20 years as I write, but they are still on the road every day, carrying people of all ages to work, to the store, or to new accomplishments over the horizon. Businesses provide parts, mechanics make a living, magazines flourish, and clubs gain new members. Triumph is a living marque.

The car business is hard on people and families. I have had my foot on the gas for more than 40 years, and my family deserves special recognition for patience and understanding. My sons Geoff, Tim, and Drew; my daughter, Jennifer; and, always, my wife, Carol Ann.

Over the years many friends and associates have contributed, directly and indirectly, to making this book a worthwhile project: Dave Allen and Alan Bethell, who got me into this; Chris Andrews, a real friend; Bruce and Jimmy McWilliams, the all-round enthusiasts; Kas Kastner, Bob Tullius, and Joe Huffaker, who gave us the victories we needed; Graham Whitehead, who brought me back and backed me up for over 20 years; Mike Dale, whose personal example inspires others to do their damnedest; John Dugdale; Lyman Gaylord, always there and always ready; Ed McCauley, who helped companies and people stay together; Marty Chanes; James Groth; Bob Timmerman; Dorothy Deen and Jim Sitz; Bob Burden; Dick Langworth and Graham Robson, whose Triumph history is *the* basic reference work. To the dozens of other friends, coworkers, and just plain Triumph people out there, if you search for your name and come up empty, you are not forgotten! I hope that the book will help you remember some of the good times we all enjoyed.

After my kids started to grow up, when I went into storytelling mode about family or work or racing, they would listen and when it was over they would say: "Write it down Dad!"

This time, I did.

—*Michael L. Cook,*

Foreword

By J. Bruce McWilliams

Mike Cook's story of the rise and fall of Triumph automobile sales in America is a remarkably detailed personal journal, spanning more than 20 years with this relatively small English company. At its zenith, Triumph never produced more than 140,000 cars a year, a modest number, of which a large percentage were sports cars. Most of these were sent to North America, making Triumph, for a time, the largest seller of such models in the United States.

In Mike's account of one man's role in establishing a small company's place in a huge American market, he captures the difference between marketing imported cars versus domestics, remarkably dissimilar propositions. Those in the trenches of the earlier years of the "foreign car" movement were true enthusiasts, sometimes to the point of fanaticism. From senior executives to secretaries, everyone was a believer. Technical merits, performance abilities, and aesthetic appeal of the marque were matters of serious conviction to be pressed on just about anyone willing to listen, and they were the only topic of conversation among the initiated. Weekends at racetracks, where sports cars laid their competitive prowess on the line, were the order of the day.

If not racing it was rallying. SAAB's outright and team wins of the 1958 Great American Mountain Rallye in Vermont established this virtually unknown, and certainly peculiar, little two-stroke in the American market with an instant reputation for performance on ice and snow, setting it on its way to sales success. Triumph's first official U.S. competition entry was in the GAMR with a team of TR2s, in which it scored a class win. The usefulness of competition for promoting the sale of imported cars was demonstrated again and again, and Triumph's constant successes leap-frogged it to the top of the sales charts.

Bruce McWilliams at the 1963 New York International Automobile Show. *Plain English Archive*

Triumph's racing activity is but one component of the Mike Cook story. The book is a chronicle of the caring attitude for the fortunes of Triumph that always led him to go beyond the call of duty. That he was not unique in this derives from an essential fact of the imported car movement, which he exemplified. Tiredness never entered the equation: there was a mission to carry out. If a car had to get moved from one car show to another or between back-to-back dealer meetings, Mike got the job done, despite the hour, the distance, or the prevailing weather.

There was something of a David and Goliath attitude at work in the early days. It often caused the imports to do bold things the domestics would have regarded as unthinkable. Their unconventional, often sophisticated, and sometimes whimsical advertising and promotion are a case in point. Raw economics drove them to find ways to gain maximum effect from skimpy advertising and promotional budgets, and the pioneering spirit of their people led to independent thinking. Lean organizations limited the layers of approval that so often hamper bold programs, so that bright minds were able to exercise their imaginations. For imports, sales development was tantamount to psychological warfare between themselves and the domestic mass marketers, many of whom looked upon import enthusiasts as more than a little mad! Some of our efforts raised the benchmark of automobile advertising and promotion and, themselves, became the subject of editorial and news coverage, adding to their effectiveness. Besides, it was fun to be the tail that wagged the dog.

In time, evolving dynamics of the American market on the one hand and sickness at the core of manufacturers on the other, caught up with companies such as Triumph. They became obliged to practice a sort of sleight of hand to hype sales. In quick and low-cost ways, they had to supply a measure of excitement to the introduction of new models. They were heavily dependent on paint jobs that made the shape look different, flashy tape and throaty exhaust systems, to inject the visual and acoustical impact so necessary at new model launch time. At the same time, quality and technological improvements had begun to flood in from Japan, offering a new kind of competition. Ever-increasing U.S. government regulations became an incredible burden, all too frequently deflecting the use of resources in unproductive ways. There was no end to them! An automobile company producing 11 different models with a scant staff of 13,000 workers just couldn't keep up.

The spirit in the ranks remained, but Triumph engineers who should have been working on development of new models were spending most of their time responding either to new government regulations or government assaults for alleged violation of previous ones. At one point, NHTSA slapped nearly 30 charges against the five companies comprising British Leyland—Austin, MG, Jaguar, Rover, and Triumph—for alleged violations of federal safety standards. Response required thousands of man-hours on car and component testing and preparation of a quarter-million pages of reports and charts. Engineers and other senior company executives made repeated trips from the UK to Washington to appear before NHTSA officials. More than a year passed before the affair wound up, *with only minor fines in some instances*. But the true price was horrendous.

Mike's story of his Triumph years is a well-documented journal. A sense of failure never creeps in. He was there through most of it, playing roles in advertising and public relations, and producing company publications. Mike is still doing his best to set the record straight on Triumph in America for Triumph owners, enthusiasts, and anyone with a serious interest in automotive history.

Introduction

In 1949, when I was a high school sophomore in Cincinnati, Ohio, imported sports cars were rarely to be seen on the road. I was lucky to have a neighbor who took me riding in his alloy Jaguar XK 120 roadster! In high school and college I learned about MG and other British marques, and even test drove the new Corvette and Thunderbird, but $250 for a 1939 Ford sedan convertible was all I could afford. Flush with graduation money in 1955, I fell for a 1951 Humber Hawk sedan with a sunroof, but the car's rich red leather and bronze paint couldn't make up for the bog-slow performance. I was still hoping for a sports car.

My enthusiasm for imported cars led me to a part-time sales job at Lancett Motors, a Citroen, Panhard, Renault, and Triumph dealer in Reading, Ohio. The only franchise of the four that provided proper parts and service back-up was Triumph. It had the country covered under a number of territorial distributorships, each of which appointed and serviced its own dealer body. European Motors in Detroit was the Triumph distributor for Ohio, and it got parts to the customer in a reasonable time. Decent service was important, because Triumph was expanding its U.S. product line. Alongside the TR3s on Lancett's lot were the Triumph 10 sedan and station wagon, derivatives of the British Standard 10 models.

I was driving a VW Beetle at the time, but a British roadster was more my style. I had looked at Sunbeams, and test drove a Jaguar XK 120 coupe, but in the spring of 1957 I swapped my VW and $400 for a 1955 Triumph TR2. Good-bye blue sedan, hello refrigerator white sports car. It was a pivotal moment in my life.

My new mount had disc wheels and rear fender skirts (the British called them "spats"), which made it look a bit like an XK 120 from a certain angle. Inside

With the exception of the dark interior and right-hand drive, this car is identical to my first British sports car, the 1954 TR2. The rear fender "spats" gave the TR a Jaguar XK 120 look, but most owners removed them. Note the long doors, which go to the bottom of the body, making exit beside a high curb virtually impossible.

appointments were pale ivory seats, tan carpets bleached and dyed white (the previous owner really liked white), and a white dashboard. Gauges included a large tachometer and speedometer behind the wheel, and smaller round fuel, oil pressure, water temperature, and charge gauges grouped in the center of the dash. This car was well prepared to inform the driver.

Seats in the TR2 were comfortable, if thinly padded. Severe bumps allowed one's posterior to smack the floor. The driving position was legs out, arms out (not all TRs had adjustable steering wheels). A good relationship of seat and wheel allowed the average driver to see easily out of the shallow windscreen.

If done correctly, the top was easy to raise; the side curtains popped in quickly, and the interior was quite free from drips in normal rainstorms. Wipers worked fine, but the defroster effect from the noisy heater was feeble. Fortunately, there were turn signals, operated by a lever above the horn button. Hand signals would not have been possible, because the side-curtains had no sliding windows, only a zipper that gave outside access to open the doors via a pull cable.

Never mind the limited creature comforts. The car was quick, it handled well, especially after I added Michelin X tires, and it improved my social life. In impromptu traffic light drag races, I quickly found that nothing domestic could touch it, not even the vaunted Oldsmobile Rocket 88, which was an easy mark. Only when a Plymouth Fury appeared beside me at a light one day did I discover, at the cost of a speeding ticket and a week's suspension of my license, that the TR could be beaten.

In the TR, I cruised to SCCA races on air bases at Columbus and Akron, visited Indianapolis, and left an echo of lovely four-cylinder noise from the straight pipe on every major highway in Ohio. That straight pipe earned me another ticket, this one for "excessive noise," and cost me points with my girl-friend's parents! It was my habit to pass her house on the way home at whatever hour of the day or night,

The only photo of your author in his first Triumph, taken in Glendale, Ohio, in the summer of 1957. My mother is with me, kerchiefed against the wind. After I departed for New York, she frequently drove the noisy little TR to the local grocery store. *Cook family*

downshifting for the 90-degree left-hander in front of their house and accelerating flat out down the street toward my driveway. The racket was enough to break windows.

Yet fast driving and noise were part of the scene. We sports car drivers were a fraternity, cheerfully waving to every sports car we passed on the road. We were united in our love for the cars and the top-down tradition we were in the process of establishing.

After buying the TR2, I joined the Triumph Sports Owners Association and started receiving the *TSOA Newsletter*, a small publication produced for the Triumph company by Paul Thurston, a PR agent with offices in Rockefeller Center. In my job as sales representative for a Cincinnati emblem jewelry firm, I saw an opportunity to sell lapel pins and car badges to the Triumph club. Invited to be best man at a wedding in New York, I took along my sales bag. With the newlyweds safely off on their honeymoon, I called first at the TSOA office and then at the Standard-Triumph Motor Company (STMCI) offices at 1745 Broadway on the corner of 56th Street, hoping to nail down a new account.

Although I didn't make a sale, I met several nice people at Standard-Triumph. Later, when I made my decision to leave home and try for a job in New York, I wrote a letter to Alan Bethell, President of STMCI, applying for a job. The following summer, after I had been working in New York for five months at a small advertising agency, I was called down to Broadway for an interview and hired to be Assistant Advertising Manager and Executive Secretary of the Triumph Sports Owners Association.

In the middle of 1958, I was a comparatively late arrival at an established, thriving company. Triumph exports had been traveling the roads of America since the first British car companies got back into production after World War II. After marketing small numbers of cars strictly through independent distributors for several years, Standard-Triumph established the Standard-Triumph Motor Company, Inc., in New York in 1954 to handle the burgeoning TR sports car sales volume. By the time I approached their receptionist, they had already moved to larger offices twice and were marketing a car that was becoming a house-hold name in the United States, right alongside MG and Jaguar.

CHAPTER 1

Triumph Takes Off

British firms had learned immediately after World War II that they had to "export or die." The British government restricted supplies of things like sheet steel, unless most of the finished products were going on board ships to earn dollars. With the British Isles still devastated from the war, the potential sales volume for any new sports car was very small at home anyway, but vast in the lucrative U.S. market.

The newly formed Standard-Triumph Motor Company, under Sir John Black, made a start on a new postwar Triumph range with the 1800 roadster and sedan, announced in 1948. A few of these, and the later 2000 versions, were imported to the U.S. but it was really with the start of TR2 production in sight that Standard-Triumph began organizing sales and service facilities in the United States.

The first U.S. offices were in California, established in 1953 and managed by Denton Massey, a polished British gentleman remembered by contemporaries for his enthusiastic use of his expense account. However, financial statements from the time showed the company was making money.

By October 1954, Massey had been recalled and a new western regional manager appointed. Alan F. Bethell was only 30 years old but destined to be Triumph's president in the United States just three years later. Bethell had joined Standard Motors in England in 1940 as an engineering apprentice, doing road tests and inspection. It was not long before World War II beckoned him into the army. He served for four years in the Far East, attaining the rank of warrant officer, and rejoined Standard-Triumph in 1947.

Completing his apprenticeship, Alan became a regional service manager, first in the UK and then in Europe. Later, traveling the Middle East, Africa, and the Far East as a regional sales manager, he recalls having to source parts locally to keep both Standards and Triumphs functioning. His effective efforts as a regional manager brought an offer from the company chairman, Alick Dick, to take charge of Triumph's nascent operation in the western United States. It was a very big promotion and he quickly agreed. Although the sports car craze was nationwide, California was the place where sales initially took off, accounting for over a third of national sales volume for Triumph and other British manufacturers.

By the end of 1953, Standard-Triumph dealt with only one distributor in the West, Cal Sales.

Alan F. Bethell, addressing a distributor meeting, was president of Standard-Triumph Motor Company, Inc., from 1956 until August 1961. His style and personality made the company a very pleasant place to work.

Dorothy Deen, president of Cal Sales Inc., was a highly capable chief executive in the 1950s, when women seldom held top jobs in business. She took good advantage of her looks and personal style to help market Triumph products like the TR10 estate wagon and sedan. *Road & Track*

Founded by Dorothy Deen and her father, Arthur Anderson, Cal Sales controlled Triumph marketing west of the Mississippi through an agreement made directly with Sir John Black. Typical of the distributors appointed by European manufacturers, Cal Sales invested in major facilities to support Triumph sales, stock parts, handle warranty claims, etc. It performed all functions usually done by the manufacturer in the home territory.

Representatives like Alan Bethell worked as advisers and liaison between company and distributors. In his trusty TR2, he kept moving between the various locations, selling cars, checking on service and parts operations, and watching out for the interests of the parent company. Sales were few to start with. In 1954 only 972 Triumphs were registered in the United States. In Bethell's peak year as president, 1960, sales totaled over 17,000. Bethell's activities in

Cal Sales was heavily involved in bringing the short-lived Doretti sports car to market. This is actress Terry Moore in a publicity shot for the 1954 Third International New York Motor Sports Show. The Doretti, which used Triumph drivetrain and other mechanical components, was approved by Standard-Triumph and listed in company brochures. The styling was quite different from the TR2, but the Doretti used a near copy of the experimental Triumph TRX grille, shown in Chapter Two. *Automobile Quarterly*

the West were so effective that he was asked to take charge of Standard-Triumph's overall operations in the United States, based in New York. He took over in 1956 but continued to travel extensively.

Alan was on hand when Cal Sales opened its new buildings in Gardena, California, on July 15, 1957. In a 1992 interview, he told me his philosophy on appointing independent distributors. "Appointing distributors was the accepted way of doing things in those days. You selected them with care and gave them support and supervision. In the 1950s there wasn't enough market yet to justify the investment needed to set up factory distribution. It was up to me to make sure the distributors did their job. I made Cal Sales work." While distributors were initially essential for cash poor UK manufacturers, times became more prosperous and eventually the importing companies bought out the independents, often at great cost, in order to gain full control over U.S. operations.

Dorothy Deen had begun her experience with imported cars like many other Americans, by owning an MG-TD, but she turned her enthusiasm into a business. With backing from her father, she and a partner, Paul Bernhardt, started an imported car accessories company. Named Cal Specialties, the company sold luggage racks, wind wings, aluminum valve covers, and other items dear to the hearts of sports car nuts of the time. The brand name was Doretti, a sort of Italian corruption of Dorothy. Her father was an engineer who had earned a good living from projects as diverse as engines for model airplanes, Whizzer motorbike engines, and steel tubing. His interest in sports cars equaled his daughter's, and he drove Triumph-powered Morgans.

Anderson also imported steel tubing into the United States. While in England negotiating a business relationship with Tube Investments Ltd., he was introduced to Sir John Black. The encounter between the manufacturer and the sports car enthusiast led Anderson to start Cal Sales to sell TRs. Cal Sales also provided the name and took on distribution for the Doretti, a low-volume roadster built with Triumph running gear by Swallow Coachbuilding, a Tube Investments subsidiary. Swallow, started by William Lyons in the l920s, was the predecessor of Jaguar.

The new Cal Sales announced the Triumph TR2 and the Doretti at the same time, in January 1954, at the Ambassador Hotel in Los Angeles. Interestingly, the announcement also included the Standard Vanguard, a 2-liter, four-door sedan, and the Vanguard Cadet, a specially named version of Standard-Triumph's very basic four-door economy car (see Chapter Two).

Unfortunately, the Doretti's life was short. Although it had style, it was heavier than the TR2 and offered less performance at a higher price. After just two years, Tubing Investments stopped production.

Cal Sales opened a new sales, service, and parts complex in Gardena, California, in the spring of 1957. John Warren, left, export sales director of Standard-Triumph International; Alan Bethell; Dorothy Deen; and Walter Danielson of Cal Sales get ready to smash the champagne bottle. Cal Specialties was another of her corporations, which marketed sports car accessories under the "Doretti" brand.

Only 275 were built, and the Doretti is now a collector's item.

Cal Sales was on its way and began developing facilities for its multiple operations. In mid-1957, the company held the grand opening of its complex in Gardena, California. The facility housed offices, parts, service departments, and Cal Specialties, which had its best customer in-house!

The Eastern half of the country was the territory of Southeastern Motors, based in Hollywood, Florida. Cal Sales, with the energetic Dorothy Deen always on the lookout for publicity, had a national profile. Southeastern was not well known and is not well remembered. Like Cal Sales, it had been awarded its franchise directly from Standard-Triumph and had established a network of dealers. However, not even the people who dealt with them can remember why they faded away or exactly when. The circumstances are unclear, but by some time in 1957, Southeastern Motors was gone. The Eastern territory was divided, initially among six new independent distributors. Later, as some of Cal Sales' enormous territory was carved away, the total reached eight. Company brochures show that Cal Sales still controlled 18 states, including Texas and California, as late as February 1958.

On August 11, 1958, I started work in the Triumph offices at 1745 Broadway, the company's third U.S. headquarters. The first office had been established at 99 Park Avenue in 1954 by Christopher E. Andrews, a long-time Standard-Triumph employee with a great deal of export experience but no prior knowledge of North America. It was a special administrative assignment, and having rented space, hired staff, and retained legal counsel, etc., Chris went back to England. He would not return until 1963, to take over U.S. operations as president.

Mainly a financial and shipping operation concerned with customs brokers, port authorities, etc., the first New York office employed only about five people. However, increasing sales and the paperwork necessary to deal with the larger pool of distributors called for more staff and more space. A new office was rented in the Chanin Building on East 42nd Street. Alan Bethell was put in charge at that time, although not yet with the title of president. Edward McCauley joined the company as accounting manager at the Chanin Building in May 1956, working for Treasurer Richard Soppet. Ed remembers Bethell being in charge with a title roughly that of vice president for sales.

The operation moved to Broadway at the beginning of 1957, coincident with the opening of the New York showroom by Genser-Forman Triumph Distributors, Inc., whose territory was New York, New Jersey, and Pennsylvania. The showroom, located on what was then "auto row" on Broadway and 56th Street, had offices upstairs with convenient expansion available over a Fiat showroom in the building next door. Eventually, we also had space above the Buick showroom one block south on the corner of 55th. One of the earliest Triumph dealer/distributors in the United States, Fergus Motors, was only a few doors away but no longer franchised. Owner Joe Ferguson was a brother of Harry Ferguson, whose tractor business had contributed so much to Standard's success.

As a TR2 owner back in Cincinnati, I had partaken of the sheer joy generated by sports car ownership in those days. At driving events, on rallies, or crowding some bar on wintry evenings, sports car club people got more fun out of life than anyone else. It was delightful to find that the sports car camaraderie existed in full measure at Standard-Triumph in New York. Indeed, the entire imported car industry

was like that—people selling products they liked, driving the cars on weekends, attending car events, racing, and enjoying life on four wheels. Sadly, I had to sell the Triumph to finance my move to New York. Yet a car was hardly necessary in the city, and I got plenty of opportunity to drive my new employer's vehicles for business and pleasure.

My new boss, Dave (David R.) Allen, had come to Triumph from the Sports Car Club of America, where he had been editor of the club magazine, *Sports Car*, and had been in charge of publicity. A soft-spoken, unflappable man with a pipe perpetually tucked in his mouth, he had become friends with Alan Bethell and shared the same birthday, Christmas Day. When the job of advertising manager at Triumph became vacant in late 1956, Alan hired Dave.

Whether any company is a nice place to work or a dismal environment is determined by the attitude of top management. Triumph was fun because Alan Bethell's bubbly personality and friendly attitude made it so. Bethell allowed his employees to make many of their own decisions, lending guidance but never criticism. He enjoyed his job and he wanted his employees to feel the same. Typical of the way Bethell worked with everyone was a newspaper clipping that arrived on Allen's desk one morning. The headline read "Pope returns in Triumph." A note from Bethell was attached, saying: "You goofed again! Which model?"

Although my salary had jumped quite nicely when I left my small ad agency copywriter/gopher job to join Standard-Triumph, it didn't run to expensive restaurant lunches. Groups of us frequented places like the Shandon Star, an Irish pub still on Eighth Avenue south of 56th, where a meatloaf sandwich and a glass of beer cost 45 cents including cole slaw and pickles. Another spot, usually reserved for payday, was Frances Bell on 55th near Sixth Avenue, where a sit-down, three-course meal (soup, chopped steak with vegetables, pudding) cost 95 cents. The flamboyant waiters were all actors waiting for a part on Broadway. Frances herself, at least 80 years of age, presided at the cash register with a smile for everyone. The building now houses the Jazz Museum.

A popular spot for the upper executive group was the Park Sheraton Hotel, on the corner of 56th and Seventh Avenue, where a club sandwich and a martini was about $3! Similar prices prevailed at the Carnegie Tavern across Seventh, then an unpretentious bar/bistro. For a real feast, there was the Carnegie Delicatessen on Seventh between 55th and 54th. Their hot pastrami is still the best in Manhattan.

Walking down Broadway took me past the Packard showrooms at 61st Street, where the oil-stained wooden floor held the final sad models of the mighty marque. They were Studebaker bodies with flashy chrome and gold Packard lettering tacked on. The

A gathering of British Automobile Manufacturers Association members' cars in the Tavern On The Green parking lot in New York, prior to setting off for the British Press Trials at Lime Rock Park, in Connecticut, in May 1959. Triumph TR3s are in the first and second row and the TR10 estate and sedan are third and fifth from left in the back row.

atmosphere was funereal; footsteps in the showroom echoed off the high ceiling, and no salesman appeared to serve the occasional tire-kicker. The paint was peeling from the tall, neon-lettered Packard sign in front.

From the Packard showroom and a few used-car places above Columbus Circle, Broadway became auto row below 59th Street. The General Motors Building stood on the corner of 57th with showrooms at street level. Chrysler, Dodge, Buick, Fiat, Borgward, Renault, Gogomobile, and others shared space with Triumph between Times Square and Columbus Circle. The crowded showrooms of the imports showed where the public preference was going and more than balanced the loss of Packard, Hudson, Nash, and others that had not managed to keep up.

Most import offices were still in Manhattan, usually combined with showrooms in the same building. The British Motor Corporation/Hambro showroom was on 57th between Sixth and Seventh Avenues with MG, Austin-Healey, Morris, and Austin cars on display. Jaguar was also on 57th, closer to Fifth Avenue. Further uptown was the Rootes showroom, on the corner of 60th Street and Park Avenue, where Hillmans, Sunbeams, Singers, and Humbers were available. Max Hoffman's BMW showrooms were at 57th and Park and the Frank Lloyd Wright–designed Mercedes showroom was at 56th and Park, where it still is today. Down at 46th and Park was Charles Kreisler's multifranchise dealership, where most British cars were on display, including oddities like Berkeley.

The foreign car business was highly competitive, and manufacturers and importers strove to take commercial advantage of every sales opportunity.

However, the British manufacturers enjoyed a uniquely cordial trade association relationship. The British Automobile Manufacturers Association (BAMA), a subsidiary of the Society of Motor Manufacturers and Traders (SMMT), had more than 30 members, including GM, which was importing Vauxhall for Pontiac, and Ford, which had a serious British Ford sales operation separate from its regular dealer body. BAMA had some clout.

Each year, BAMA held events, such as the Press Trials at Lime Rock Park, where members of the automotive press tried everything from TRs to Bentleys on the track. All association members participated in the expenses and furnished vehicles to be driven. Other BAMA exercises included British Inter-Marque Trophy Day, a gymkhana/slalom competition in which local sports car clubs were invited to participate. In the West, BAMA sponsored Press Trials at the old Riverside Raceway, Vacaville, and others.

Director of BAMA, and reporting direct to SMMT (Society of Motor Manufacturers and Traders) in London, was John Dugdale, who would become a good friend. John had worked for Rootes in Latin America and New York, then switched to Jaguar and was its western manager for several years. Later he would go back to Jaguar as U.S. advertising manager, but from 1958 through 1966 he dealt with all of the British auto manufacturers and parts suppliers as the central organizer of many significant events. His book, *Jaguar in America*, tells the import story from that unique perspective.

My first assignment at Standard-Triumph was to take over the Triumph Sports Owners Association (TSOA), the club that I had joined when I bought my TR2 and which had always been run in the United States by an outside agency. Since then, Triumph had gone through a general agency upheaval and decided to bring the TSOA operation in-house. Hence the need to hire me!

The TSOA had been founded in England in 1955 by Standard-Triumph to act as a clearing house for information for owners of the new Triumph sports car and to provide technical assistance to owners who wanted to develop the car for competition. The original TSOA Handbook refers to the club being founded by "The Triumph Motor Company (1945) Inc.," indicating a desire to separate the sporty TR from its staid Standard brethren.

The TSOA *Handbook* contained specifications, a series of information sheets concerning mechanical modifications, and the promise of a regular newsletter. In England, the newsletter appeared erratically, but in the United States, once it had been determined that Triumph should set up an American branch of TSOA,

a mostly successful attempt was made to issue a monthly publication. It was my job to take the previously mimeographed, 8-by-10-inch newsletter and turn it into a properly printed publication with photos. My first issue came out in October 1958.

The TSOA was a company-run organization and membership was free to Triumph owners. Thus, even in 1958, membership was high—near 10,000—and it peaked at over 15,000 before we finally started charging annual dues. Company-run organizations often have newsletters that seem more like corporate brochures, but we managed to stock the *TSOA Newsletter* with performance hints and club news, not just product ads. TSOA was also the organizing body for the Triumph Rallies of Europe, not competitive events but European tours for buyers who took delivery of their new Triumphs at the factory.

There were local Triumph clubs all over the country already, some of which are still going strong today. Although the original British TSOA had expected to emphasize the technical aspects of the TR and supply information about racing, most of the American owners used their Triumphs as regular cars, commuting, going on vacation, and just driving. So, my first year's issues of the *TSOA Newsletter* covered how to install hub bearings, how to erect the top, articles on European Rally success, U.S. sports car racing results, and a series of "can you top this" letters from families determined to drive around in a TR2 or 3 with more children than anyone else. The record still appears to be two parents plus five kids, the oldest of whom was nine. (Safety concerns were different then—the Corvair was two years in the future, no one had heard of Ralph Nader, and the first federal safety and emissions regulations were still nine years away.)

That was the scene when I arrived at Triumph. There were over 700 dealers nationwide, and they had four Triumph models to sell. The TR3 was sold as either a convertible or a hardtop. The Triumph sedan and estate wagon, known as "TR10s," filled out the showroom. Our competitors from England were MG, Austin-Healey, Sunbeam, Morgan, Lotus, and Jaguar. Fiat, Alfa, Porsche, and others weighed in from Europe, but there were no imports yet from Japan.

MG had the edge in history and a humpy little two-door from Wolfsburg was setting new sales records, but Triumph was the fastest-growing make in the sports car field. TRs weren't pretty but they were solid, reliable, roomy for a two-seater, and had the gutsy 0–60 acceleration that Americans loved. They qualified very well as "cute little sports cars" and that's what the country was buying. I joined the company when the cars were quite popular. To get there, Triumph had taken a long and interesting road. . . .

The Long Buildup to the TR BICYCLES TO BANKRUPTCY

Many car companies started out making horse-drawn or people-powered conveyances. The first Triumphs were bicycles, built beginning in 1887 by the Triumph Cycle Company, founded by Siegfried Bettman. A German who had emigrated to England and settled in Coventry, Bettman started putting motors on his successful bicycles in 1902 and became one of the most successful manufacturers of two-wheelers.

In 1923, Triumph went from two wheels to four. The first model produced was a two-seater roadster marketed with emphasis on styling and quality. Triumph was an industry leader in the use of hydraulic brakes, first installing them in 1925. Note that Ford did not use hydraulics until 1939, and Jaguar not until 1949! In 1927, Triumph jumped into the highly competitive "light car" market with the Super Seven. This small Triumph was priced well above the contemporary Austin and Morris Sevens, but it offered style,

finish, and equipment that justified the price, and the hydraulics gave it the only good brakes in its class. Triumphs became known for peppy engines and attractive styling. But despite the success of the bicycle business, Triumph had nothing like the financial reserves of its competitors, Austin, MG, Morris, and others. Production was low and there was never enough in the marketing budget.

Triumph offered a wide range of models, and Triumph chassis, especially the Super Seven, were often used by custom roadster builders like Gordon England. The Super Seven attracted a following of enthusiasts who put the little cars through near-impossible tests. Super Seven owners drove nonstop across the United States and Australia, setting a variety of nonstop speed and distance marks. Supercharged Sevens challenged Austin and MG on the racetrack, but without support from the factory. Triumph management preferred the all-round performance and

A 1937 Triumph Gloria "four-light" saloon. The number of "lights" in this case means the number of side windows. This car was known for good handling and road performance; the chassis was designed under the supervision of Donald Healey, and it reflected his international rallying experience.

A nice overhead view of a 1937 Triumph Gloria Southern Cross, four-cylinder roadster. This car had been fully restored at the time of the photo, a publicity shot for the 1973 New York International Auto Show.

durability demonstration of rally competition. Donald Healey, just beginning his career, competed with Super Sevens in British and European rallies with great success, beginning in 1929.

All of these sporting successes and Triumph's great popularity Down Under led to Triumph building factory-bodied sports cars called Southern Cross, starting in 1932. Southern Cross and, later, Vitesse models were built in many variations in the 1930s, based on the four- and six-cylinder Gloria chassis, launched in 1933. The Southern Cross, a two-seater, looked something like a broad-shouldered, muscular T-series MG. The Gloria Monte Carlo was a high-performance, four-seat tourer. In 1936, Triumph was making over a dozen different models of various sizes but production was only around 2,000 units a year.

Donald Healey was hired as chief engineer in 1935. He continued to drive existing Triumph models in international competition but also turned his talents to a car that would increase the public interest in Triumph. He conceived a supercharged 2-liter, twin overhead cam engine, to be mounted in a rakish, lightweight two-seater sports car, a potential rally winner. The engine was based on a contemporary

2,300-cc Alfa Romeo and built with Alfa's permission and cooperation. Styling also followed the appealing Italian car. In an interview with *Road & Track* many years later, Healey defended the use of another firm's design as the only way a company like Triumph could afford to engineer a new and complicated high-performance car.

The Dolomite was capable of over 110 miles per hour and had acceleration figures comparable with performance cars built 50 years later. Healey drove it on the 1935 Monte Carlo and collided with a train, destroying the car but leaving him and his navigator unhurt. Later that year, the Dolomite project was canceled for lack of funds, after three prototypes and a total of six engines had been built. One prototype survives today in a private collection. While the car did not reach production, the name did, and Triumph built a number of Dolomite sedans and tourers until the start of World War II, and then revived the name briefly in the 1970s. The marketing emphasis on performance continued with a line of cars named "Vitesse," French for "speed."

Triumph production and sales coasted down in the last years before World War II, even though the

Sir John Black—Father of Standard-Triumph

Sir John Black, known universally as "Captain Black," did not believe in doing things slowly once he had an idea. The title came from his military service in World War I and was appropriate for a man whose management style usually consisted of giving orders and expecting obedience. He went to work for the Hillman motor Company after World War I Married one of Mr. Hillman's daughters, and made his reputation in the industry as an ambitious and efficient manager. He was hired by Standard Motors in 1929 to direct an expansion program and by 1934 was running the company.

Sir John Black shows the new 1947 Standard Vanguard to Field Marshal Montgomery. "Monty" is wearing his trademark beret. The car is a left-hand-drive export model, many of which went to Canada.

The name "Standard" had been chosen by the company's founder, R.W. Maudslay, to indicate that his products had interchangeable parts, a rare quality in the early days of car manufacturing. An obsession with reliability and quality performance characterized the company throughout the 1920s and early 1930. Black encouraged adding and element of performance and modern styling. Starting in 1935, the various sizes of Standard cars became known as "Flying Standards," indicating both up-to-date body styles and good road performance. There was even a 2.8-liter V-8.

Standard had more than enough engineering and production capacity, which led to an association with William Lyons' S.S. Cars, later to become Jaguar. Lyons needed both chassis and engines for his first cars and turned to Black to supply them. In the beginning, S.S. mechanical components were virtually 100 percent Standard, including engines, gearbox, and rear axle. this arrangement lasted until Jaguar started to build its own chassis, and Black decided to sell the Jaguar engine tooling to Lyons in 1946. Another customer was Morgan, which started buying Standard engines in the late 1930s.

The Jaguar connection was profitable but, much more important, it stimulated Sir John Black to think about adding sporting cars to the Standard product line. He saw how fast Lyons' company was growing and was eager to get into the lucrative performance car market segment. Acquiring the Triumph name, long associated with speed and excitement, gave him exactly what he needed to begin his own sports car project. The one Standard engine for which Jaguar had not purchased the tooling was the 1,776-cc unit, just the thing, in his mind, to power the first in a new range of Triumphs.

Black ran Standard-Triumph as chairman and managing director until the end of 1953. At that point, despite his sterling record of producing profits, his board determined that his dictatorial ways had become detrimental to doing business. While he was recuperating from injuries suffered in a crash while a passenger in a new Doretti, the board of directors came to his home and unanimously demanded that he resign. He did so, effective January 4, 1954, and Deputy Managing Director Alick Dick was named Managing Director at the age of 37. Royal Air Force Marshall Lord Tedder later became chairman.

A 1939 Standard Twelve, last of the prewar "Flying Standards." The chassis of the similar Standard Nine was chosen as the basis for the first TR-2, 15 years later. *Plain English Archive*

The first postwar Triumph was this 1800 Roadster. Built in traditional style with aluminum panels over wood frames, it also had a "dickey seat," known over here as a rumble seat. The car was first powered by a 1,776-cc Standard engine but later, renamed "2000," it had the Vanguard 2,088-cc unit. Underpowered with either engine, it was a tourer, not a sports car. *Plain English Archive*

overall quality and performance of the company's products had never been better. The ever-hopeful management, better engineers than businessmen, had sold the profitable bicycle and motorcycle businesses to raise cash for the car side, investing in production facilities that sat idle, waiting for orders that never came. As guns began firing in Europe and Britain prepared for war, Triumph went bankrupt and the assets were sold.

Triumph fans and former employees held out hope that the company might be resurrected after the war, because the manufacturing facilities and quantities of parts still existed. People like Donald Healey were eager to make a new start once the conflict was over. But a 1940 German air raid destroyed or damaged much of Coventry, including the cathedral and the Triumph buildings. At the end of the war in Europe, the dormant Triumph company was owned by Thomas Ward Ltd., of Sheffield. Ward simply wanted to get rid of whatever Triumph assets were left. All they had was the name.

The Triumph 1800 and later 2000 Renown sedans carried the razor-edge theme almost too far. They were more formal in style than most Rolls-Royces. A small number of limousine models were produced with a longer wheelbase and more passenger legroom. They enjoyed brief popularity, but the dated appearance and modest performance meant they went out of favor quickly.

A Merger and a New Beginning

In October 1944, a purchaser stepped forward. Sir John Black, chairman and managing director of the Standard Motor Company, wanted to add a sporting line to accompany Standard's successful but staid family cars. With minimum negotiation, the legal details were completed and Triumph had a new home. Shortly afterward, the Standard-Triumph Motor Company, Ltd., was born.

The new combined corporate name would be reflected in the products. With nothing left of the prewar cars, new Triumphs would be built from scratch. They would use Standard components mounted on new chassis and clothed in unique body shells. A small group was assigned to work on new Triumph concepts while production of Standards resumed. At first, like the other British manufacturers, Standard built the same cars that had gone out of production in 1940. However, at the beginning of 1948, Standard became one of the first British manufacturers to introduce an all-new car.

The first Standard-built Triumphs were announced at the end of 1946 and they were a com-plete departure from the designs of the old Triumph company. One was the 1800 Roadster, which featured a bench seat for three plus a two-passenger "dickey seat" (rumble seat) and was certainly the world's last production car with that feature. The Roadster styling, by Frank Callaby, was a sort of modernized 1930s look with a tall chrome radiator grille set back between bulbous front fenders and flanked by huge headlights.

The Triumph 1800 sedan, although on the same chassis, bore no resemblance to the roadster other than the grille. Styled to Black's preferences by Walter Belgrove, the only senior Standard-Triumph employee who had worked for the original Triumph company, it had the "razor-edge" styling beloved of British limousine coachbuilders. It had very gracefully curved front fenders that swept down to vestigial running boards and then merged with the rear fenders. In contrast, the sides were flat and the roof and window area rectangular. The trunk was also a box, and the best overall description of the look of the car would be "square."

Both 1800s were powered by a version of the 1,776-cc overhead-valve four-cylinder engine, which

The 1947 Standard Vanguard posed dockside with HMS *Vanguard,* one of the most famous battleships of World War II. A few Vanguards were sold in the United States, but far more went to car-starved Canada in the late 1940s. This one is a prototype. Although it has a Royal Automobile Club badge, it is missing the center hood trim, and it lacks parking lights.

Standard still supplied to Jaguar for its lowest-priced models. The chassis was fabricated from steel tubing and used Standard independent front suspension, transmission, and rear axle. Both cars had three-speed column shifts. Body construction was "coachbuilt," using aluminum panels over ash wood frames, except for the fenders, which were steel.

The 1930s retro look of the roadster and the imposing formality of the sedan won mixed reviews from the car magazines and the public. One criticism of the cars was lack of power, but, at the beginning of 1948, the Vanguard, first Standard car able to take on North American, would solve the problem. Not only did it jump-start Sir John Black's export efforts, it provided the essential component that would make a true Triumph sports car possible—the engine.

Parts from Here and There

Standard shredded the established image of the British family sedan with the Vanguard, named for the British warship. It could seat six in a pinch, and it had a decent-sized four-cylinder engine and a real trunk. A fastback, styled to appeal to North American tastes, it was short for its width and resembled a 1941 Ford that had been pushed in a foot or so at both ends.

Rugged, roomy, and with enough power to challenge the Fords and Chevys, the Vanguard sold well in Canada, and a few were imported to the United States by Fergus Motors in New York. Despite its power, however, the car's dumpy appearance put off buyers. Standard at first merely added a heavier chrome grille and new interior appointments. A more elaborate restyle, Phase II, had a squared-off front and more normal trunk extension, now looking even more like a British attempt to make an American car. By late 1953, Standard-Triumph in the United States was planning to launch the Phase II and, later, a further restyled Phase III through its new distributor/dealer network in North America. The Vanguard was being touted as a serious contender in the U.S. family sedan market.

Looking at the photos, you may wonder why they bothered, but it wasn't unusual for a British car company to plan the launch of a new sedan in America. In the 1950s, though sports cars got the publicity, sedans contributed significantly to the British leadership in overall imported car totals, starting with Austin, which had sold up to 8,000 cars a year here as early as 1948.

The four-cylinder engine that moved the Vanguard so well had wet sleeves and rugged components and was perfectly suited to the tractors that Massey-Ferguson contracted with Standard to build. The gutsy 2-liter added pep to the Triumph roadster and sedan, now named the 2000 and Renown, and was the logical choice for Triumph's new TR2 sports car.

Sample Vanguards and TR2s were brought into both East and West Coast ports in late 1953, and the new Standard-Triumph Motor Company, Inc., was announced at the same time. Standard-Triumph and Cal Sales organized a Western press announcement at the old Ambassador Hotel in Los Angeles. On

hand were a TR2, Vanguard Phase II, and Vanguard Cadet—a rebadged Standard 8 economy model, on which even a passenger-side windshield wiper was extra. Sir John Black, deputy chairman and managing director of Standard-Triumph International, the UK parent, made the announcement, telling journalists that public introductions would be made at the Los Angeles Auto Show in January 1954 and the New York International Automobile Show in April. He said that all three cars would be available for sale after the New York show.

In fact, the Vanguard and Cadet never went on sale. During or immediately after the New York show, management decided not to market the Vanguard or any car with the Standard name in the United States. Apparently a group of distributors and their leading dealers (and probably some knowledgeable Standard-Triumph employees in America) finally convinced the company that the cars would not sell. The big Vanguard offered nothing unusual in appearance, specification, or size compared to the Fords and Chevys that were its

The Tractor Connection

Much of the cash needed to finance the postwar expansion of Standard and Triumph came from a fortuitous alliance between the company and Harry Ferguson, designer of a practical, lightweight farm tractor. Ferguson had previously contracted for the tractors to be built by David Brown in England and Ford in the United States. However, in 1945, he was looking for a new supplier to build the tractors, while Ferguson retained the marketing rights.

Sir John Black just happened to have a large factory available at Banner Lane on the outskirts of Coventry, used during the war for aircraft engine production. He and Ferguson completed a deal in August, and things went forward with such speed that the first tractor came off the line in July 1946. From then until Standard-Triumph left the tractor business in 1959, tractor production often exceeded car volume. Profits from the steady sales enabled Standard-Triumph to pursue car projects.

The first Standard-built Fergusons were powered by Continental engines. However, once development of the Vanguard had begun, plans were made to use a version of the new sedan engine in the tractor, and this went into effect around the time of the Vanguard announcement in late 1947. From this grew the legend that the Triumph 2-liter sports car engine had

Sir John Black, in the driver's seat, with Harry Ferguson. This 1946 photo shows the first Ferguson to come off the line at Standard's Banner Lane factory. The smiles are appropriate. Ferguson had found a new partner to build his tractors, and Black had found a source of income to enable his company to finance its postwar expansion. *Plain English Archive*

been developed from a tractor powerplant. It was the other way around. The first time the engine appeared under the bonnet of a Triumph was in 1948, when the Triumph 1800 Roadster and Saloon became the "2000." With changes in displacement, manifolding, and cylinder heads, the rugged unit would power TRs until 1968.

The Vanguard Luxury Six Estate. Last Standard car built, it had facelift styling by Michelotti and stayed in production through 1963. It was the first Standard-Triumph car to use the wonderfully smooth 2-liter six that later powered the GT-6 and, enlarged to 2.5 liters, the TR6. These cars were set up for U.S. district service managers and carried mechanical component assemblies and tools for use in dealer service schools.

competition. At $2,250, it lacked even the price advantage that had helped to sell the much smaller Austins and Ford Anglias.

The Vanguard, if plain, was at least well equipped. By contrast, the stark little Cadet did not even have an outside trunk opening or roll-up windows, and performance, with 803 cc, was woeful. At a time when the price of gasoline was hardly a factor in the cost of running a car, few Americans would sacrifice all comforts for the sake of 40 miles per gallon, even for a suggested list of $1,387.

Not only did the company drop the Vanguard marketing plan, it named Alan Bethell and his team to run its future North American programs. From 1954 until 1958, Standard-Triumph concentrated its American efforts on sports car sales. Instead of depleting resources in an effort to sell unwanted sedans, Standard-Triumph now had funds available to properly develop and market a Triumph car that would ride the crest of the sports car movement and sell as fast as they could make them.

The TR2 had its own unique chassis frame and bodywork but the drivetrain and suspension came from various Standard and Triumph vehicles. The car used the Vanguard engine and a four-speed version of the Vanguard transmission. The rear axle and the front suspension came from a unique little Triumph sedan called the Mayflower.

Announced in 1949, the Mayflower was, like the 1800 roadster, a unique exercise in automotive engi-

The Triumph Mayflower was a unique example of Sir John Black's passion for razor-edge styling. About the same size as a VW Beetle, the Mayflower had more passenger and luggage space but was underpowered. Over 30,000 were made, but not enough people thought it was cute, and production stopped after three years.

neering . . . only more so. It had basically the same dimensions as a VW Beetle but the styling of a razor-edged Rolls-Royce limousine. It was boxy, which meant it could carry four adults in real comfort, but the upright styling—fine on the larger Renown—drew doubletakes and perhaps a few chuckles when applied to a car just under 13 feet long.

The Mayflower was supposed to open up North America for Standard-Triumph, but this was merely Sir John Black's opinion, unsupported by market research. In fact, about 4,000 of them were sold, almost all of them in Canada. Fergus Motors imported them into the United States but they did not catch on, for several reasons. One was timing. The American driver was-

n't ready for economy cars in 1949 any more than in 1954, especially when the Mayflower cost nearly equaled a much-larger Plymouth or Ford. Contemporary road tests indicate that just about everyone who drove it for a period of time came to like it. Potential customers taking test-drives, however, found the three-speed gearbox awkward, the power negligible, and the looks at best controversial.

The Mayflower was a reasonable success on the home market. By the time it was canceled at the end of 1953, over 30,000 had been built. For North America, however, its major contribution to Triumph history were the suspension and rear axle it bequeathed to the TR2.

3 Birth of the "TR"

Sir John Black named the prototype Triumph sports car "TRX" in 1950, setting a naming pattern for 18 years of Triumph 2-seaters.

Modern-looking and curvaceous, the TRX was a complex car full of fault-prone hydraulic and electric systems. Three prototypes were built, and the car was shown at the Paris and London Motor Shows in 1950, with good reactions from the press. The high costs required to tool up and build the TRX kept it out of production, but it served a good purpose. It kept the Triumph sporting image alive while the company sought a less expensive way to enter the sports car market. The TRX grille design even reappeared on the short-lived Swallow Doretti of 1954.

The two-letter TR appellation hung on, although not right away. When a much simpler two-seater was

First Triumph to use the initials "TR," this is the TRX of 1950. Three prototypes were built, with electrically operated top, on-board jacking system, and other advanced features. It used the first twin-carburetor version of the Vanguard 2,088-cc engine. Potential high production costs killed the project.

The Sports 20 TR, as unveiled to the public at the Earls Court Motor Show in London in October 1952. The front is similar to the eventual production TR2. The parking lights would move from the top of the fenders to the front, below the headlights. The rounded rear is obvious and the spare wheel can just be seen, in its well in the rear panel. A two-tone Triumph Mayflower is visible in the background.

hurriedly designed and assembled for the 1952 Earl's Court Motor Show, it was designated "Triumph Sports 20TS." Later, after the production car was christened "TR2," it was retroactively named the "TR1." Almost immediately shortened by the public to "TR," regardless of number, it became the world's second-best-known sports car name (after MG) and ran on through "TR8" before Triumph sports cars ended in 1981.

The motoring public first saw the progenitor of the TR2 at the London Motor Show in the fall of 1952. It had been created to a strict budget and the designers had been told to use as many available components as possible. Thus, the engine came from the Vanguard, the gearbox was a four-speed version of the Vanguard three-speed, front suspension and rear axle were Mayflower parts, and the chassis was based on a modified and reinforced 1939 Standard Flying Nine frame.

Bodywork was extremely simple with no compound curves. Some of the most characteristic TR touches like the external hinges for bonnet and trunk were that way because they made the car less expensive to produce. Although the front of the show car looked quite like the eventual production TR2, there was no trunk. Behind the seats, the rear

Wearing a manufacturer's license plate and dirty from road testing, the TR prototype sits in the service area at Standard-Triumph in Coventry. The hood emblem is shaped like a shield and features the Triumph world with a field of stars behind it. It appeared only on this "TR1" and on the first prototype TR2.

This might have been the TR4! Michelotti's first styling exercise on a Triumph chassis was this TR3 "dream car" of 1957. Far too modern and American for British tastes, it nevertheless got Triumph management thinking. The shape of the windshield and the separate glass rear window with open roof section predicted the TR4 hardtop. *Road & Track*

panel curved gently down to a full bumper. The spare wheel was half-embedded in the panel and the fuel filler pipe ran through the center of the wheel. As the photos indicate, it was a good try but had no sports car dash to it.

After the Show, Standard-Triumph invited Ken Richardson, a well-known racing technician/driver who had been with BRM, to do testing. His input resulted in extensive redesign and strengthening of the TR chassis. The public's opinion of the prototype had made it obvious that a new rear treatment was needed. While Harry Webster supervised the chassis modifications, Walter Belgrove led the styling team to re-create the car aft of the doors. The new design included a proper trunk and a separate compartment for the spare wheel and tools, accessible from the rear. The full bumper was gone, replaced by simple, vertical bumper guards, a la Jaguar XK 120.

Ken Richardson was hired by Standard-Triumph to do testing in the TR Prototype. He stayed on to become the competitions manager. He drove the TR2 prototype on its Belgian record run in 1953. The car used a metal tonneau cover as well as the undershield. The car still has the unique globe and stars emblem.

This photo has been used many times, but it never loses its appeal. In the morning mist, Ken Richardson urges the TR2 down the Jabbeke highway, reaching for the highest speed attainable. He and the little white two-seater set a standard of performance that TR sports cars would strive to match for the next 27 years. *Plain English Archive*

The resulting car, officially named "TR2," was displayed at the 1953 Geneva Motor Show in March. In May, during speed testing on the Jabbeke motorway in Belgium, the TR2 distinguished itself by topping 124 miles per hour in racing trim with undershield, metal tonneau cover, and racing screen. Even with the top up and side curtains in, it still did over 114! It had taken just a short few months to turn the crude prototype into a salable sports car. A legend was ready to be born.

The TR2 was obviously ready to do the job Sir John Black had intended. After the indifferent attempt to sell the 1800/2000 roadster and sedan and the false start with the Mayflower, Standard-Triumph finally had a car to compete with MG in the North American market. The distributor organization in the United States was waiting. With the start of 1954, Triumph began to make its mark in the sports car field.

Triumph Stands Out

At a time when it seemed some manufacturer was releasing a new car every couple of weeks, the first Triumphs stood out as something unique. The styling did not compare with MG's vintage appeal nor with Jaguar's years-ahead curves. Lacking chrome trim, it was called homely, even in slickest form with fender skirts. It was fast, but the steering and handling did not match an Austin-Healey 100 for precision. The colors put people off. Aside from British Racing Green and black, there were no strong shades. Tan, gray,

This early TR2 lacks the rear fender skirts and has MG-TD-type taillight lenses. The reflectors on the rear fenders may have been for some market other than the United States. It was not a beautiful car, but the performance outsold the looks! *Plain English Archive*

pale yellow, white, mauve, and a tomato-soup red called "Geranium" (with top and tonneau to match) made potential customers long for something bright. Yet it was relatively comfortable, sturdy, and reliable, and driving it was exhilarating.

When Cal Sales took on the Triumph line, Dorothy Deen began a campaign to persuade the Standard-Triumph marketing people to change the colors to something more appealing. She had no success at all and began repainting cars on her own in Ferrari red, bright yellow, and other shades. Many were two-toned, using the seam between inner and outer fender sections as the dividing line. The Cal Sales two-tone TR2 race car was driven at various times, by the likes of Phil Hill and Richie Ginther. Her persistence eventually paid off, and Triumph came to offer one of the best selections of colors in the industry.

Marketing Joys and Traumas

TR2s and TR3s had "fly-off" handbrakes that operated backward. To set the brake, you pulled up on the lever and pressed in a button on the top. To release, you pulled hard enough for the button to pop up and then released the lever. Anyone trying to release the brake by pushing down on the button wasn't going to drive away any time soon. My father managed to set the brake at an intersection while test driving my car and sat there for 15 minutes, before giving up and walking home.

Importers trying to break into the American market had problems educating their customers, but overseas management also had an attitude. The fly-off brake was confusing to most Americans, but management didn't change it until the late 1960s. Other anomalies like the manual choke, side curtains, and button-on tops would also have to be dealt with sooner or later.

The show chassis exhibited at Earls Court in 1953 after the TR2 was already in production. Note that it is left-hand drive. Over 80 percent of TR sports cars were exported to Europe and North America. While the British were the best at designing them, few in the war-devastated British economy could afford the luxury of a sports car. With modifications to track, etc., this layout was used right through the TR6.

These are 1956–1957 TR3s rolling off the final assembly line at Coventry, with tell-tale "Export" stickers on the windshields.

While I was still scorching Ohio roads in my TR2 prior to moving to New York City, Standard-Triumph had been making significant moves in both product development and establishing its business in the United States. The two distributors named at the beginning of 1954 had grown to six. Five of them divided the eastern half of the country, while Cal Sales handled the West from its Los Angeles base via a network of regional offices in San Francisco, Portland, Vancouver, and Houston. Over 500 dealers stocked Triumphs, and parts were available at every distributorship.

The company made steady changes to the TR2 as soon as they were perfected, without waiting for the next model year. It also made changes with new models. My TR2 had painted hood and trunk hinges. The TR3, first available during 1956, had chrome hinges. The awkward, hard-to-adjust interi-or hood release mechanism was replaced by Dzus fittings at the front corners of the hood with the 1955 model year, released in October 1954. They were operated by the "T-Key," which had been standard equipment on the TR sports car from the beginning. Both the trunk lid and spare wheel compartment had the Dzus fitting.

The 1,991-cc engine with its twin SU carburetors stayed essentially the same through 1957, but the factory added electric overdrive to the option list along with a removable hardtop and wire wheels. Another change, unseen but beneficial to brake balance, was the installation of 10-inch drums on the front. (The rear drums were left at 9-inch.) Physical changes were few, but an important one was the move to short doors after the first 3,500 cars. The original doors, as on my car, reached to the bottom of the body, making it impossible to open them when

This May 1957 publicity photo was taken in Washington Square Park, New York, before the vehicle road through the park was closed to traffic. So equipped, the TR3 was sold as a "hardtop model" at $2,790 vs. $2,625 for the plain roadster. The shorter door is clearly visible, still with no exterior handle.

parked next to a high curb. The rear edge of the doors was constantly being chipped and repainted.

The TR3 was officially announced at the beginning of 1957, after 2-1/2 years of TR2s. It is most easily recognized for having the first real TR grille—an egg-crate affair replacing the simple metal grid at the back of the TR2 opening. However, a group of transitional models lacked the new grille and had only a chrome strip around the sides and bottom of the front opening. Nearly 4,000 of the first 1956 TR3s had drum brakes at the front, replaced by Girling discs later in the year. It was the first installation of disc brakes on a volume-production car. TR3 engines were rated at 100 horsepower instead of the TR2's 90.

The most useful creature comforts were the optional rear seat, which actually could be used for children, and new side curtains with sliding plexiglass windows. No longer did the owner have to undo a zipper and scar up his hands reaching inside to push the cable door lock release—simply slide the window forward and you were there. A fresh-air intake on the cowl aided ventilation.

In January 1958 the Triumph TR3A would arrive in New York's Broadway showroom. This model recorded several Triumph "mosts"—most years built, most cars built, most creature comforts, and, certainly, most remembered.

On my final day at Lancett Motors in Ohio, I saw the last of the 1957 TR3s and the first of the new TR3As sitting side-by-side. Most noticeable was the new front panel with a low, wide, anodized aluminum grille and the headlights set farther back. Much more impressive were the real, outside, locking door handles! The front bumper was sturdier and more attractive. Even the side curtains had new flat brackets, replacing the old inch-thick sockets, which were hell on elbows.

Triumph dealers were having few problems selling the TR3. However, Standard-Triumph and other sports car producers were constantly trying to expand their potential market in the United States. The most readily available way to do this was to market small sedans and, after the aborted Vanguard launch had faded from memory, Standard-Triumph introduced the Triumph 10 sedan and station wagon. Getting

The Triumph badge with "10" at the top shows up well in this 1958 TR10 estate wagon publicity shot. The wagon came with the cream-colored paint around the windows and sold for $1,899 at the port of entry.

away from depending on sports cars as the sole source of sales volume and profit was a struggle that only one British manufacturer, Jaguar, ever won, but many felt they had to try.

The American car manufacturers had managed, over the years, to create full product lines under every nameplate. You could get a Chevrolet badge on anything from a pickup truck to a snazzy convertible. Not the imports. Most of the early imported cars, especially the British, made their mark through a fad for a single model. MG became a household word via servicemen returning home with TC sports cars purchased in Europe. With Triumph, it was "TR." The name became so pervasive that one major corporation, TRW, Inc., ran a national ad campaign announcing "We Are Not A Small British Sports Car"!

Although a third of the sales were still in sunny California, Triumph volumes dipped in the winter months and the dealer organization wanted more different models with the magic Triumph name. Although most Triumph dealers had multiple fran-

chises that included Fiat, Renault, Volvo, or other sedans, they tended to sell what was hot, and the "TR" was on a steep rise in popularity. The Volkswagen Beetle had also become popular and with it the idea of the economy car. Triumph dealers reasoned that a small sedan with a Triumph badge would be their ticket to increased sales.

Standard-Triumph responded by upgrading what it had. The stark little Standard 10 sedan and station wagon, built with a few deluxe touches like roll-up windows, heaters, and vinyl seats, got a "Triumph 10" badge, and a new TR was born! Well, not quite. The slab-sided, tallish little cars were reasonably reliable and could keep up with traffic, but they were almost too homely to be cute. A clever advertising campaign promoted them as family cars, but they were too basic in styling, equipment, and comfort to attract many buyers. The little wagon could hold quite a bit of cargo with the rear seat folded down or removed, and some dealers promoted it as a fleet vehicle for local deliveries.

Even with gas at 35 cents per gallon, fuel economy was the primary selling point for small imported sedans. In June 1959, Alan Bethell handed $27 to model Kitty Flint, all she needed for gas and oil to drive the TR10 sedan from New York to Los Angeles.

Cal Sales' Los Angeles Auto Show exhibit in 1958 had a pair of two-tone TR10s. The sedan was gold and white, the estate bright red and white—anything to make the little cars more attractive in the showroom. *Dorothy Deen*

The TR10 estate was marketed on its capacity, and the ad campaign made use of this couple in various situations. With the rear seat folded it really could carry a lot.

Ability to park in tight spaces was a selling point for the TR10, as this couple proves. Even in 1958, it wasn't unusual to see a Model A Ford in regular use. Supermarket posters offer coffee cake for 31 cents, chicken at 35 cents per pound.

The "TR10s," as they were known, were the last Standard cars to be marketed in America, and they accomplished a couple of things. The Gold Star 948-cc engine was the unit from which the Triumph Herald economy car and 1,147-cc Spitfire sports car engine would be developed. The little cars also filled a gap in TR showrooms until America received the Herald, not to be announced in the UK until late 1959.

Sitting at my desk above 56th Street in the autumn of 1958, my main concern was promoting reservations for the 1959 Triumph Rallies of Europe, producing the *TSOA Newsletter,* and working with my boss on publicity for the Triumph team entry at Sebring. The offices vibrated with a satisfying buzz of activity. Sales were good, the cars were good, and the economy was good. It was a time when the prospects for the sale of imported cars in the United States seemed limitless.

In 1958, *Sports Cars Illustrated* (now *Car and Driver*) picked a typical suburban family and gave them a TR10 sedan to drive for three weeks as their regular transportation. The conclusion was a signal to Detroit. The test family endorsed the Triumph and said: "This is all you need!" *Reprinted by Standard-Triumph*

We gave a family a car for three weeks, and told them . . .

"Don't call us, we'll call you!"

Illustration: Don Curnelius

by John Christy

4 Triumph Marketing Takes Shape

By the end of the 1950s, the American consumer knew there were things like sports cars and economy sedans, but not much more than that. The designation "imports" was not yet common. They were all "foreign cars." For many consumers, any sedan smaller than a Ford was an Austin or Volkswagen and any two-seater was an MG. The various importers had to battle for recognition. In doing so, they used some familiar methods and some not so familiar.

Normal print advertising in newspapers and magazines was a major segment. Importers frequently relied on radio, using television when they could afford it. Auto shows were swamped with requests for

"Any Time Is Triumph Time" was Triumph's show theme for 1959. Here it is at the New York Coliseum, where Triumph had prime space at the top of the escalators. A TR3 chassis is suspended above a huge sundial, and the individual cars are backed by display units with action photos on one side, signs of the Zodiac on the other.

exhibit space from 15 or 20 importers at a time, and it was sometimes difficult to get space because so much of any show's floor area was allocated to the domestic manufacturers. The imports were tucked into corners, lower floors, and hallways, but they often attracted more of the crowd than Detroit's cars.

One show that did not slight imports was the New York International Automobile Show, run by the Charles Snitow Organization. Conceived in the early 1950s, the New York Show started out in the Grand Central Palace on Lexington Avenue and moved to the New York Coliseum when it opened in 1957. The British had supported the show from the start and were given the prime exhibit space at the head of the escalators on the second floor of the Coliseum. Although the "main" exhibit area was on the first floor, the design of the building channeled the crowd from the front door directly to the escalators, to the fury of the American exhibitors and others who were on the first floor.

Stepping off the escalator, show visitors were immediately immersed in a world of imports, with Triumph and British Motor Corporation (Austin, MG, Austin-Healey, Morris) immediately ahead; Jaguar and Rootes (Sunbeam, Singer, Hillman, Humber) just beyond; and Rolls-Royce/Bentley, Aston-Martin, and Rover further along. Filling the rest of the second floor and the third floor balcony were Fiat, Renault, Peugeot, Alfa-Romeo, Mercedes, and BMW, along with less familiar names such as Auto-Union, DKW, Borgward, Citroen, Abarth, and others.

Although the Chicago show always drew more visitors, perhaps because admission was only a dollar, New York was the center of import activity and always featured a parade of new models, show cars, and stunts. In 1959 the Triumph exhibit was built around the theme "Any Time Is Triumph Time," featuring a TR3 chassis mounted on a pole in the center of an enormous sundial. The time theme continued with Zodiac displays denoting the four seasons at each corner of the exhibit. All cars displayed were powder blue. Another touch was the use of two sets of identical twins as show models.

Standard-Triumph sales during 1958 had totaled more than the previous four years put together. Alan Bethell's message to distributors and dealers at the beginning of 1959 noted that Triumph was the first import to offer a line of sedans, station wagons, and sports cars all under the same marque name. He urged, "Let's make 1959 Triumph's greatest year yet!" The first nationwide distributor meeting was held in New York during the International Show and was attended by several representatives from Standard-Triumph in England.

When I joined Standard-Triumph, the advertising agency was Chester Gore, Inc., but it was on the way out. Late in 1958, it was announced that the account had been awarded to Doherty Clifford Steers and Shenfield, a medium-large agency with offices in New York and Los Angeles and clients like Kimberly-Clark and Seagrams. Through many corporate changes at Triumph and a couple of mergers of its own, this agency held the Triumph account for more than 10 years. The original account team included Harry Ireland, senior vice president; Bob Kelly, account supervisor; Bob Doherty, account executive; Pieter Fischer, assistant account executive; and Bob Petrocelli, art director. The team put together a series of campaigns with real character and marketing strength.

Doherty Clifford disappeared years ago as a separate agency but survives partially in the huge Needham, Harper & Steers combine. Chester Gore remained active in the ad business, as head of his agency, until his death in April 1997.

Ad shoots were "real" in 1959, and this shot has the TR3 moving along with an actual herd of horses. The models later confided that they were really nervous that the horses would overrun the low-slung TR. All of these ads emphasized performance, handling, and the safety of (front) disc brakes.

Main Street...Turnpike...or Track...

"Shop and go" driving starts to be fun in a TRIUMPH TR-3. You'll find its quick responses make light of heavy downtown traffic. Its nimble handling makes parking a snap...and there's ample room for plenty of bundles just behind the front seats, or in the large lockable trunk.

America's #1 sports car value

The TR-3's 100 horses love exercise. And high-speed thruways won't tire them *or* you. The TR-3 is built to take car-killing road competition. It is surprisingly *comfortable*, too. Solid suspension and contour seats combine to make the miles enjoyable.

The TR-3 has taken first-in-class in practically every major European rally during the past five years. Special competition equipment for the TR-3 is available through all 700 TRIUMPH dealers. Today call your local TRIUMPH dealer for a test drive!

TRIUMPH TR-3 ONLY $2675*

*U. S. Ports of Entry, plus state and/or local taxes. Slightly higher West Coast. Overseas delivery available. Standard-Triumph Motor Co., Inc., Dept. E-90. 1745 B'way, N.Y. 19

This 1960 ad emphasized performance and comfort in a different way, still treating the TR as an everyday, all-round car. This "racing" scene was shot in a parking lot, with the author driving the second car in the picture.

Sports car marketers like Standard-Triumph had different advertising and promotional themes, but they all arrived at similar conclusions about basic media strategy. A pattern developed that held good for the industry for many years. Even at 1959 prices, television commercials were beyond the budget of most importers, so very careful studies were made of the print media available.

Customer surveys of the time indicated that the sports car buyer was likely to be male, college-educated, married and usually in a well-paid, professional job. His interests were broad but sports and current events played a big part, and a large percentage were car enthusiasts. The results of these surveys plus advertising agency recommendations produced a media list in the late 1950s that holds true for many imports 50 years later.

In July 1958, *Triumph News*, our publication for dealers, listed Triumph's advertising schedule for July

and August. The media list included *Saturday Evening Post, Holiday, Time, Sports Illustrated, New Yorker, Esquire, Sports Cars Illustrated* (now *Car and Driver*), *Road & Track, Motor Trend, Sports Car*, and *Sunset*. The survivors from that list are still good media buys for a sports import in the twenty-first century.

In those days, when import buyers were out of the mainstream and ad dollars were short, it was vitally important to target potential customers accurately. The advertising sales staffs of magazines like *Time* fully realized this, and named import market specialists who worked very closely with the advertising managers to develop rifle-approach campaigns aimed directly at real prospective buyers. In 1953 the *New Yorker*, through the efforts of ad specialist Don Lawder, pioneered an annual imported auto buyer survey which, carried on by Bill Conrad, Arnie Gittleman, and others, became a standard reference work in ad agencies and corporate advertising departments.

As time went on, *Newsweek, US News & World Report, Fortune*, and other news and business magazines joined the import media roster. Making sure of catching the businessman/buyer at both ends of his day, Triumph and other import ads were frequently seen in *Playboy*, which had the famous auto writer Ken Purdy on its masthead, and later in *Penthouse*. Nobody was yet using the word "lifestyle," but our target consumer's preference was for possessions that would contribute to enjoying life, and a sports car was the central acquisition in the list.

DCS&S's first campaign was touted to the dealers as the "Biggest Advertising Campaign in Triumph's History." Print ads featured headlines like "Hardtop to Beat" and "New Fun at 50" for the TR3. The sedan and estate wagon were sold on a low-first-cost, low-upkeep basis, with strong emphasis on British craftsmanship. Both campaigns placed the cars in "realistic, believable situations."

Going back through the files, I found internal memos complaining of lack of agency attention, lack of creativity on certain cars, and excessive costs. Hindsight says that we were probably getting our money's worth. The agency's performance reflected the client's attitude. Its poorest work was on cars in which we, the company people, had the least confidence. The TR3, TR4, and Spitfire always had good, hard-hitting ads. The Triumph 2000 and the Herald campaigns were well executed but missing some of the enthusiasm that made the TR ads shine. All of us knew that the TRs made the most money and were market leaders, while the economy cars and the mid-priced sedan lacked the TR's established reputation and had tough competition.

TV exposure was considered essential, but air time was very expensive. We supplied prerecorded radio commercials but dealers had to put their own

At 56th Street and Broadway in Manhattan, the Triumph showroom was highly visible. The face of the building was covered in reddish tan tiles, against which the bright red, lighted TRIUMPH lettering stood out well. Alan Bethell, left, is shown here greeting Tully Brammer, who traveled the country by TR3 with promotional trailer, representing North American Van Lines.

TV spots together. To get on the tube, importers became pioneers in providing products as prizes on the first wave of TV game shows. Triumphs and others starred on *The Price Is Right* almost from the beginning. *Triumph News* advised that the TR10 estate wagon would appear as featured showcase prize on the daytime *Price Is Right* three days in November 1959. The appearance drew over 1,200,000 responses from the viewing audience.

An additional 20 million viewers saw the TR3 on *The Dick Clark Show* as part of a promotion sponsored by Beechnut gum. Later, millions more watched Triumphs appear as prizes on *Masquerade Party*, hosted by the inimitable Bert Parks.

A good working team was in place at Triumph on Broadway. Alan Bethell was in his third year as president; Guy Fox was vice president, sales; Dave Allen headed advertising and public relations; D. Peter Snow was in charge of service; and Dick Soppet was treasurer. The staff was expanding as sales increased and we would soon be taking additional office space,

first by breaking through a wall to expand into the building next door on Broadway and then adding a floor in a decrepit building at 1733 Broadway on the corner of 55th Street.

We all pitched in to whatever tasks needed to be done, but we were busy enough that I was getting more and more advertising work to do, and an assistant was needed to cope with the TSOA. Three were hired and resigned in three years! First was Cliff Jahr, who left to write advertising copy and later became a free-lance writer and author of some fame before his death. Next was Al Ashley, who fought New York valiantly for a year before returning to the Midwest. Last to arrive was Fred Gamble, who would leave his mark on Triumph racing before moving on to Goodyear.

A Hint of Unknown Peril

After the launch of the TR3A and the TR10 sedan/estate wagon duo in 1958, for the moment Standard-Triumph had nothing to do but sell cars. In

Triumphs lined up awaiting shipment to the United States. Most are TR3s, but there are a number of TR10s. The roadsters were shipped with windshields and front bumpers removed. Shipping damage was high in those days, before the "roll-on, roll-off" ships made transporting cars across the ocean so much more efficient.

Released at the end of 1958, this press photo shows Alan Bethell congratulating Dorothy Deen on Cal Sales' 10,000th TR3 sale. By the end of 1959, Cal Sales' total would top 15,000.

Unloading a TR3 from the SS *George Lykes* at Pensacola, Florida. Cars were loaded and unloaded by crane, which sometimes took days instead of the few hours it now takes to drive a shipload of cars onto the dock.

the office, we were hearing about the new small sedan, the Herald, which would be announced in England at the Motor Show in October, but we would not be seeing that car until March 1960. Our main concern was moving the products we had now. Three new distributors were appointed, bringing the total to nine. The new territories were created in part by reshuffling the Jarrard Motors territory and carving away several Midwest states from Cal Sales. In New England, Foreign and Sports Cars, Inc., went out of business and a new organization, Triumph Distributor of New England, was created. The list was completed with the addition of distributors in Alaska and Hawaii in early 1960.

Standard-Triumph and its U.S. subsidiary were on top of the world. TR production had reached 450 units per week, a far cry from the 10 or 20 envisioned by Sir John Black only five years before. The TR3 was the leader in U.S. sports car sales, topping even MG, and the TR10s were selling, often because of creative sales promotions by local dealers. We knew there were exciting new models in the pipeline and there seemed to be no clouds on our sales horizon.

Yet, it was a fateful year. During 1959, Alick Dick, Standard-Triumph's managing director, engineered the sale of the Ferguson Tractor manufacturing business to Massey-Ferguson. In New York, any of us who actually were aware of the transaction found it interesting but not significant. It was known that cash would be needed to develop and market new models like the Herald, so the elimination of the Ferguson business looked like a good source of funds. Cars, not tractors, were the company's future. It was unthinkable that the loss of the tractor income might be the start of problems for the company from which it would never recover. Yet, so swift was the decline that, only a year later, Standard-Triumph would willingly give up its independence in an acquisition by the Leyland Group.

The Competitive Spirit

In March 1959 we weren't thinking of future disasters. Corporate minds were much more likely to be enjoying the frequent success of Triumph teams in the famous European rallies. The Alpine, the Monte Carlo, the Tulip, the Liege-Rome-Liege, the RAC International . . . all were events that challenged cars and crews in ways not thought of in the United States since the pioneering cross-country runs held early in the century. Under the direction of Competitions Manager Ken Richardson, Standard and Triumph cars had been competing with great success in these car-killing rallies since the advent of the TR2. TRs were class winners, team prize leaders, and top-10 overall finishers on a regular basis.

Given this record, it was a natural for Standard-Triumph to make an official team entry of four TR3s in the first running of the American International Rally. Organized as a U.S. version of the famed Monte Carlo Rally, the American International had eight starting points in the United States, Canada, and Mexico, with all competitors converging on a common finish in Las Vegas. Triumph's team was highlighted by the presence of CBS newsman Walter Cronkite, always a sports car enthusiast, with navigator Stu Blodgett, a regular on the sports car rally scene. The other three cars were handled by Bob Halmi and Lou Batori; Denise McCluggage, with navigator Eleanor Halmi; and Doug Kennedy, editor of *True* magazine, with Alex Thompson.

Bob Halmi was Triumph's regular photographer for advertising and PR and is the same man who became a well-known film and TV producer, listed on the stock exchange as Robert Halmi, Inc. He was also a competitor in TRs in various European events, and drove the leading American entry in the 1958 Monte Carlo, sharing the ride with Doug Kennedy. Bob, now in his 70s, is chairman of Hallmark Entertainment and

Lou Batori, left, and Bob Halmi tune in the short-wave radio used to keep accurate time on the American International Rally. The rally team cars were mechanically stock, but had some suspension mods and carried a spare wheel and tire on the trunk lid. A headrest was provided for the navigator.

Not the pits at the races, but a Howard Johnson's on the New Jersey Turnpike. Mike Cook, left, and Mike Jackling posed with three of the American International Rally team cars en route from Columbia Triumph Distributors in Maryland back to Manhattan. *Bill Greehey photo*

famous for producing TV miniseries such as *Scarlett* and *Lonesome Dove*.

Lou Batori, an avid amateur rallyist, was in the electronics business and equipped the team cars with the latest timing and communications gear—Avion odometers and short-wave radios for time signals. Eleanor Halmi was Bob's wife and thoroughly familiar with rallying at all levels. Denise McCluggage was already a racing star in Europe and the United States and had competed in some European rallies. Thompson, Kennedy's navigator, was another SCCA amateur rally expert.

Four of us flew down to Washington, where the TR hardtops had been prepared by Columbia Triumph Distributors, experienced through running its own racing team. The cars had all the suspension modifications for good handling but used basically stock engines for reliability. Finished in Sebring White with double blue racing stripes down bonnet and trunk and blue numbers, they were an exciting sight on the New Jersey Turnpike as we drove north, each with an extra spare wheel bolted to the trunk lid.

Denise McCluggage had confessed to Dave Allen that she had never actually driven a Triumph so he assigned me to take a car to meet her in midtown

Manhattan and show her how the TR worked. I found myself trying to teach a racing professional, used to winning in exotics like Ferrari and OSCA, how to drive a garden-variety English sports car in city traffic. After a while, I shut up and just enjoyed the drive. Denise and I are still good friends.

Thirteen cars started the rally from New York, leaving at precise intervals from Sardi's, the famous old New York theater restaurant on West 44th Street. The day was a cool October 13, and the first car off left at 3 A.M. What a thrill watching Walter Cronkite drive off in the car I had just chauffeured from Washington, D.C.! The wind whistles down 44th Street with bone-chilling force in the fall, and Sardi's did a roaring business, with emphasis, for once, on coffee.

The Triumph team made the first leg on time, arriving in Asheville, North Carolina, without penalty and set off on the second leg, destination Fort Smith, Arkansas. Bad weather hit hard, and in the midst of fog and rain, the Cronkite/Blodgett car slid off the road near Cleveland, Tennessee, and rolled over into a lake! Unhurt, the intrepid pair got the car towed out and hauled into town for a cleanup and oil change. Unfortunately, the sleepy service station attendant who did the work didn't get all the water out of the engine, and the bearings went away shortly after they got back on the road.

With Cronkite and Blodgett out, the other three cars still constituted a team. Eleanor and Denise were rear-ended by another car in the fog, when they pulled back onto the road after swerving to miss a dog. They suffered both whiplash and a 100-point penalty, but the other two TRs were still "clean." On the last leg, from Santa Fe to Las Vegas, the rally went time-speed-distance, requiring frequent, very accurate speed changes. The first Triumph team to arrive in Vegas was the two women, with Denise driving much more cautiously than her usual style and Eleanor only lifting her eyes from her calculator when she had to massage her neck. The team won the Best Foreign Manufacturer Trophy; Best New York Starter; Third in 1,600–2,000-cc Class; Seventh Overall; and the Ladies' Prize.

Another Triumph team entry that set the juices flowing was the three TR3S prototypes that went to Le Mans in June. Using a special twin overhead cam engine, the TR3S was a rugged-looking car with extra body width to accommodate a 4-inch increase in track. However, racing luck was poor, as two of the cars retired early with fan failure, the blades shearing off and going through the radiator. Knowledgeable Triumph people have been asking ever since why racing cars had fans in the first place! The third team car, driven by Peter Jopp and R. Stoop, was called in for removal of the fan. After that, it ran until halfway through the 23rd hour, when the oil pump failed. When it retired, it was leading its class, and was sixth overall.

The TR3S was, supposedly, a prototype of a production car to sell alongside the TR3 at a higher price. Rumors were widespread enough that the July 1959 *TSOA Newsletter* contained this caution at the end of the Le Mans story: "May we say again that the TR3S will not be put into production or sold to the public until the successful completion of their development period. Nor will they replace the TR3. They, instead, will be a more powerful addition to the Triumph sports car line."

Another Triumph team established eight new Federation International Automobile (FIA) Class E (1,600–2,000-cc) records at Monza in Italy. Set with a TR3, driven by a team of students from Cambridge University, the records included 5,000 miles at an average of 102.5 miles per hour.

As 1959 came to an end, sales figures showed that the TR3 had passed MG for the lead in U.S. sports car sales for the first six months of 1959. The competition between the two for top honors in this sales battle was always fierce. Triumph had no trouble out-doing MG in overall marque sales—the MG sedans usually did not sell as well as the Triumphs, but the MG people made certain that sports car volume was reported separately and they nearly always won that battle. This rivalry was deeply rooted and continued even after the two marques were both being sold under the British Leyland banner.

I had helped the TR sales total by purchasing a new TR3, which was delivered in the spring. British Racing Green with a tan interior and wire wheels, it was the perfect car for a bachelor. Although parking is always at a premium in New York, I found a space in the Mecca Garage for just $35 per month. The company gave us a good deal on car purchases, and a number of employees would buy a new car every year, selling it at a profit and buying another one. One of these was Elsie Dorn, supervisor of the STMCI Billing Department, who bought her fourth TR and picked it up on TR Rally Number 2 in 1960. Her picture appeared in the *Triumph Dealer News* as an employee with true brand loyalty. Six years later, her Powder Blue TR3 became my first race car!

Press Trials and Tribulations

Earlier, I mentioned the many and various activities of the British Automobile Manufacturers Association, known as BAMA. BAMA was a subsidiary of the Society of Motor Manufacturers and Traders (SMMT) in England and had a mission to promote sales of British cars and automotive products of all kinds in the United States. It had been founded in the early 1950s and was based first in Washington and then, as British car importing activity centered itself around New York, in Manhattan. Late in 1958, John Dugdale left his position in charge of overseas delivery sales at Jaguar and became the executive vice president of BAMA, with new offices in Canada House on Fifth Avenue.

BAMA was unique in actually presenting the British auto industry to the public as an entity under one banner. Members who were direct competitors still fought each other for every sale, but cooperated on mutually beneficial events. The BAMA publicity operation generated good press coverage and managed to keep the focus on the cars so that all members got a share of the coverage. BAMA took advantage of publicity opportunities wherever possible at events like the Royal Visit of Queen Elizabeth and Prince Philip to the Chicago International Trade Fair of 1959, where eight BAMA members, including Triumph, set up special displays.

One of the most successful UK press events hosted by the SMMT was the Press Trials, staged at the Goodwood track near London. All the UK manufacturers brought cars to the Trials and, teeth gritted, let the motoring press loose with them. Accidents were few, even after a lunch that offered a certain amount of alcohol, but mechanical abuse was rampant. Despite misgivings on the cost of rebuilding the

A Royal Visit to the Chicago International Trade Fair of 1959 attracted eight members of the British Automobile Manufacturers Association as exhibitors. Chicago Mayor Richard Daley accompanied Queen Elizabeth II and Prince Philip as they toured the show.

CEOs of British car firms' American operations line up in front of their products prior to the start of the British Press Trials at Lime Rock Park, 1959. Shown, left to right, are Dick York, Rolls-Royce; Gordon Munro, Rover/Land Rover; Jo Eerdmans, Jaguar; John Panks, Rootes; Alan Bethell, Triumph; and John Dugdale, BAMA executive.

test cars, the BAMA members in New York authorized "British Press Trials" at Lime Rock Park in Connecticut, and I had my first experience there in May 1959.

BAMA Press Trials were also held in Toronto and at various tracks in California. The turnout was always excellent and the problems few. BAMA sponsored them for several years and then switched to "British Inter-Marque Trophy Day," a low-key autocross type of competition staged in places like the parking lot at Roosevelt Field shopping center on Long Island. Involving local sports car clubs and guests who were potential customers, the Inter-Marque Trophy Days were fun, but there is still nothing like a real racetrack!

For us in New York, the Trials were an enjoyable excursion, calling for a pleasant drive up to Lime Rock on Thursday evening, arriving at the Wake Robin Inn, The White Hart, or another hotel in time for dinner, and getting an early night in preparation for final car-cleaning Friday morning.

A drivers' meeting was called at 9 A.M., laying down rules of conduct—no passing in curves, no more than 70 miles per hour on the straight, pay attention to the flags—and then there was a rush for the cars. Each manufacturer had a parking area in the paddock and all keys were held by the manufacturer's representatives. To drive, the guest went first to a large board that held passes for each available car. A

Walter Cronkite gets a ticket! Al Burns of Triumph's sales department provided the photo op by putting on a London Bobby's uniform and writing up Mr. Cronkite during the British Press Trials. Cronkite was an avid sports car fan and raced a Lotus at the Lime Rock track.

driver got a pass and then went to a manufacturer's rep for the keys. The rep also explained the shift pattern and handling characteristics and asked the drivers to exercise caution. Around the track, flag stations were manned by members of the Sports Car Club of America, and they had more and more signaling to do as the day wore on.

The fastest and most sporting cars, like Jaguar, Triumph, MG, and Sunbeam, were commandeered first, with the slower-moving writers ending up in stately sedans like the Rover 105 and Humber Super Snipe. It was also possible to be chauffeured in grand style through the esses in a Rolls-Royce—the Rolls people couldn't quite get up the nerve to let the press drive the Roller themselves.

We all worked hard to persuade the most important auto and business writers to attend. There was lots of one-upmanship going on, with one company bringing a prototype or new model, another having a famous driver on hand, and others bringing in entertainment or other personalities. Thus, in 1959, Walter Cronkite was on hand with Triumph. Our staged stunt of the day was to pose Cronkite in a TR3, being handed a ticket by a London "Bobby"—actually Al Burns of our Sales Department in costume.

From 9 A.M. until lunch, activity on the track was heavy. However, fast driving can be tiring work and there was soon a long line for the buffet, set up under a large tent on the shady side of the paddock. We were concerned with alcohol, but it was socially impossible not to offer a drink with lunch in those days, so we compromised. Anyone planning to drive in the afternoon could have one beer. Guests who wanted a second one were relieved of their driving credential before they were served.

In the afternoon, the crowd of writers gradually thinned out, as people completed testing all of the more interesting machines or left early to make Friday evening commitments, knowing how heavy traffic would be. This left time for the manufacturers' people to drive each other's cars, which was fun and very useful in gaining hands-on knowledge of competing products. In the 1962 Lime Rock Trials, for example, I belted around in a Mini-Cooper, following Bob Burden, the advertising manager of British Motor Corp., who was driving our Triumph Sports Six convertible.

Wear and tear on the cars was expected. Replacing brake pads and shoes after the event was the norm, and new front tires were often required. We

First publicity photo taken of the TR3A. The model is Gretchen Dahm, who became quite closely associated with Triumph, working at auto shows several years in a row and posing for numerous advertising and PR shots. She also bought her own TR3 and became president of the Manhattan club, called the Triumph Motor and Petrol Society.

were aware that many members of the press had a heavy foot on the gas but, in 1960, I found out they had a heavy foot on the other pedals as well. On the drive home, the clutch pedal fell off due to a broken weld at the pivot point under the dash. Unwilling to break a date that evening, I drove 60 miles back to the garage in Manhattan with only one or two problems, such as stalling the car in the middle of Broadway in front of a bus!

1960 Begins With the Herald and Ends With Leyland

The main event of the 1960 model year for Standard-Triumph was the announcement of the Herald, a new economy car to be built in sedan, coupe, and convertible form. Styled by Michelotti, a rising new Italian designer, the Herald went against the modern trend by having a separate chassis, and

The cadets at West Point get to drive cars only for the final three months of their senior year. Every year there is a grand delivery day with all manufacturers delivering cars to the parade ground for their proud, uniformed new owners to pick up. In 1960 cadets took delivery of at least two truckloads of TR3s. The historic Thayer Hotel is in the background.

Standard-Triumph was good at display cars and this Herald coupe, sliced down the middle, served very well to demonstrate the car's features. The driver was relaxed in comfort but pity the poor girl stuffed into the tiny rear seat with her head jammed against the window!

The Herald coupe seemed an ideal, peppy little family sportster, with a back seat perfect for two kids and adequate for even two adults for short jaunts. Perhaps a forerunner of cars like the Mazda MX6 and Nissan 200SX of the 1990s, it did not come close to their performance and was dropped in favor of building more of the four-seater convertibles. What a great little car it would have been with the later 1,500-cc engine from the 1973 Spitfire!

was touted as having easily replaceable body sections. It was well ahead of its time in having safety features such as a collapsible steering column, and it had a unique front structure that lifted up to expose the engine and front suspension.

Standard-Triumph chief Alick Dick had pinned the future of the firm on increasing car sales volume and market share, and he was counting on the Herald

to create a major portion of the increase. Much of the huge cash nut from the Ferguson tractor transaction went into paying off the costs of developing the Herald and the necessary facilities to build it. The company took over the Royal Albert Hall in London for the announcement, putting on a full-scale theatrical production entitled "Greet The Day." Original music was written and recordings passed out to the

Left to right, Bill Greehey, Mike Cook, Francis Gentle, and Mike Jackling, the U.S. Herald Build Team, lined up with their do-it-yourself coupe kit. This shot was posed for the record after the road show was complete and before the car was turned over to Genser-Forman Distributors. For ease of assembly, the sun visors and mirror were a unit, the floors were attached to the firewall and rear body sections, etc.

guests. One rests in my files, a rather scratchy 33-rpm testimonial to corporate ambition.

The U.S. launch of the Herald would be my first experience with a major new model press announcement. My involvement was a dual one. In addition to working with Dave Allen and the public relations agency on the announcement, I was part of the Herald Build Team. This four-man group would be the star act at the introduction, actually assembling a Herald coupe on stage for the press' first look at the new car. The other team members were Bill Greehey of our Warranty Department, Francis Gentle from the Service Department, and Mike Jackling, who worked for our office manager but was also involved with sales. All three had joined the company within months of my arrival.

The Build Team concept had been a huge success at the UK press introduction and was repeated in every major world market for Triumph. Our team

performed at the press launch and at nine different distributor meetings and, as a sort of grande finale, built the car on national television during the NBC *Today Show* with Dave Garroway. I missed that performance, being away on the Triumph Rally of Europe. Alternate team member Frank Pinnington from the Sales Department filled in.

The U.S. launch was in Palm Springs, California, at the beginning of March. Boeing 707s were just going into service and only a few of our group had even seen one, let alone had a flight, when we boarded at Idlewild (now Kennedy) Airport.

We had nine Heralds for the press introduction, all flown in for the occasion. The Herald had been in production for nearly a year, and the modifications for the U.S. market were simple in 1960, consisting of specifying the luxury trim and putting the wheel on the left-hand side! Other than that the cars were the same worldwide. Yet, after months of planning, we

Hard at work on the assembly during the Palm Springs press meeting in the El Mirador Hotel ballroom. The hardtop is being fitted by two team members, while the grille and front valance are attached by the other two. Most assembly was with welded-on studs and wing nuts.

Job completed. Cook is at the wheel, Greehey, Gentle, and Jackling behind the car. Except for the obvious joint in the lower quarter panel, it looked like a regular Herald. In fact, instead of breaking it up for parts, Genser-Forman welded it all together and put it on the road as a company car for its field service rep!

had only those nine cars to cover a press group numbering more than 40. It was my first experience with the way British car companies met deadlines—sometimes at the last minute, sometimes not at all!

One Herald needed even more careful handling: it was a convertible, one of the very first made. A four-seater, to be promoted as a family sports car, it would be the key vehicle in the presentation. Those of us from the American company who would be transporting, breaking in, and otherwise handling the new cars, were warned to be extremely careful with our one drop-head.

Once again, in those days, there was no transporter to take the precious little group of Heralds the 90 miles to Palm Springs. Bright and early on Monday morning, we picked up the cars at the airport, made sure the tanks were full and set out at a careful 50 miles per hour. In addition to everything else, the cars had to be broken in. We had two days to do it before the Wednesday evening start of the meeting.

The drive was uneventful but one sedan had a noisy differential. Another had a persistent rattle. All of the cars felt tight and desperately needed road miles to make them ready to perform for the press. During the rest of Monday and all day Tuesday, we drove, accomplishing the break-in and laying out a test route as well. It was not uneventful. Francis Gentle nearly terminated his career with the company by trying a high-speed turn on a gravel road and sliding off the road into some rocks, damaging the

One of the press-launch Herald sedans, just off the American Airlines DC-6 freighter at Los Angeles airport. The shipping tag is still attached to the central bonnet handle. U.S. specs included the rubber-covered bumpers, which were optional on Heralds for the rest of the world.

The first Triumph Herald convertible in the United States. It arrived by plane direct from England so we had to do press and advertising photography on site at Palm Springs, hiring a local model. This powder blue car was featured in a number of advertising shots.

rear quarter of a Herald coupe. So there were now eight test cars.

After the day's driving, Gentle and others worked the cars over, tightening, checking, and tuning, but they had no facilities for major mechanical work. Thus, I was dispatched back to Cal Sales on Tuesday afternoon to see if their service shop could do anything with the noisy sedan differential. The visit gave me my first meeting with R. W. "Kas" Kastner, then Cal Sales service manager, but otherwise it did not solve the problem. The car needed a new ring and pinion, and the spare parts stock had not yet arrived. I drove back to Palm Springs with the differential still howling, and we were down to seven.

At the launch meeting, there was no stage. The guests faced the disassembled Herald coupe, laid out on the floor with a podium to one side. After an introduction by Dave Allen, John Warren, export sales director of Standard-Triumph, explained the positioning of the Herald as a world car and a replacement for all previous small sedans made by the company. The

last Standard economy cars had been built. From now on, it would be Triumph only.

When Alan Bethell went to the podium, our Build Team lined up behind the car at attention, ready for the signal. When it was given, the clock started and we went to work. While Alan covered the features, we assembled the car bit by bit. We attached body sections, installed seats and battery, and hooked up hydraulics and wires, while Alan discussed the independent suspension; the unique forward-opening hood, which revealed not only the engine but the front suspension; and safety items, like the crushable dash made of compressed fiber, and the collapsible steering column. Members of the audience craned their necks and even stood on chairs to see the process. When we closed the bonnet and stood back, Alan marched from the podium, entered the car, sat down, and twisted the key. The engine roared to life and he demonstrated the Herald's famous "lock" (turning circle) of 24 feet; by driving it in a circle in front of the press who applauded boisterously. We were a hit!

We sent the press away happy. There was virtually universal approval of the Heralds by the auto writers, who praised the handling and thought the performance peppy despite climbing to several thousand feet during the testing. Even the lone convertible survived, although not helped by John Warren having driven it on the test roads using every gear to the limit and every rpm the little twin-carb 948-cc engine could muster, while Bethell rode shotgun with a pained expression. Obviously the warnings given to the break-in crew didn't apply to the boss.

Back in New York, we all plunged into getting ready for the Herald's debut at the New York International Auto Show. Our Build Team still had several appearances to make, and I had the additional pressure of preparing to host the Triumph Rally of Europe in May. After that, in June, Triumphs would be displayed on the BAMA exhibit at the British Exhibition, a very prestigious trade show. On hand were Alick Dick, still the authoritative CEO full of plans for the future, and Air Marshal Lord Tedder, board chairman of Standard-Triumph.

Financial Disaster and a New Direction

In 1959, leaning heavily on the TR3, Triumph sales had been right on 23,000, a figure they would not match for another 15 years. In 1960, for the first time since the TR2 arrived, sales turned down, dropping to around 18,000. The Herald's performance was

The 1960 New York International Automobile Show was the first public display of the Herald in the United States. Based on the theme "A Year of Triumph," it had a Herald chassis on one side of the central turntable, a TR3 chassis on the other.

especially disappointing. Although it had features, room, and looks, it didn't catch the consumer's fancy the way the VW Beetle had. Part of the problem was the American compacts—Corvair, Falcon, and Valiant—which had more room and power for a price very close to the Herald's. Another part was a drop in enthusiasm for sports cars and imports in general.

Lord Tedder, Standard-Triumph chairman, did an extensive trip to the United States in 1960, stopping at Disney Studios, where he had a tour guided by Walt Disney himself. A couple of Heralds and a horse were thrown in for good measure. From left, Joe Smith, western service rep; Cornelius "Connie" Yeras, western sales rep; Disney; and Tedder. There's no mention of why they are holding rifles. In the background, some filming was going on.

Prince Philip, center, hands in pockets, officially opened the British Exhibition in New York in 1960. He visited the Triumph exhibit and spoke with Standard-Triumph Chairman Alick Dick, who is standing next to the Herald with hands behind his back. Whispering in Philip's ear is Lord Rootes, who may have been urging Philip to visit the Rootes display in the background. Others in the photo are Alan Bethell at far right and Dave Allen, second from left. Martin Tustin is behind Dick.

While the new-car market was soft in the United States that year, in England it became a disaster. Things beyond Standard-Triumph's control, such as new government restrictions on credit purchases, reduced the company's sales projections by 50 percent. Flush with cash from the sale of the tractor business in 1959, Standard-Triumph had gone on a buying spree, acquiring a small empire of supplier firms. The rest of the money had gone to help pay off things like the all-new, five-story assembly plant where the Herald was built. In just over a year, the tractor money was gone, and Alick Dick was actively looking for a partner or someone to buy the company.

Dick had spoken on occasion to Sir Henry Spurrier, head of Leyland, and his ace sales manager, Donald Stokes. Leyland was looking to expand beyond the world of trucks, buses, and other commercial vehicles, and Standard-Triumph, smallest of the UK independent manufacturers, looked good. Leyland made an offer late in 1960, which Standard-Triumph

Standard-Triumph flouted convention on the assembly line by sending many of its cars down the line sideways. This endless stream of Herald Coupes from 1960 is a good illustration. Later, a similar setup in the all-new assembly hall could mix various models with the same or similar chassis. Thus, Heralds, Spitfires, GT-6s, and Vitesses shared a single assembly line.

accepted. In April 1961, the company officially became part of Leyland Motor Corporation.

Looking back, it's amazing how little was made of the merger in the U.S. organization. Obviously, STMCI's financial difficulties were not part of everyday discussion around the U.S. offices, but the fact of the merger offer and acceptance was known. I was also vaguely aware that, without the Leyland takeover, Standard-Triumph would have been in serious trouble. But the situation seemed very far away from Broadway and 56th Street. This territorial separation from corporate affairs was encouraged by the factory. Even though we were selling most of the TR3s produced and making pots of money for the parent company, we sometimes felt we had no more status than some South Sea island distributor selling a dozen cars a year. It was frustrating, especially when better communication between New York and Coventry about specific market requirements was badly needed.

Like any corporation, we were unwilling to disseminate bad or confusing news. The Leyland merger—or purchase, as it actually was—was deemed to be hard to explain, so it was ignored in company publications. The *Triumph Dealer News* didn't mention the deal until June 1961, when the shareholders had approved the sale. They gave the story three paragraphs. The *TSOA Newsletter* never mentioned it.

At the end of the summer 1960, our big news was the buyout of Cal Sales by Standard-Triumph. After seven years of steadily increasing sales and handsome profits, the sudden downturn in 1960 and the uncertain outlook for future sales made Triumph's largest U.S. distributor pause and reflect. It wasn't alone. Standard-Triumph first discussed taking over distribution from Southeast Triumph Sales, Inc., operated by Wendell Jarrard. I asked Ed McCauley if Standard-Triumph was really interested in buying out distributors in a year when sales were dropping so fast. His response covered all the ground.

"The actual starting point (of the takeovers) was that business was so awful that the distributors just wanted to get out. Whether it was Alan Bethell's recommendation, and people in the UK decided with him that we should make it easier for the distributors to go, or whether it was simply decided that they should be taken out because they wanted to get out, I don't remember.

"It was a snowball thing. We started talking to Jarrard, and then to Cal Sales, and then to Houston, and I started bouncing around the country and lived out of a suitcase for six months! I'd be one place and get a call from Alan to say when I was done there could I go and see so-and-so. One time I went from Pensacola to Los Angeles to San Francisco to Portland, Oregon, and was gone three weeks. It was about July 1960 that we started talking

to distributors, and it was nine months to a year before we were done."

At the time, there had been juicy rumors going around the New York office that we were buying everything in sight from each distributor at highly inflated prices; not just cars and parts, but furnishings, etc. I asked Ed. "We just bought their assets. I don't remember any sweeteners or anything extra. There were no big payments based on future car sales. It's just that when we got into big arguments, we would give in more easily than they would. At Cal Sales, if someone had put an ashtray on the table I would have said, 'Five dollars!'"

All of the distributor takeovers were significant, but Cal Sales had been by far the largest contributor to Triumph's success. It had delivered more than 15,000 TR3s by the end of 1959. In a 1996 biography that appeared in *Automobile Quarterly*, Dorothy Deen said the timing of the buyout was good. She felt it was time for her to move on to different things. Standard-Triumph was interested in handling distribution in-house, and so the relationship was severed amicably.

Alan Bethell immediately announced formation of the Standard-Triumph Southeast and Western Zones. These used the same buildings and locations as the former distributors—we simply took over leases. New zones followed in rapid succession: Southwest, based in Houston; Central, based in Detroit; and Northeast, based in Boston. The Columbia Distributors territory was folded into Central. The only independent distributors left were Genser-Forman in the East, Midwest Triumph Distributors in Chicago, the distant Vail Motors in Hawaii, and Nu Car Sales in Anchorage, Alaska.

Alan Bethell's official statement on the distributor acquisitions said that it was "primarily designed to bring us closer to our dealers and to the buyers of our cars, and to broaden present sales and service facilities." This was more than empty PR. I asked Ed McCauley if he thought the company was better off with direct distribution.

"Not being in marketing, I have to take somebody else's word as to whether it was a good thing," he said. "I thought distributors were on average no better or worse than doing it yourself. We certainly believed that it was financially sensible not to try to support two organizations on the tiny profit margins available in those very inexpensive cars."

As 1960 ended, sales were still spiraling downward, and no experts were prepared to say when the spiral would turn up again. A Christmas note from Alan Bethell complimented all of us on our contributions to the company but enclosed no bonus. We were all concerned about the serious sales situation, but it was hard to believe it would be more than a momentary hiccup.

The Triumph TRS team cars, ready for the start at Le Mans in 1961. Larger than TR4s, with a longer wheelbase, they were powered by a twin overhead cam engine of 1,998 cc. They took the team prize and beat all other British cars, with the lead car finishing ninth. Competition Manager Ken Richardson is squatting on the pit rail talking to some journalists.

The TRS twin-cam engine, nick-named "Sabrina" for its prominent front cam covers. The engine used rare dual-choke SU carburetors and developed over 140 horsepower in mild tune.

Besides the Herald launch and the distributor takeovers, we had been excited about the good showing of the Triumph team cars in international rallies and at Le Mans. The Le Mans cars were the "TRS," an all-new car that used the twin-cam engine first installed in the "TR3S" in 1959. Once again, the company was careful to say that these were experimental cars, intended for racing, not production.

Actually, the twin-cam engine had originally been intended for production but was complicated and expensive to build. The horsepower advantage it offered did not outweigh the benefits of sticking with the tried and true overhead valve four. The body styling of the TRS was intriguing, giving hints of the TR4 to come and looking quite a bit like the TR6, which was nine years in the future.

The TRS engine is often referred to as "Sabrina," the name of a popular and sexy British singer/entertainer. In the twin-cam layout, the forward ends of the camshafts had prominent, domed covers. The Sabrina nickname was applied to these for the same reason that the round, pointed bumper guards on Cadillacs were named "Dagmars" after the well-endowed actress.

A news tidbit appeared at the bottom of the last column on the back page of *Triumph Dealer News* for December 1960. It said: "With the opening of the new Standard-Triumph factory at Malines, Belgium, Triumph became the first British automaker to establish its own plant within the European Common Market. Heralds in all three models are rolling off the assembly line to be sold in Belgium, the Netherlands and Luxembourg. This will later be followed by assembly of TR3s, a top-selling sports car in Belgium for some years."

The Belgian plant functioned for several years and even produced Spitfires for the U.S. market in the mid-1960s. Owners who have a car with a Belgian ID plate should not assume the car was purchased overseas. It may have been part of a regular shipment at a time when the Spitfire was very popular and in short supply.

The TR4 Arrives and Leyland Asserts Control

Although total sales were down, Triumph had moved up from eighth to sixth place in overall import car sales at the end of 1960. However, market pressures were increasing, and 1961 looked like a tough year.

Sales of imported cars had risen to a point where American unions were beginning to fear loss of jobs related to the car industry. Politicians took up the cause and, by 1961, "Buy American" was frequently seen on bumper stickers and in advertising. As sales dropped, British importers fought back with publicity campaigns to demonstrate the contribution the imported car industry was making to the American economy. Using figures developed by BAMA, in a widely circulated press release, Alan Bethell pointed out that Britain was buying over $152 million in U.S. goods while shipping only $73.8 million worth of products to this country. The list of purchases by British firms included many automotive items such as dies, tire-building machinery, stainless-steel sheets, painting equipment, and spark plugs. Bethell concluded that ". . . any plan to help the American economy by curtailing the import of British cars would probably have the reverse effect. It would reduce demand for American-made materials and components for cars."

Bethell said that imports were actually creating jobs in America and summed up by saying: "Few Americans will buy products from abroad that duplicate American products. Many cars from Britain, for example, have met needs not otherwise satisfied by United States manufacturers. British automotive sales in this country are mostly sports cars and economy cars of types not directly competitive with domestic vehicles."

Such PR efforts had some effect. The highly respected syndicated financial writer Sydney J. Harris devoted a column to the subject, in which he called the Buy American campaign silly.

As the new zone and regional offices struggled to get more Triumphs into showrooms, Guy Fox left the company, and Dave Allen took over the national sales responsibility. Named vice president, advertising and public relations, during 1960, he now became vice president, sales and advertising. With Sales Manager Bob Law and Dealer Development Manager John Tidwell, he began an exhausting series of dealer meetings, covering the country to discuss ways to sell more cars. Prices were sharply reduced—18 percent on the Herald sedan and 10 percent on the coupe. The convertible and the TR3 were counted on to sell at better profit margins. The latest TR3 ad asked "Is the TR3 the Stutz Bearcat of the Sixties?" and showed one couple in a TR3, another in a real Stutz, dressed in 1920s bearskin coats, etc. A huge showroom poster supported the campaign.

A showroom sales promotion kit featuring a full-sized photo cutout of Dave Garroway had been distributed during 1960. In 1961 the budget would no longer allow using Garroway or purchasing any TV time, but sales promotion efforts continued. A portfolio of Robert Riger drawings portraying a sports car rally appeared in *Sports Illustrated*, and copies of these sketches were made available as gifts for people who test drove a Triumph. The company also made a lot of publicity out of a cover on *Time* featuring "Big Jim" Moran, a Triumph dealer in Chicago, although it must be said that he made the cover based on his prowess as a Ford mega-dealer.

A boost was given to the Triumph performance image when a Herald coupe won the Tulip Rally in Holland overall. The TRS team, back at Le Mans, won the Organizer's Team Prize, and one finished ninth overall. The three TRs were among only 22 finishers out of a field of 55 and beat all other British entries. However, this was the last official race for these cars, and any thoughts of production were soon put to rest with the announcement of the TR4 that September.

Triumph made third place in overall import sales in the month of June, but the total was only 1,185 units. Even that was higher than average in a year that would see only a few more than 12,000 cars leave Triumph showrooms. That was a third less than in 1960 and just over half of the 1959 total. Lack of interest in overseas delivery sales, plus budget problems, forced the cancellation of the two planned 1961 Rallies of Europe. However, the company maintained top-quality sales and service facilities.

Dave Allen worked long hours and traveled constantly in the effort to keep sales up. I fell heir to much of the day-to-day contact with the advertising agency. My assistant left the company and we were fortunate to replace him, almost immediately, with

Fred Gamble. Hired to run the TSOA and edit the *Newsletter*, Fred was not a trained writer but an international racing driver. Fed up with the racing life, Fred was ready for an "inside" job.

By September 1961, we were deep into planning the announcement of the TR4. This car, based on a modified TR3 chassis, but with wider track and a completely new body, seemed to answer most of the criticisms of sports cars without taking away the benefits. It had roll-up windows, a snug, rain-proof top, effective interior ventilation, fresh-air heating, and a big trunk. However, it was still a two-seater with excellent performance from a larger four-cylinder engine; it had an all-synchromesh gearbox, disc brakes, and fine road-holding; and it still looked like a real sports car. We had high hopes for it.

Although Rootes had beaten us in the creature comforts department by announcing the plush little Sunbeam Alpine as a 1960, we were comfortably ahead of MG, who would not show the MGB until the spring of 1962. In addition, we were covering all bases by continuing to sell the TR3 as a "TR3B" with the larger engine and all-synchro gearbox of the TR4.

The Publicity Division of the ad agency, under Dick Fehr, had reserved the Shawnee Inn resort, owned by band leader Fred Waring, as the site for the press announcement of the TR4. Newspaper and magazine writers would be invited during the first week of October to see and drive the car and hear the company's marketing plans for 1962. Considering the state of the imported car market, it would be the most important product announcement in Standard-Triumph's U.S. history.

With my mind full of thoughts about the TR4 meeting, I arrived at the office on a Monday morning in late August to find that Leyland, after five months in control, had decided to run Standard-Triumph its way. Dave Allen was gone. Alan Bethell was gone. In various positions in New York and at the Zone offices, a total of 16 people had been let go. In England, before the year was out, close to 300 managerial staff would be fired. Alick Dick, kept on as CEO following the Leyland takeover, had been asked to resign on August 17, and virtually the entire Board of Directors was replaced at the same time. A long-time Leyland executive, Stanley Markland, was put in charge at Coventry.

At 1745 Broadway, the new president was Martin J. Tustin, who had been a Standard-Triumph executive since 1956. He was a member of the Board and general manager of Standard-Triumph International, the overseas sales operation. Prior to that, he had been at Ford since 1933, with a break to serve as a flight lieutenant during World War II. A familiar face to us at STMCI, he had been in our offices for several months with the title of "resident director." Ensconced in a corner office, Tustin had not taken a visible part in

day-to-day operations, but the number of meetings he held with Bethell, Allen, and others were an indication of his authority. In the Leyland restructuring, he lost his seat on the board but was made president and CEO for both the United States and Canada.

Joining Tustin as new vice president, sales and service, was D. Peter Snow, who had been national service manager. Another ex-RAF man, Peter's North American automotive career had started with Hambro Trading in Toronto, from which he was transferred to become general sales manager at Hambro Automotive, importer of MG, in New York. He then joined Nisonger Corporation, the U.S. importer of Smiths instruments and other products, and left there in 1956 to join Standard-Triumph.

Third man on the executive committee was Ed McCauley, who had been made treasurer after the departure of Richard Soppet earlier in 1961. Having started in 1954, Ed was the senior in terms of service and an excellent anchor for the volatile Tustin and sometimes impulsive Snow.

The advertising and public relations functions fell to me. In one of those mysterious corporate changes that are never really communicated to the employee, I was given a small office, and all advertising and PR matters were routed my way. I took on all normal relations with the advertising agency and the agency public relations staff and, after a few weeks' initial shock, started to act like an advertising manager. There was no change in title nor, for several months, even an increase in salary! Despite suggestions and requests, even after a small salary increase finally came about, my business card continued to read only "Advertising and Public Relations," lacking the magic word "Manager." After a couple of years, when I needed to order new cards, I told the printer to make it "Advertising Manager." He did, and that was it. I had promoted myself, but I could never figure out a way to give myself a raise as well!

The Leyland purchase of Standard-Triumph had been very low key and had not caused any waves. The abrupt change in North American management caused an uproar, with rumors flying that Standard-Triumph was losing so much money that it would be closed. Negative stories appeared in the press. Dealers besieged the zone offices and distributors with requests for assurance and more information. A statement was obviously needed and one was issued to all North American dealers by Sir Henry Spurrier, chairman of the Leyland Motors board. It was paraphrased in *Triumph Dealer News*, which wrote:

He emphasized the firm intention of Leyland to continue operating Standard-Triumph International as an automobile firm, and to continue plans for expansion in the near future.

What does this mean to the American Triumph dealer? It means a future with an assured supply of Triumph cars and parts, the sports cars most in demand in today's market. The TR4, soon to be in your showrooms, has a prospect list that includes every sports car owner and potential owner in your area.

The new models mean everything to you from more sales to better credit availability. Show the Spurrier statement to your bank or financing company manager. He may have read the bad publicity in the business magazines and be concerned. Point out that Standard-Triumph is in business to stay, and you are too.

Accompanying this article was a company statement that confidently predicted an upturn in Triumph sales due to the TR4 and a year of steady improvement in 1962. A market analysis by *Automotive News* was quoted, predicting a "firm and profitable year for imported cars in 1962." Dealers were also promised imminent delivery of literature and showroom kits for the new model, which had already been publicized extensively in the car magazines.

Quite amazingly, all of these predictions came true! In that panicky September, we were headed into the launch of a very important new Triumph, with an untested management team and a sales network full of misgivings about our corporate future. However, in just a few months, things would begin to turn around. The TR4 was a hit, the imported automobile market seemed to have bottomed out, our organization was functioning, and we were poised to move to new offices. After a rough start, the decade of the 1960s began to look less murky and more like the rosy future we all hoped for.

Before the year ended, Bob Tullius began to make himself felt on the Triumph scene. With his TR3 and a brand-new SCCA competition license, he won a couple of races in the latter part of the season. Armed with these results and a salesman's gift of gab (he sold Kodak Verifax machines for a living), he kept calling me and then my assistant, Fred Gamble, who took care of racing matters. Bob simply demanded that the company give him a TR4 to race in 1962 or else "he would beat the pants off your TR4s with my TR3." Finally, the telephone calls became so urgent and so long that we agreed to meet with Bob if he would come to New York. He arrived in midafternoon and made an impassioned, two-hour pitch. Partway through, we adjourned to the bar of the Fuji restaurant, next door on 56th Street

There, relaxed by Kirin beer, Fred and I had a wonderful time listening to Bob expound his theory of an amateur racing team with highly professional management and car preparation, all funded by corporate sponsors. It was a unique vision and Bob was a pioneer among competitors in taking a corporate marketing approach. None of us, including Tullius, knew it, but Group 44 was born that afternoon on a bar stool at the Fuji.

Of course, in the midst of corporate turmoil and without a meaningful budget for racing, we told him no, but there was no stopping Bob. After carrying out his threat and beating the TR4s in the early 1962 events, Bob got his TR4, and thus began another pleasurable and long-lasting relationship.

This is Bob Tullius, doing a victory lap at the old Marlboro, Maryland, racetrack in 1962. Yes, his first winning TR4 was black. This is how he looked only a few months after pitching Standard-Triumph for a car—a winner, just as he promised!

5

Cheaper Than Staying at Home! THE TRIUMPH RALLIES OF EUROPE, 1957–1962

"Get a Triumph TR3, tour Europe 28 days, for much less than it costs to stay home!" That's what the ad in *Road & Track* said and, between 1957 and 1962, a select group of U.S. Triumph enthusiasts confirmed it.

Fly the Atlantic on a charter with First Class service. Pick up a gleaming new TR at Mecca (the factory), and take a 3–4 week excursion through up to 10 European countries. Stay in top-class hotels; enjoy free sight-seeing tours and lavish cocktail parties. Never worry about luggage—there's a van. Never worry about the car—mechanics will check it and wash it every night!

The Triumph Rallies of Europe were a dream vacation. The Triumph Sports Owners Association (TSOA) members who went on them could not believe their good fortune, as they paraded in and out of cities like Rome and Paris in a line of 30 or more multicolored Triumphs. Originally conceived by Dave Thomas, a Triumph dealer in Long Beach, California, as a tour for a small group of friends, the Rally concept was endorsed by Dorothy Deen, head of Cal Sales, the western Triumph distributor. It was further polished and refined by Alan Bethell, then president of Standard-Triumph in New York. After a meeting with Dave Thomas, Alan called British Overseas Airways Corporation (BOAC, now British Airways) and confirmed that chartering a plane for the trip was possible.

What Alan had in mind, of course, was not just the sale of a large group of TRs. Any profits were going to be eaten up by the organizing and extra service that would be required to take care of the groups of visiting Americans. It was the

publicity he wanted, both in the media and word-of-mouth. Once he had a plan and a budget, he went straight to John Warren, S-T sales director, and got an immediate go-ahead.

The first event was offered to TSOA members immediately with departure at the end of April 1957. To sign up, the member went to a Triumph dealer, ordered a TR3 for delivery in Coventry, and specified that it was for the Rally. Not a TSOA member? Sign up on the spot! Payment for the airfare, hotel, and tour portion was sent direct to the TSOA in New York. Total cost, including TR3, was about $3,000 with another $1,000 for a second person.

Originator Dave Thomas sold so many Rally cars that he was, for a time, the world's largest Triumph sports car dealer. With wife, Nell, he went on four Rallies, including Number 1 and the final TR4 event.

Party All the Way

It was party all the way on the 1957 trip, beginning with a reception at the Park Lane Hotel in New York and continuing overnight on BOAC's newest, the propjet Bristol Britannia. After 11 hours in the air, time-lagged Rallyists stepped off the plane to find their cars lined up in neat rows on the tarmac at London's Heathrow Airport and the British press there in force.

Photos and interviews done and luggage stowed, the tour set off for its first party on British soil, at the Bull Inn, Gerrard's Cross, Buckinghamshire, en route to Coventry. Later groups went to the Royal Automobile Club country club outside London. RAC membership was one of the "perks" of the Rallies, and the

TRs parked outside the cathedral in Pisa with the famous tower leaning in the background. *Mike Cook*

badge was on every TR, to receive the salutes of RAC's uniformed road patrolmen.

Tanked up (take that to mean what you will), the Rally group left the Bull Inn and went to Stratford for two nights at the Shakespeare Hotel. No worries about luggage—the tag system worked out by Poly Travel, which contracted for the land arrangements, worked perfectly, even when there was more than one hotel.

The cars got their first routine check and wash. The next day, one hapless driver bounced his TR3 off a lorry within the factory grounds, but found it waiting for him, good as new, after lunch. The day finished with a long afternoon drive to Dover, where the White Cliffs Hotel welcomed the sleepy Americans. They found a tray of refreshments in their rooms with a note from the management: "To decide to visit the White Cliffs and risk it, surely deserves a sherry and biscuit."

A ferry trip to Boulogne awaited them the next morning. At the French port, the entire Rally group was diverted to a special parking area and taken into a Customs building, where they were surprised to find the Mayor of Boulogne and other officials presiding over a welcoming champagne reception. It was the first of many such parties on the trip.

The Classic Rally Route and Some Variations

The 1957 Rallyists entered Austria from the north, via Germany and went to Vienna, looped through Switzerland back to France, and thence to England. Later trips followed the "Classic" Rally route, which included France, Monaco, Italy, Austria, Switzerland, Germany, and England, with variations that included Spain and Yugoslavia.

The TR4 Rallyists in 1962 crossed from Dover to Ostend, visited Brussels, Weisbaden,

High in the Italian Alps at Cortina d'Ampezzo, site of the 1956 Winter Olympic Games. Tops went up here as the Rally Group took the pass into Austria. *Mike Cook*

and Berchtesgaden; and then passed through Salzburg and Vienna into Yugoslavia. They reversed the Classic tour by entering Italy at Trieste, and stopping at Venice before Rome.

Only 12 cars toured Scandinavia in 1959, landing at Prestwick and sampling Scotland before ferrying overnight to Denmark. Sweden, Germany, Holland, Belgium, and France were on the menu before the return to England. All TSOA Rallies had a preoccupation with food, and the Thomases brought back a 4-foot-long sandwich menu from Oskar Davidsen's in Denmark.

Rally plate, TSOA badge, and RAC badge stand in front of one of the many souvenirs given Triumph Rallyists. It's a silk head scarf printed with images of current Standard and Triumph products, a Herald to the left, TR3 at right. *Mike Cook*

In 1958 a "Rally East" was followed by "Rally West," subjecting Europe's tourist attractions to two groups of American sports car nuts only one week apart!

Looking for Lunch and Other Adventures

After its champagne welcome, the 1957 TSOA group set out for Brussels, but soon found it was approaching lunchtime. One item not included in the rally price was lunch, so a stop for bread, cheese, wine, fruit, etc., was in order for most Rallyists, and *Le Picnique* became a Rally tradition. Nonpicnickers sampled local restaurants along the way, often brightening a town square with colorful TRs.

Lunch handled, the Rallyists forgot break-in rules and raced down the Jabbeke highway for an overnight in Brussels. The next day was entirely in Germany, ending in Darmstadt. The restored town center was surrounded by blocks of wreckage, reminders of World War II air raids, then only 12 years in the past. The late David Hebb, writing for *Sports Car*, described the postwar Hotel Zur Taube as having hallways "as uncluttered as the passageways in a battleship." By a variety of routes, Rallyists toured Germany the next day, most arriving very late at Regensburg, from whence they journeyed to Austria.

After the rally, a number of newspapers, prompted by Triumph PR man Paul Thurston, ran stories on Rallyists. Articles appeared in *Sports Car*, the magazine of the Sports Car Club of America, and several car magazines. The Rallies, and the desired publicity, were off to a good start.

The Southern California group leaving Los Angeles for New York and the very first TSOA Rally of Europe, in 1957. At left, in the white coat, is Dorothy Deen, then head of Triumph's western distributor, Cal Sales. To her left, in bow tie, is Dave Thomas, Long Beach Triumph dealer who conceived the Rally idea. Next to Dave is his wife, Nell. Note the landau irons on the TR3 hardtop. *Plain English Archive*

In 1958, Dave Allen, Standard-Triumph's advertising manager, hosted Rally West, which departed from Los Angeles, changed planes in New York, and landed in London, encompassing two nights without sleep. The visitors were welcomed outside Brighton by the mayor, riding in a 1906 Standard, and paraded into town.

Sadly, one couple was hospitalized in Brighton, victims of a head-on with a bus. This may have been due to fatigue and driving on the unfamiliar left, but it calls up a fact about the Rally groups. In general, the participants were not sports car enthusiasts when they signed up, and many were people in their 50s and 60s trying a sports car for the first time. Most were looking for an interesting vacation and found the idea of driving a sports car through Europe exciting.

In 1957, 1958, and 1959 the Triumph Rallyists landed at Heathrow Airport and stepped off the plane directly into their new TRs. This is the arrival scene in 1957, with pipers playing away and reporters covering this new method of selling British cars. *Plain English Archive*

The 1958 group went cross-Channel to Dieppe the following morning and on through France toward Spain, stopping at Rouen and trying the Le Mans 24-hour circuit on the way. A 1957 participant had overturned his TR doing a hot lap in the wrong direction but, while he continued the trip as a temporary passenger, his car was returned to Coventry, rebuilt, and delivered to him several days later!

In 1958 the Rallies went to Spain and were treated to a sumptuous reception by the Triumph distributor in Madrid—Don Carlos, Marques de Salamanca. En route to Valencia the next morning, one young driver shot off a turn and wrapped his TR3 around a pole. He and his passenger went to the hospital, while the Spanish police arrested Dave Allen. As the official representative, he was, in the eyes of the Spanish law, responsible for the accident, and he cooled his heels in a cell until the Marques could get him out. Spain under Franco was an oppressive place, contrary to the spirit of the Rallies, and the parade of TRs did not return.

Monte Carlo was always a stop on the Classic route and members of the 1958 group

Many Rallyists were surprised they couldn't order automatic transmission. Every Rally, on the first day, shattered the peaceful English country silence with the noise of clashing gears as Buick-trained Americans fought their gearboxes. Accidents were few but after 1959, Standard-Triumph stopped delivering cars to tired drivers at Heathrow and, instead, had them waiting at the first night stop.

First stop for refreshments on the 1957 Rally was the Bull Hotel. Most tops were down, despite the usual English weather. *Plain English Archive*

TRs wait for the Dover-Ostend ferry in 1962. The second car in line is a TR3B. *Plain English Archive*

could look down from their hotel windows and watch practice for the Grand Prix. Our 1960 tour encountered the Standard-Triumph Tulip Rally team of Herald coupes, madly flashing lights as they roared past. It was still the heyday of international rally competition for Triumph, and a TR3 won its class in the Tulip that year.

Rallyists found the very formal Monte Carlo Casino a place where James Bond would feel right at home, but money was just as easy to lose there as in Las Vegas.

From Beer and Sausage to Wine and Cheese

The 1960 Rally missed touring a wine cellar, but those who went on earlier events treasured memories of wandering through labyrinthine cellars, pausing at intervals to taste another delicious vintage. The 1957 group went to Clos de Vougeot Castle, whose owner, M. Jean Morin,

also owned a TR. Nell Thomas remembers walking "miles underground" and estimates 29 glasses of wine before lunch! Despite being served cheese puffs between tastings "to absorb the alcohol," the Americans needed to be guided to lunch, but they somehow managed to drive on to Dijon for the night.

After adventures in Italy, Austria, and Switzerland—with a crash in each country (none with serious injury)—the long, straight roads of France were frustrating to drive on a Sunday. The longest day's travel we had, 400 miles, was done at France's weekend 70-mile per hour speed limit. However, the run into Paris from the rendezvous point made up for it. Led by dashing gendarmes on motorcycles, the Rallyists paraded into the city at high speed. The gendarmes cleared the way but didn't linger for stragglers. Usually, the Triumphs were safely parked in a guarded area on the Right Bank,

Ready to leave Rome, 1960. The devious exit route confused everyone and most didn't see each other until dinnertime. *Plain English Archive*

The Triumph service engineers hit a hay cart in Switzerland in the Vanguard Luxury Six. They were not injured. The wagon was stocked with spare parts, but few were needed. *Plain English Archive*

within sight of the Eiffel Tower. In 1959 they were left on the outskirts because of civil unrest in France. Dave Allen remembers gendarmes posted on street corners carrying machine guns.

In two days, Paris was covered, from the Eiffel Tower to the Sacre Coeur, from the Champs Elysee to the Louvre, to the famous Flea Market. Some visited the Folies Bergere, all went to the Crazy Horse, and all were hung over as the line of Triumphs streamed along the highway in the direction of Calais. There, they boarded the TSS *Halladale* and sailed toward the White Cliffs.

Which Was the Freebee?

Normally the usual "arrangements" prevailed at British customs. However, in 1960, Rally Number 2 participants arrived in London to find that, if they hadn't packed everything in the car, they had nothing to wear that night and a five-hour round trip to Dover by bus the following morning. Customs had decided to go by the book, and refused to clear the souvenir-crammed baggage without the owners present.

On Rally Number 1, my tour, the baggage van missed the ferry! The apprentices had enjoyed Paris nightlife even more than the Americans and only one, the slow one, was competent to drive the fatigued Atlas van. Although they caught the next boat, I had to leave one of the service engineers in Dover to watch out for them and make my first trip into London, unguided, at rush hour. Full of pride at managing

Dave Allen posed this shot in Italy, 1959. *Plain English Archive*

to find the place, I entered the Picadilly Hotel to discover the entire Rally group assembled in the lobby. The "arrangements" had failed again.

The hotel had overbooked and, with the Covent Garden Flower Show on, could not accommodate everyone or find alternative hotels. I had to convene a meeting in a side room, call for volunteers, and split up three couples

into male and female groups to share two rooms. Other volunteers took rooms without bath, and two couples shared a suite. It was only for the first night, but it certainly depressed everyone's spirits.

After a day crammed with sightseeing and shopping in London, our last TR trip was London to Coventry on the new MI Motorway. Previous Rallies had to use the old A45 on which, as Paul Thurston wrote in *Road & Track*, "British drivers . . . insist on passing a 15-mile per hour model with a 16-mile per hour model whenever a clear patch of road appears."

MI had no speed limit in 1960, and I found the TR would do about 112 in OD fourth. Foot on the floor, I was irritated to be passed by a 3.8 Jaguar doing at least 125. A few miles later, my good humor was restored as I passed the 3.8 parked off to the side issuing clouds of steam.

Lunch was one last party, followed by individual and group photos and removing the last personal belongings from the cars before they were taken away to be shipped back to the States. Some people returned to London by train. The rest of us took a prosaic bus trip back to London with a stop for tea under an ancient oak at the Duke of Bedford's estate.

The following morning, the bus to take us to Heathrow was late. There was a frantic scramble to put everyone in taxis with me handing out 10-pound notes so the Rallyists wouldn't have to

End of the line for a new TR3 and some happy Rallyists in 1960. The assembly line was not automated. Bodies moved along the overhead track by manpower! *Plain English Archive*

The 1962 tour watches a shiny TR4 leave the line, followed by a TR3B, still in production at that time. Claude Isaac, the Poly Travel courier who accompanied most Rallies, is third from the left. *Plain English Archive*

pay their own cab fare. Why the rush? There was plenty of time to make the plane but no one wanted to miss BOAC's farewell party.

So it ended as it began. The Americans floated aboard the plane in a haze of champagne and British goodwill, clutching one last bag of souvenirs and Duty Free. They also carried prints of the photos from the day before, silk scarves, Wedgewood cigarette boxes, and other bric-a-brac from Standard-Triumph, BP, and BOAC.

Beginning in 1957 with six countries and 2,500 miles in two weeks, by 1960 the basic Rally hit 10 countries and covered over 3,000 miles. Articles in *Sports Illustrated*, *Road & Track*, and *Esquire* made the publicity goal a fact, and Triumph dealers benefited greatly. Of the Rally group, although some went back, with relief, to their automatic Roadmasters, many bought Triumphs again and became lifelong enthusiasts.

Dave Allen reports that a 1959 Rallyist, just before boarding the plane for the trip back, said to a Triumph executive, "I can't figure out whether the Triumph people gave me the car or gave me the trip . . . because I sure feel like I got one of them for free!"

And that's exactly how it was.

3,500 mls. around Europe in 24 days in a TRIUMPH TR3.

Author and car at the end of the 1960 TSOA Rally. Dent came from rear-ending an Opel in downtown Innsbruck. Photos were always taken when the cars were turned in, developed overnight, and given to the Rallyists before they boarded their flight back to the United States. *Plain English Archive*

CHAPTER

6

A Promising Decade Ends with a Question

"The new edition will mean a fuller way of life for many who have adored the TR3 . . . if I liked real comfort in a sports car and didn't have a guilt complex about indulging myself, I'd be first in line."
Cameron Dewar, *The Boston Herald*

TR4 to the Fore!

As the pale sunlight of an early October afternoon highlighted the gold showing on the trees bordering Route 46 in western New Jersey, I pushed the Vanguard Luxury Six Estate as fast as I dared. I was en route to Fred Waring's Shawnee Inn on the Delaware, where the 1962 Triumph TR4 would be unveiled to the American press. My passengers were all automotive journalists who alternated between looking at the speedometer and lighting yet another cigarette as we zipped along the old two-lane highway. Interstate 80 is the preferred route to Pennsylvania now but, in 1961, it was just another dotted line on President Eisenhower's emerging national limited access highway system.

Fred Waring's Shawnee Inn was the site of the U.S. TR4 press introduction. Al Burns, left, and Peter Snow of Standard-Triumph help a pair of journalists get used to the new car. *Plain English Archive*

66

Bob Fendell of the old *New York World Telegram*, and Bill Hackman of the *Rochester Democrat and Chronicle*, prepare to go off on their test run. Larry Vinci of Triumph stands at right, and Dick Fehr, PR man from Triumph's ad agency, is behind the car. Group at rear includes Cameron Dewar of the *Boston Herald*, left, and the author, next to him. *Plain English Archive*

Heartfelt sports car enthusiasm of the sort expressed by Cameron Dewar, in the quote above, was commonplace in 1961. In succeeding years the guests at automotive press gatherings became ever more cynical about engineering, manufacturing, management, country of origin, or whatever they could find to demean by excess criticism. Not then. Triumph's reputation was excellent and our cars well known for performance and durability. The press expected our new car to be a world-beater, and if there were some items to be criticized, the criticism would be in the context of an overall positive review. You had a chance to prove yourself.

New car announcements are perennially at resorts, usually where a good golf course is available for press relaxation after an arduous test-drive. Fred Waring's Shawnee Inn was beautiful, close to New York, and nearly empty in early October. Waring and his orchestra, the Pennsylvanians, were famous throughout the country for their popular dance music.

There was no question that the reporters would be impressed. The TR4 appeared to take care of virtually every objection ever raised about the TR3 and

other British two-seaters in terms of comfort and utility. Most compelling to several writers was the fresh-air heating/ventilation system, a real departure from British tradition. The styling was modern and far less utilitarian than the TR3. Triumph also had a nation-wide network of dealers, several parts warehouses, and a strong sales and service training program.

It was just over a month since Martin Tustin became president, but he did not speak to the press in generalities. He began by describing the four-year TR4 development program, and then said that while the TR4 was all-new it was based on eight years of successful TR production, so the customer could be confident there would be "no bugs to iron out." He discussed Triumph's all-new, fully automated assembly plant, which had computer stock control and television monitoring of body selection and the assembly process.

He also predicted 1962 sales 50 percent higher than 1961. "Ninety percent of our sports car production goes to the U.S. and Canadian markets, so you can understand why a thorough survey of American preferences counted most heavily in the development of the

One of the first U.S. publicity photos of the TR4, showing a white roadster and a red car with white hardtop, an option that was soon dropped. Fred Gamble posed with the cars. *Plain English Archive*

TR4," Tustin said. In fact, Tustin knew as much as anyone in the company about the new sports car, having been the ramrod behind the program in the UK, working with designer Michelotti and the engineering staff.

After a technical rundown by Peter Snow, the journalists hopped into the test cars and tackled the narrow, twisting roads of eastern Pennsylvania. The reaction was uniformly positive, ranging up to ecstatic. Most enthusiastic was one unskilled editor who put a TR4 in the ditch while trying to demonstrate his driving ability. He raved about the car while enduring the glares of the Triumph service people who had to fix the body damage and the PR people who had to figure out how to accommodate reporters at the next meeting with one less car. We crossed our fingers against accidents like this, because the factory had managed to send only around eight preproduction press cars to cover a series of meetings nationwide. For one reason or another, there were never enough cars for any press launch.

My return trip to New York was in a rented Chevrolet station wagon that roared noisily but slowly away from stoplights and leaned steeply in turns, but my journalist passengers weren't noticing. They were all discussing the competitive merits of the new TR4 against MG, Jaguar, Alfa Romeo, Volvo, etc. Comments from some of their stories indicated how important they considered the new TR to be in the sports car market.

Bob Fendell of the *New York World Telegram and Sun* praised the "increased precision of the steering" and predicted, "Mother is likely to preempt it for going to the shopping center." The *Newark Sunday News* auto editor, Bob Taylor, liked the heating/ventilation system, calling it "a new British sports car with man-sized

ventilation." Josh Hogue of the *San Francisco Chronicle* was delighted with "this handsome companion to the TR3 . . . here is a car that should go places." It was clear that if we could get enough of the new car, Tustin's sales prediction would come true.

The Shawnee meeting was followed by press gatherings in Aurora, Illinois, and Monterey, California, and then by a string of zone-distributor-dealer meetings in all territories. Still breaking in to my new job, I stayed on the East Coast, but attended the Genser-Forman Triumph Distributors dealer meeting at the Hotel Astor on Times Square, the Boston dealer gathering, and several auto shows. The dealer reaction was unanimously enthusiastic. For once, a car company had produced exactly what the dealer body had asked for. All that remained was to build enough to fill the orders.

The TR4 had an advantage over the TR3 in terms of production. Although the first few were built on the old TR3 assembly line, by December TR4s were rolling off a modern, 200-yard-long line in the new plant that also housed Herald production. By February 1962, the *Triumph Dealer News* reported that 4,000 had been built, the majority of which were shipped to the United States. With the imported car market back on an upward trend, we needed all the cars we could get. Our national advertising included the usual auto and business magazines, plus a deal with National Airlines to place TR4 advertising on one million of the airline's ticket envelopes.

Major Triumph Moves—Across Manhattan and on to the Racetrack

Late in 1961, a questionnaire was mailed to Triumph racing competitors, asking their comments on expenses, Triumph's potential as a race winner, and what they felt was needed to help make the car more competitive. The meeting with Bob Tullius had helped create this new interest in racing. It was also inspired by racing enthusiasts Fred Gamble and Kas Kastner, Triumph's Western Zone service manager, who had been 1959 West Coast Class E Champion in a TR3.

The response from Triumph competitors came down to this: What they needed was options, money, and information. The company set out to deliver all three. The few factory competition options, such as alternate rear axle ratios, heavy-duty shocks, and sway bars, were made more widely available through dealers. Special items, such as racing camshafts and alloy wheels, were sourced in the United States. and marketed through the Triumph parts system. Technical information was available by phone from both Gamble and Kastner, and the first of a series of Triumph Competition Preparation Handbooks was published, covering modifications to both TR3 and TR4.

The money requirement was the most difficult. The Sports Car Club of America affected a "pure amateur" attitude and specifically ruled against sponsorship of its members' racing activities or any suggestion of prize money. Gamble and Kastner came up with the concept of "expense money." The top three Triumph finishers in SCCA national category races would be eligible for payments to cover "expenses for the next race." No mention was made of their previous finishing position, so it wasn't prize money. No decal appeared on the car, so it wasn't sponsorship. The payments—$100 for first, $50 for second, $25 for third—seem small, but they could make a tremendous difference in the 1962 racing world. At that time, a set of racing tires cost $100 or less, and decent motel rooms could be had for $15 a night.

Not only did the gimmick work, it was eventually copied by virtually every competing importer. When SCCA finally saw the light and began to allow sponsorship, the Triumph Competition Support Program continued to be the most effective way to keep the most TRs on the racetrack. It remained part of the marketing program for the next two decades, until there were no new Triumphs left to sell.

With sales surging and Triumph's new parent, the Leyland Motor Corporation, wanting to show some class, the Triumph offices "above the store" at Broadway and 56th Street, had to go. Ed McCauley, a veteran of three moves prior to the Broadway location, once again sought new space in a more upscale part of town. We ended up still on the corner of 56th Street but four blocks across town on the seventh floor at 575 Madison Avenue. Sharing our floor was a new market research company, Daniel Yankelovich & Associates, which would become one of the

biggest. Also in the building was the fledgling *Madison Avenue Magazine.*

My hastily erected cubicle in the old offices had 5-foot-high glass-topped partitions and was referred to as a "piggy pen" by our statistician, Maureen Dunne. On Madison Avenue, I had a real office, small, to be sure, and farthest in distance from Tustin's luxury corner, but facing Madison Avenue with a big window. Looking down, I could see traffic that still moved two ways on Madison, as it still did on Broadway.

There was a lot to see in the new neighborhood. In our exploring, we soon found that it was possible to sneak into the IBM cafeteria in their building across the street and enjoy a good meal at a reasonable price! However, to do it, you had to be wearing a white shirt and dark suit—IBM allowed no colored or striped shirts and no sports jackets.

The move brought us closer to our advertising and PR agency. Doherty Clifford Steers & Shenfield was a block west and five blocks down at 530 Fifth Avenue. Most of the advertising media we used—*Time, Newsweek,* etc.—were only a short cab ride away. In those days, when the two-martini lunch was a standard with advertising sales people, we were in the heart of the uptown lunch district, and it became easy to see why so many people in advertising management were a bit soft around the belt-line.

We were also in the center of the imported car industry in Manhattan. Only a block away, on Park Avenue and 56th, was the striking Mercedes-Benz showroom, designed by Frank Lloyd Wright. Across Park was Hoffman's New York showroom, full of exotica but concentrating on BMW and Fiat. Hoffman had been bought out of both the Mercedes and Jaguar distributorships, but he was now the national distributor for BMW and had the Eastern territory for Fiat.

Rootes Motors displayed Hillmans, Humbers, Singers, and Sunbeams at Park and 60th Street, while further south, at Park and 46th, Charles Kreisler's dealership featured Rootes cars, MGs, and others by BMC, and oddities like the tiny Berkeley sports cars, powered by motorcycle engines. Jaguar was just around the corner on 57th Street. We all felt as though we had finally arrived in a real New York location. The 575 Madison offices would be our base for four exciting years.

I have mentioned the Park Sheraton Hotel as a favorite lunch spot for Triumph people working on Broadway. We had one last blast there in late fall. Invitations arrived in the mail, at home, to all of the Standard-Triumph New York employees, from Alan Bethell. To celebrate his new job as national sales manager for American Motors, he was hosting a cocktail party at the Park Sheraton immediately after working hours. All of us who could, nearly everyone, attended and spent a couple of hours once again enjoying Alan's wit and personality. Others who had exited the company, like Dave Allen, now advertising sales manager for *Sports Cars Illustrated* magazine, were also there. It was a classic gesture from Alan, who went on to become vice president, marketing, for AMC. Alan later left AMC to join Eaton, Yale and Towne, from which he retired as one of four division managers and a board member. After several years as a consultant he retired again, to live aboard his sailboat, alternating between the port of Mentor-On-The-Lake outside Cleveland and "somewhere in the Caribbean."

The Manhattan showroom stayed in the 1745 Broadway building for several more years, until British Leyland Motors bought out the Genser-Forman distributorship. A 45-story apartment building now occupies the site of the last Triumph showroom in Manhattan.

The TR4 was on the auto show circuit. After being shown at Boston, San Francisco, Detroit, and Los Angeles, it now debuted at the big shows—Chicago, at the beginning of February, and the April International Automobile Show in New York, still the premiere showcase for imported cars in North America. There, we surprised the press by not resting on the TR4 as our only new item for 1962.

Although all dealers approved the TR4, many had liked the TR3's lower price and traditional sports car appearance, and wanted both cars to sell. Triumph fulfilled their dreams with the TR3B, announced at the New York Show. The TR3B was a great way to use up overstock of TR3 components and keep a low-base-price sports car for one more year. TR3Bs theoretically all had the TR4's 2,138-cc engine and all-synchromesh gearbox, but some were built with the 1,991-cc TR3 engine.

In all the excitement over the TR4, the company had not forgotten the Herald, which was also prominently displayed at New York. Early in 1962, we began phasing in the Herald 1200, actually 1,147-cc, replacing the old 948-cc unit. This added enough extra torque to make the car much more competitive in traffic and should have given it more strength in the marketplace. However, the Herald never lived up to its potential, leaving most of us wondering why. The Herald convertible, with smart style and four seats, was a real bargain in open cars and had no competition anywhere near it in price.

Part of the reason the Herald did not sell better lay in the company's heavy emphasis on the TR series. Although we spent adequate amounts to promote the 1200, we did not really get behind it. Sports cars made more money and were easier to sell, so the Herald was always an afterthought. The dealers followed the same philosophy.

A First Racing Championship for Tullius and Triumph

In the spring of 1962, Bob Tullius ran his first official race for Triumph. No, he didn't have a sponsorship contract, the company name didn't appear on his driving suit . . . even the "Group 44" team name was still in the future and the TR4 he drove was Powder Blue. Nevertheless, Standard-Triumph had provided the car for him to race. In

Selling the first Herald 1200s was a difficult tast because there was virtually no visible external difference from the original 948-cc cars. This early 1200 can be distinguished only by the lack of a handle in the center of the bonnet. Later 1200s had U.S.-made full wheel covers and different grilles.

One of the first TR4 ads with the UN building as background. New Yorkers will notice that the ugly Con Edison power plant has been airbrushed out of the skyline to the left. Bob Halmi shot the photo at about 6:15 A.M., just as dawn was breaking, and the light on the car was provided by a pair of kerosene lanterns. Although put together by the U.S. agency, this is a Canadian ad for *Maclean's* magazine and has Canadian prices and logo. The U.S. logo had Triumph in both wings. *Plain English Archive*

The TR-4 wins its first medal...standing still

Triumph's new sports car won its first gold medal only six days after its introduction. A first prize for coachwork at the famous Earls Court Show, London. The TR-4 took this one standing still. No wonder. For $2875*, the TR-4 gives you comfortable bucket seats, thick carpets, an ingenious and completely rain-proof top, new roll-up windows...and a collection of luxuries you used to find only in marques costing thousands more. How will the TR-4 do on the road? Let's put it this way: its companion, the TR-3, won more silverware from rallies than any other car in history. The TR-4 has even more power—plus higher torque, wider track, more sensitive steering, synchromesh on all forward speeds. So stand back! As for fun: the TR-4's responses are much brighter and quicker than any ordinary car's possibly could

be. And it's quite a feeling when you're going 40, to know you could be doing 110. Get a test drive at any of the Triumph dealers in every province. And also be sure to try the Triumph Herald economy car ($2200*).

The Triumph Herald Convertible—the economy car by sports-car engineers.
*P.O.E. East, Standard-Triumph (Canada) Ltd., 1463 Eglinton Ave. West, Toronto 10, Ont.

STANDARD TRIUMPH
(CANADA) LIMITED
VANCOUVER · TORONTO · MONTREAL

Ad No. 5465
Maclean's—May 19, 1962
This advertisement prepared by Doherty, Clifford, Steers & Shenfield, Inc.

doing so, one story came to a conclusion and another began.

After his meeting with Fred Gamble and me in New York late in 1961, Tullius called at least once a week, promoting his driving talents, encouraging me to think of sports car racing as an advertising medium, and virtually demanding that the company send him a TR4. In the early part of the 1962 racing season, he made good his threat to use his TR3 to beat the TR4s that were just emerging onto the race tracks of the United States. He won some early season events in the South, then came to New York to press his case in person. Bob spent most of an April afternoon reiterating his racing marketing concept. He was persuasive, even more so because he was proving he had the talent to win races in our cars. However, we were still in the financial depths created by the very poor sales year in 1961. The TR4 and the improved Herald had not arrived until late in the year, and sales figures were just beginning to get back to what we considered normal. I would have liked to have recommended that we hand a new TR4 to Bob, but in a choice between backing an unknown race driver in amateur racing and buying another page ad in *Time*, the magazine would win every time. After another two-hour meeting, Bob left. This time we were too busy even to go for a beer!

The next day, Martin Tustin called me into his office. This was his way. Where Bethell would pop out of his office and go to see people to discuss the day's problems, Tustin usually stayed at his desk, summoning subordinates as required. This day he blew a cloud of cigar smoke at me and said, "I've decided to let Tullius have a car! See that he gets one from the next shipment. There's a race in three weeks! Now get on with it."

The abrupt dismissal left me no time to ask questions. I went back to my office and ordered the car—any color, any shipment, just get it! Later, on my way to lunch, as I passed through the reception room, Shirley Massey Rubin, for years the Triumph and, later, British Leyland, receptionist/phone operator, said something about "Bob Tullius hanging around." When I demanded to know what she was talking about, she told me that Bob had not left the building after his meeting with Fred and me. He had waited in the reception room until Tustin came out to go home, buttonholed him, and gave him an abbreviated version of the marketing pitch. Tustin, either impressed or anxious to get home, gave in.

Bob Tullius on the starting line at Marlboro, Maryland, in the black racer rebuilt from two wrecks. Bearded Ed Diehl leans on the roll bar. This may have been the car's first outing. Bruce Kellner, in the dark driving suit behind the door of the other TR4, was a very successful competitor in TR3s and TR4s and gave Tullius lots of competition. *Plain English Archive*

A month later, several of us traveled to Lime Rock Park to see Bob's first race in the TR4. He and his close friend and mechanic, Ed Diehl, had been able to do only a few things to the car—principally transfer components from Bob's race-ready TR3. The car was not quite ready and, about three-quarters of the way through the race, Bob could not hold off Arch McNeill in a Morgan, and had to be content with second place.

Two weeks later, practicing for the race at Lake Garnett, Kansas, Bob swerved to avoid exhaust system parts falling off a Porsche and lost control. The blue TR4 hit one tree going forward, spun around, backed across the track and hit another tree, burying the tree into the rear of the car almost up to the gas tank. Bob was unconscious after the first hit and very lucky—the second tree prevented the car from going straight into the lake.

Basically unhurt, Bob dragged the wreck back to Ed Diehl's Virginia shop and the two considered their next move. Triumph would buy some parts, but there was no question of another new car. Since "parts" in this case would have to include a new chassis and most of the body, some important decisions had to be made. Ed had access to another TR4 wreck that had a reparable frame. They inspected both cars, nodded to each other and got to work. A few weeks later, a new race car emerged from Ed's shop. If Powder Blue hadn't been bad enough, this one was black!

There was a good reason for the color. The body of the car was so rough from the hasty repairs and switching of components from one wreck to another that only a coat of rather dull black paint could hide most of the flaws. Bob once admitted that the frame had required such strenuous effort to straighten it that the wheelbase had come out nearly 89 inches, an inch too long! Maybe the stretch brought good luck, because Bob fulfilled his promise—he won the 1962 SCCA Class E Production championship by a convincing 24-point margin. It was the last time he ever raced a Triumph in any color other than white!

Our new emphasis on racing had to have the blessing of the parent company, which had recently been ambivalent about competition. Following the Le Mans team win with the TRS in 1961, the Standard-Triumph Competitions Department had been abruptly closed, and all personnel, including the stalwart Ken Richardson, had been dismissed or reassigned. Lack of budget was the reason, with the new Leyland management determined to balance the books. However, the closure was brief. Once the TR4 had been launched, the marketing potential of rallying and racing the new car appeared to be good. A new competitions group was set up, concentrating at first on European rallies where the TR3 had been so successful.

Our major problem in gaining approval for a racing program was to educate the UK management about

This is the Sports Six convertible in a U.S. publicity photo. The revised bonnet, four headlights, and chrome bumpers instead of rubber were the main features that distinguished it from the Herald. The car also had larger tires and chrome trim rings on the wheels. No, the body fits weren't that bad—the door is open! *Plain English Archive*

North American sports car racing. European competition followed a strict displacement class system that usually allowed only the most exotic cars to be race winners. Under the SCCA performance class system, which grouped cars according to their overall performance potential, a good-handling car with a small engine might be placed in the same class as a car with a much larger engine but crude suspension. The TR4, with its good power and average handling, was a potential champion and the UK people gave the thumbs up.

Triumph's First Six for the United States

The abrupt changes in the U.S. market's appetite for imported cars had most of us in the business pretty dizzy. In 1960 came the plunge, 1961 had been flat, but 1962 saw a return to the volumes of 1959. Our new sports car was selling very well, but the Herald was lagging and the TR3B, which some dealers had thought was an essential base-price sports car, wasn't moving. The Herald 1200 was still deemed not to have enough power, and neither the TR3B nor the TR4 had a back seat. The factory's latest four-seater exercise looked like a promising addition to the range. It was the Vitesse Convertible, which we renamed the Sports Six.

The Herald chassis had looked extremely adaptable from the beginning, and all sorts of possible sports models were considered for it. Once the company's latest engine, a 1,600-cc six, was ready, the engineers dropped one into a Herald chassis and found it a very happy combination. They launched both sedan and convertible versions but the United States took only the soft-top. A new hood with four headlights distinguished the car, but the important change was the jump in horsepower. The Herald 1200 had 43 horses, the Vitesse 1600 had 70!

The first Sports Six announcements said that automatic transmission would be optional. In fact, there was one car with automatic which members of our U.S. management group test drove for several days each. In those days, when the words "sports car" and "automatic" were mutually exclusive in the minds of enthusiasts, we reacted the same way we had to an automatic TR3 a couple of years before. We were unanimous that the automatic took all the character (and a significant amount of performance) away from the car, and the option was dropped.

With the new engine and other items like walnut interior trim and wider tires, the car cost Standard-Triumph so much to build that a premium price was necessary. The Sports Six was initially priced at $2,499. The Herald convertible was only $1,949. Although it had many features that improved it over the Herald, most potential customers only noticed two extra cylinders and two more headlights and felt they weren't worth $500. They were right. The Sports Six was truly overpriced and did not sell, even though the list price had been dropped by $150 to $2,349 by the end of 1962. It should have been a good lesson—that the potential customer will evaluate a product based on his own perception, not what the manufacturer tells him about the product. In the case of the Sports Six, it did not help that our management didn't have enough confidence in the car to budget for adequate advertising.

The 1200 arrived unheralded. *Triumph Dealer News* did not announce the new Herald until a statement to dealers from Martin Tustin in April 1962, despite the fact that it was an important event beginning in late 1961. I have no recollection of any special press meetings or announcements—the car just arrived. Although it replaced the original Herald, there was hardly a ripple, despite the significant improvements. *Road & Track*, for example, felt that the extra displacement turned the Herald into an all-purpose car instead of one that was only useful around town at low speeds. Tustin urged dealers to get customers to drive the car as proof. Part of the reason for the delayed promotion of the 1200 may have been that we had excess stock of 948s to sell first! However, once again, the marketing budget was being reserved primarily for the sports cars.

The same message from Tustin touted the TR3B at $2,365, certainly a very good deal. He made it sound as though the TR3 and TR4 would coexist in showrooms for years to come, but also said, "Other new models are now in development for early release

in the U.S. market." Those of us inside the company knew that the next new model would be the Spitfire, and that the TR3B would have only a brief sales life.

Poor marketing support for sedans was also a habit at British Motor Corporation, where management concentrated on MG and Austin-Healey. Jaguar did it better. Knowing its customer group was older, Jaguar divided its budget more equitably and sold large numbers of sporty and luxury sedans alongside its XKs and E-types. One Jaguar advantage, of course, was that its sedans had power and comfort that equaled and often bettered the domestic American products. In the small sedan field, only the VW Beetle was engineered for continuous high-speed highway driving, and it certainly was the best built of the imports.

Only a month after the move to Madison Avenue, I left my office late on a Friday and met Peter Snow on the way out. "See you Monday," I said. "Not here, you won't!" he responded gruffly. He had been abruptly let go for reasons never made clear to me, leaving the company temporarily without a sales or service executive.

The sales chair at Standard-Triumph was a bit of a hot seat. Two sales managers had been hired to work under Guy Fox but lasted only about a year each. Neither left much of an impression, other than the famous "garlic memo" authored by the second manager, two pages about personal hygiene distributed to the people manning the stand at the New York Auto Show. After Guy left, Dave Allen had his short tenure as sales and advertising vice president, and then the sales portion of the title passed to Peter. He was succeeded by Richard Roth, who had been the first Standard-Triumph Central Zone manager in Detroit. A veteran of many years at Chrysler Corporation, Dick Roth had joined Triumph in September 1960 as a regional manager and became zone manager in January 1961. He brought a lot of automotive sales smarts to the job and could be excused for once exhorting a meeting of Triumph regional managers to "Get out and sell those Plymouths!"

The final Triumph Rally of Europe was held in August 1962 over a slightly different route than the "Classic" rally. The company continued to push delivery overseas with special brochures and programs to educate dealer salespeople on how to sell cars to be picked up at the factory. At the New York dealership on Broadway, Tim Craxton, an ex-RAF pilot, led the country in overseas delivery sales. With a bushy Air Force mustache and always dressed in blue blazer and flannels, he sounded more like a travel agent than a car salesman, touting the joys of touring Britain and Europe by car.

Pursuing Exposure and Greater Owner Involvement

Tie-ins with famous personalities and products formed an important part of our advertising and marketing program. For example, we worked with

Marjorie Graner, frequently seen as a photo model and auto show spokesperson for Triumph in the 1960s, posed in this shot in front of the old International Hotel at Idlewild (JFK) Airport. A copy of one of her modeling contracts survives, showing that she was paid $40 for the shoot, reasonable money in 1963. *Plain English Archive*

Petrocelli, maker of fashions for men, on a contest in which 140 Petrocelli clothing dealers won trips to the Cannes Film Festival. On the return flight, a drawing was held and the winner received a new TR4. Showroom displays were featured in the Petrocelli stores and in Triumph showrooms. Actor Cesar Romero, Petrocelli's "Ambassador to Fashion," appeared in magazine ads with a TR4.

There were movie and TV appearances, too. *Triumph Dealer News* often published lists of TV shows in which TRs appeared. Some of these, such as *Saints*

Unloading TR4s went by the same old method—sling it out of the hold onto the dock, and hope it didn't hit anything on the way! A major damage problem came from brain fade on the part of the crane operators, who occasionally dropped cars on the dock instead of gently setting them down. These "accidents" were known to increase at times of labor unrest at the ports. Both TR3s and TR4s were shipped with windshield and bumpers removed to avoid damage. *Plain English Archive*

An original TR4 hardtop model with the steel roof removed and the "Surrey Top" fitted. This roof preceded the Porsche Targa top by about five years, but Triumph never really promoted it, perhaps because it was "either-or." The steel roof panel could not be carried in the car, and the Surrey Top was considered flimsy. *Plain English Archive*

and Sinners and *Fair Exchange,* are long forgotten. But *Alfred Hitchock* and *Leave It to Beaver* are still with us.

In that first year of the Triumph Racing Program, the company actively promoted racing as a means for dealers to advertise performance. The first competition preparation book for TR3 and TR4 had been released, and dealers were urged to get the book and offer racing preparation services to their customers. What a difference from today, when dealers are criticized for racing involvement and told to let the factory team handle it.

Along the same line, Triumph sponsored service clinics for customers, in which company and dealer technicians demonstrated proper service and repair techniques, diagnosed problems with customer cars, and answered questions on technical subjects. A program entitled "TRX," for Triumph Express Service, was offered through dealers nationwide. Basically a quick service and tune-up plan, it was intended to

help dealers compete with gas stations and independent repair shops.

Dealers were also urged to get as many customers as possible to join the Triumph Sports Owners Association. In those days of the enthusiast import buyer, the raceability of a sports car was genuinely important to its success in the showroom. Whatever car you bought was usually your only, do-everything vehicle. It was an era of one-car ownership, with only 18.1 percent of American households owning more than one car. There were "domestic buyers" and "import buyers," but few who crossed over. According to a Triumph buyer survey, 58 percent of new Triumph buyers traded in an import. Product loyalty was strong—40 percent of TR4 buyers traded in a TR2 or TR3.

I have mentioned that the Herald assembly presentation in 1960 was done on the NBC *Today Show,* hosted then by Dave Garroway. Garroway also did a couple of TV commercials for the Herald.

Unfortunately, no copies survive, but they were shot in Central Park on the cobbled arrival area in front of the Tavern On The Green. Garroway walked around the car, giving a pitch, then climbed in and drove away. It was a great spot for the little Triumph, because Garroway was well over 6 feet and had no trouble getting into the car. He received a Herald convertible for doing the commercials.

Spitfire Joins the Battle

Triumph had released three new models in a year, the TR4, the Herald 1200, and the Sports Six. Sales were returning to pre-1960 totals. Bob Tullius won an SCCA racing championship in Class E Production in the TR4. The company was third in imported car sales. We probably could have coasted for a while, but Donald Stokes, Stanley Markland, and Harry Webster were conspiring to keep the U.S.

team perspiring. In Britain, the new Triumph Spitfire 4 sports car was exhibited in the London Motor Show, and we accelerated toward a new market segment with our latest two-seater.

The company immediately denied that the use of "4" meant that there would later be a six-cylinder version but it never satisfactorily explained the use of the 4. It has been revealed since that the company had a Spitfire 6 in mind, but decided to retain the very profitable TR series, which led, eventually, to the outstanding TR6. The only official Spitfire-based six-cylinder model was the GT-6 fastback coupe.

Although the public often referred to imported two-seaters as "little sports cars," the industry did not really think of the TR4, MGB, and others as "little." Really small sports cars were few. The Fiat 1100 was one, and there were a few others, like the tiny two-cylinder Gogomobil, already gone from the market in

The Spitfire in its debut at the 1962 London Motor Show. The nonstandard hood ornament is Janine Gray, a model and film starlet who appeared in Disney's *The Lives of Thomasina* and others. Note that the right-hand-drive UK Spitfire has plain wheels and tires, while the left-hand-drive export model on the turntable has whitewalls and trim rings.
Plain English Archive

The show-prepared Spitfire 4 chassis. Based on the Herald frame, it did not need outriggers to support the body, because the Spitfire bodyshell was a rigid, monocoque unit. There's plenty of frontal frame strength. This early engine has the remote radiator header tank that was soon deleted. *Plain English Archive*

1962. The first real bargain-priced sports car was the Austin-Healey Sprite, launched by British Motor Corporation in 1958 at $1,795. Restyled in 1961, the Sprite spawned an MG Midget version for 1962. The "Spridgets" were the only cars in the market segment, but they sold well and Triumph management wanted to take a bite out of their market.

The Spitfire was far beyond the British Motor Corporation twins, bigger outside and inside, with equivalent or better performance, and amenities like roll-up windows. We had to be careful in describing it, because the cockpit was as roomy as our "big" sports car, the TR4. The Spitfire actually used the TR4 windshield, raked a bit more steeply. The styling, by Michelotti, was very smart and up-to-date, making the TR4 look slightly dowdy. The features and size of the Spitfire meant that it could not be priced down to meet the competition directly, making our sales job tricky. The Spitfire had much better accommodations for luggage and people than the Midget or Sprite, but was still

more affordable than a TR4. And, it was a perfect step up from a Herald convertible into a real sports car.

It was tough to keep a new model secret in those days, when British companies automatically launched new sports cars at Paris, London, or Geneva, despite the fact that the major market for the new cars was the United States. The Spitfire had its initial moment of glory in October at Earls Court in London, and we could only plead with publications over here to hold back their main coverage of the car until it arrived in the United States in January 1963.

Dealing with advance publicity on the Spitfire was less of a problem than it might have been, because it did not replace any existing model. It also sounded great that European countries had ordered $5.5 million worth of Spitfires, and that Martin Tustin had committed the U.S. company to more than double that—10,000 Spitfires worth $12.5 million!

It was normal at auto shows, in those days, for companies to announce huge export orders for new models, vying with each other to get the biggest numbers in the next day's papers. Tustin's order for 10,000 Spitfires created a flurry of excitement in the business press and few bothered to inquire if the factory could actually build that many for one market. It couldn't! After all, it had taken Standard-Triumph 10 years to build 100,000 TR sports cars, a birthday also celebrated at the London Motor Show.

In the spring of 1962, after Tustin announced a huge order for TR4s at the New York Auto Show, I was in his office spouting statistics about readership in an effort to get a budget increase for one of the magazines we advertised in. In his gruff fashion, he said: "Where'd you get those statistics?" I shot back: "From the same place you got the dollar figure for the TR4 order!"

Tustin chomped on his cigar, looked hard at me, and said "People have lost their jobs for remarks like that!" Then he laughed and we proceeded with the meeting. However, I had been firmly admonished to behave myself and I knew it. Tustin was known to be hard on people, especially if he thought they were slacking off. One morning, asking his secretary to get people together for a sales meeting, he discovered one individual had called in sick. He got him on the phone and said, "I'm postponing the sales meeting for one hour. Be here if you want to keep your job!" The man got out of bed and made the meeting.

Martin Tustin disdained driving a TR4 and bought a Buick Skylark convertible with the aluminum V-8 engine and four-speed transmission. Headed home, he never failed to accelerate full bore down 56th Street toward Park Avenue, smoke from the exhausts competing with fumes from his cigar. How different from Alan Bethell, who would only drive company products, importing a Vanguard Sportsman Sedan so he would have a family car.

Production capacity or not, Tustin closed out 1962 with a prediction of 30,000 Triumph sales in 1963 with a value of $60 million. He said: "The formula for continued success in the U.S. auto market

U.S. Spitfire Number 1 by the water in New Jersey. Early Spitfire tops were the "button-on" type, similar to the TR3. The top fabric came completely off and was stowed separately from the top frame. However, installation was simple, and the top was reasonably free from leaks and drafts. *Plain English Archive*

will always contain the same basic ingredients: Good products, good dealers, good service and parts, and a continued effort to maintain high standards." Unfortunately, the British auto industry only partly kept his pledge. Dealer quality and availability of service and parts were steadily improved but, by the 1970s, the industry had failed miserably to keep up in product quality and had fallen far behind in making cars to keep up with market trends.

None of these future matters were in my mind that November as I rode with a colleague in a TR4 from midtown out to the air freight terminal at Idlewild airport (now JFK) on an important mission. Awaiting me at the terminal was the first Spitfire to arrive in the United States, and I had the pleasant task of driving it back to Manhattan for a round of advertising and publicity photography.

I bounced the car off the pallet it had traveled on, attached the New York transporter plates, and set out along the Van Wyck Expressway, heading for Queens Boulevard and the 59th Street Bridge. Not having attended the London Motor Show or visited the factory recently, I had never seen a Spitfire and had to learn the car as I drove along. Bright red and very attractive, the car drew a lot of stares as I moved along the dingy boulevard under gray November overcast. It was peppy and obviously quicker than a Herald 1200. Later that day we found how much quicker when the service garage tightened up the carburetor linkage and it started running on both carburetors! I can't help thinking of the arrival of a similar new model today. Shrouded in a cover or crated, it would be off-loaded in secret into a closed van and transported to another secret location, away from all prying eyes.

After only 11 months on the job, during which he contributed significantly to Triumph's new U.S. racing program, Fred Gamble left. He joined Goodyear and opened up Europe for Goodyear racing tires. His replacement was Alan Holmes, who continued to edit the *TSOA Newsletter* and, as an accomplished photographer, made its racing coverage more exciting.

Donald Stokes, the dynamic head of Leyland Motors, our parent company, spent a day in our offices reviewing the company's accomplishments. Listening to my presentation of our advertising program, he was quite relaxed, but I was conscious of his personal force. His later performance, as head of British Leyland, was questionable, but there was no denying that he had reached his position at Leyland through his brilliance in product marketing.

The last few weeks of 1962 were frantic as we planned the launch of the Spitfire for January. Normally, we would have had a fall press preview, similar to the one for the TR4 a year earlier, but there were no cars available. Standard-Triumph had rushed a few cars to completion for the London Motor Show but now was struggling to get assembly up and running. A January on-sale date had been announced, but our press meeting could not be held until January, and the public would not see the car officially until the Chicago Automobile Show in February. Our one available car had to be used for company and distributor personnel briefings as well as for photos. The agency PR and advertising people were already fighting over photography time. We would rely on UK-printed literature at first.

Winter was coming down fast. An unexpected strike by dockworkers hit the East Coast ports. Our press meeting was slated for Fort Lauderdale, right after New Years, and was followed by other meetings in Chicago and Detroit plus the Chicago Auto Show, all dates that could not be changed. The only solution was to fly additional cars from California, where there was no strike. Another red Spitfire and a white one were flown to Florida just in time to be readied for the Southeastern dealer preview at the Dupont Plaza Hotel in Miami. The Western Zone people had grabbed the first two cars off the boat and nobody had noticed that the white one was a Hawaii car with no heater.

The arrival of the Spitfire 4 in 1963 gave the company the broader range of models the dealers needed. Nineteen sixty-two sales had been strong and 1963 promised to be better. We were looking forward to running a team of TR4s in the 12 Hours of Sebring, in March. Although we didn't know it, there would also be a new president of Standard-Triumph in the United States, and Chris Andrews' management style would have a significant effect on our daily operations.

The Italia. A Triumph for Ferrari Lovers.

The world agreed that the TR3 was a great little sports car. There was also general agreement that it was not a prime example of automotive styling. Many buyers, reveling in the handling and the power, longed to see something flashier in the driveway than the blunt little TR.

In 1959 the Italian Triumph importer, a Commendatore Ruffino, decided to fulfill these wishes by creating his own Triumph model, the Italia. He talked to Michelotti about styling and arranged for the cars to be built by Vignale of Turin. He then persuaded Standard-Triumph to supply him with rolling chassis, a very unusual accomplishment.

Michelotti, who had already designed the Herald and built the ZOOM prototype, which would lead to the TR4, did something quite different for Ruffino. His concept was a two-seater fixed-head coupe on the TR3 chassis, with bodywork resembling some of the Vignale and Farina styling efforts for Ferrari. The finished design was harmonious, with a very long hood, graceful fender arches, a Ferrari-like oval air intake with an egg-crate grille, and stout chrome bumpers. One or two touches would appear three years later on the TR4.

About 300 Italias were built. After initial interest, sales were slow. The car cost about $4,000 in Italy, when a TR3 was $2,695 in the United States. Some were purchased by Americans on overseas delivery, but most went to British or European buyers.

Sometime in 1961, Triumph changed importers in Italy and found that, in the stock they bought back from Ruffino, were a number of left-hand-drive Italias. Not about to miss a sale Triumph shipped a batch to Standard-Triumph in New York. I believe there were about 35 of them. They arrived

Show this quickly to most people and they'll pick it to be a 1950s Ferrari. This is the Triumph Italia and there is no way to identify it as a TR3 unless you look at it from either end. The narrow track gives it away. The Michelotti signature emblem is visible low down on the front fender and the Vignale flags are on the rear fender.

during 1962, showing the effects of lengthy outside storage, including faded paint and musty interiors. All were on TR3A chassis, at a time when TR3Bs and TR4s were in Triumph showrooms.

We priced them at around $3,695, cleaned them up, and got them out to dealers. Several were used by company people for a few weeks, and I drove one home one evening. It felt like a TR3 with sound-deadening, rode a little better, and was comfortable with its custom seats. Unfortunately, most of them suffered from gas fumes in the cockpit, due to improper tank venting.

Italias occasionally turn up at shows. The big problem is obtaining body parts and glass—especially the windshield, which was custom-made for the car. The design is so attractive it makes one wonder why the factory didn't consider building them as a regular production model, but there was no room in the budget or the model program for such an upscale TR. Too bad.

CHAPTER

7

The Spitfire Takes Wing

Airplanes and Battleships

The idea of a British performance sports car named Spitfire seems quite logical and, when the car was introduced, there was no explanation in the press kit or any comment in the press. As the car's popularity increased, however, a story gradually appeared. The following version is told in the 1973 Triumph 50th Anniversary press kit.

While Air Marshal Lord Tedder was still chairman of Standard-Triumph, he was approached by the head of Vickers/Supermarine, maker of the Spitfire aircraft and builder of the Viscount airliner, first to have turboprops. He asked Tedder if he would allow the name Vanguard, still in use on Standard sedans, to be used on Vickers' next passenger aircraft. Tedder agreed, on condition that Standard-Triumph be allowed to use the Spitfire name on its new, low-cost sports car.

It makes a good story, especially if you remember that the name "Vanguard" was borrowed, with British government permission, from the World War II battleship, HMS *Vanguard*. Apocryphal or not, the association with the airplane was used immediately by *Car and Driver* magazine on its cover to accompany the road test of the new sports car. Standard-Triumph later borrowed the art for a poster and used it in many ways, including on business cards, available through the company for dealership personnel. As discussed later, when the last Spitfire was announced, the famous aircraft was once again brought into play.

A large group from New York flew to Miami in mid-January for the Southeastern dealer meeting introducing the Spitfire. The dealers raved about the new car. They knew value when they saw it, and they also knew that the MG Midget/Austin-Healey Sprite twins were no match for it. It would be an important model for Triumph, because Leyland's key goal for Standard-Triumph was greater penetration of the U.S. market. The Herald, introduced just in time to meet the first American "compacts" head-on, had not done the job. It was up to the Spitfire and it was already making a big impression. Here's a quote from *Time* magazine:

"For 1963, Standard's goal in the United States is to overtake second-place Renault, whose U.S. sales last year (1962) slipped from 44,000 to about 34,000. This week, the car that Standard-Triumph is betting on to do the trick will make its debut at the Miami Auto Show. It is the Spitfire, a racy, two-seater sports car which is a little brother to the TR4, last year's best-selling imported sports car in the U.S. Priced at $2,199 in the Eastern U.S., the Spitfire has roll-up windows, road-clinging four-wheel independent suspension and speeds up to 92 miles per hour on a 63-horsepower engine. If anything can accelerate Standard-Triumph's progress, the Spitfire ought to be it."

The *Time* magazine piece mentioned the Miami Auto Show as the Spitfire's kickoff point. Actually, it was a brief sneak preview. The Miami show opened on the day between the dealer gathering and the press introduction. A brilliant red Spitfire was slipped into the Dinner Key Auditorium just before the press preview and placed on the exhibit turntable. No press release had been mailed, and no literature or press material was available at the stand. But people knew this was something special. It was new and different, and they liked it. And, if they had any questions about price, specifications, etc., there was a crowd of Triumph people on hand to answer them!

The word went out quickly, but show visitors arriving the next day were disappointed to find a Herald convertible occupying the spot where the Spitfire had accepted applause the night before. As

Car and Driver magazine featured two Spitfires on the cover of their February 1963 issue when the new sports Triumph came out. This similar photo was used for several purposes, including dealer business cards and a poster. The aircraft, AB 910, was owned and had been restored by Vickers, original builder of the Spitfires. At the time, it was the oldest known example in flying condition. The Spitfire car/Spitfire airplane idea stuck and was used 10 years later for the Spitfire 1500.

quietly as it had been slipped into the Show, the red Spitfire was spirited away, north to the Lago Mar Hotel in Fort Lauderdale, where the automotive press awaited.

Showing a new car to the public the day before the introductory press meeting isn't the usual technique, but it provided valuable market research data. The very positive reaction to the car added fire to the speeches given to both press and dealers from then on. Tustin, with his predictions of 10,000 Spitfire sales in the United States, was calling for anything up to a 60 percent increase in Triumph sales in 1963.

Discussing what he called the "look-ahead factor," he said, "With the Spitfire, we now offer the widest range of vehicles since Triumph entered the U.S. market in 1955. Each Triumph car fills a demand in a certain area of buyer interest and at a realistic price. This product mix comes from advance planning, all the way from the drawing board to the showroom."

Our U.S. executive group was augmented at the presentation by John Warren, UK sales director, and George Turnbull, production director. More than 40 newspaper and magazine writers from the eastern half of the country listened to the presentation on what the Spitfire had to offer, looked under the hood, and spent time behind the wheel. There were only three cars to drive, barely enough. Most frustrating was that, within sight from the hotel's upper floors, a cargo ship with 112 Spitfires in its hold was docked at strikebound Port Everglades. It didn't matter. The short time in the driver seat was enough to convince the auto writers than Triumph had another winner.

The cars' next stop was Detroit. Incredibly, we had determined that it would be best if the two cars were *driven* from Chicago to Detroit to meet a demanding time schedule for the Michigan dealer meeting. Al Burns, who had been the company rep at the Chicago show, along with a determined field sales rep from Detroit, climbed into the two Spitfires at the end of the Chicago show and aimed for Detroit in a snowstorm! The temperature was about 20 degrees Fahrenheit, the wind was howling, and our heaterless Hawaii car did not even have a defroster blower. Fortunately, the red car's heater worked fine. The two intrepid drivers switched cars at half-hour intervals to keep from freezing and made it to Detroit in time.

With the dock strike over, Spitfires came flooding in. By April, when it appeared at the new York International Auto show, it had contributed materially to Triumph's 30 percent year-to-date sales increase. Tustin was predicting 30,000 sales for the year, which was really going out on a limb. We soon found out why he was so fearless.

We were already doing promotional bits with the Spitfire. One of the first was the National College Queen contest, an event in which queens were elected from entries in 12 regions around the country and the finalists brought to New York, where they participated in several tests of knowledge, poise, and skill. Triumph dealers all over the country were designated as local headquarters for receiving entries in the contest, and a kit sent to each dealer contained entry forms, posters, etc.

Although strictly a commercial enterprise, run as their livelihood by a husband-and-wife team, Bob and Fran Ensworth, the contest drew a collection of absolutely lovely young women whose big test, as far as we were concerned, was a Spitfire "Safe Driving Event," held at the old reliable Tavern On The Green. All they had to do was navigate a sort of gymkhana course set up with traffic cones in the parking lot and be judged on their driving prowess.

There was a last-minute snag. One candidate had no driver's license and had not driven a car enough for it to be fair to subject her to the same testing as the others. So, the test was held and all the contestants made it through, but it did not count for points. We got our publicity, and the nondriver became the National College Queen!

Be Sure to Call Him Chris!

By New York Show time, Easter week 1963, we had all been informed that Martin Tustin was leaving New York to return to England. In fact, he was leaving the company altogether to become managing director of the Dowty group, a British manufacturer of hydraulic systems. Tustin, our president for less than two years, had been in charge through some very exciting times—the launch of four new models and the return to health of the imported automobile industry in the United States. He had assembled a new executive team at our company, including Sales Manager Richard Roth, Service Manager Bob Thompson, and National Parts Manager Andy Woods, late of British Motor Corporation/Hambro. Active in industry affairs, Tustin had served as vice president of the British Automobile Manufacturers Association.

Martin posed happily with our models at the Auto Show and departed a few weeks later. He stayed with Dowty for some time and then moved on. Sadly, he died of cancer in the mid-1970s, still a relatively young man.

A major feature of our 1963 New York show exhibit, other than the new Spitfire, was a TR4 hardtop, wearing racing numbers. We had entered a team of three TR4s in the 1963 12 Hours of Sebring in March and came away with First, Second, and Fourth in Class, as well as the best finish of any team. It was the first international race for a TR4; first international competition for Kas Kastner, who prepared the cars in the zone service shop in Gardena; and first for me as a team manager.

Christopher E. Andrews returned to New York at the end of April. As you may remember, he had established the first Standard-Triumph U.S. headquarters on Park Avenue in 1954. Recalled to England in six months after he had the organization running, he had not even visited since. His face lit up with delight when he saw our humming offices with 10 times the number of people he had hired nine years before, and more than 20 times the sales!

Chris (he hated Christopher) had been born in Kettering in the English Midlands and raised in Coventry. Before World War II he worked at Daimler, now part of Jaguar, and returned there for a year after

A bird's-eye view of the second floor exhibits at the 1963 International Automobile Show in New York. The Rootes exhibit is in the background with various Hillman and Sunbeam models. A Jaguar E-type and Mark 2 sedan can be seen at right rear. British Motor Corporation, with MG, Austin, etc., was directly to the right, out of sight in this shot. A SAAB appears to be lurking at the far left rear, but the identity of the three fastback coupes next to Rootes is a mystery.

military service before taking a job as assistant shipping manager at Standard-Motor Company. He progressed into the export area, and had been concerned with vehicle distribution in all parts of the world, so he was ready to run an overseas subsidiary.

Chris Andrews seldom dictated to his executive staff. He liked things to be done in a way he approved, but he was open to new ideas and approaches. At a luncheon immediately after his arrival, he brought all the department heads together and promised to use our knowledge and ideas to the full in running the company. He made one request of us—that we be loyal to him. This was not a problem. From the beginning Chris was the U.S. chief executive and carried that banner into all corporate meetings. It was his territory and he fought for it.

In a letter to Triumph dealers, Chris said: "Ever since my work here in 1954, the United States has been of very special interest to me. Most fortunately, my responsibilities have kept me in constant touch with the staff of STMCI and with the changing market conditions and trends in this country." Conditions were certainly changing. Imported car sales had reached near 650,000 units in 1959 but had fallen to just 323,000 units in 1962. Triumph's piece of that had been 18,000, already well up on the 12,000 sold in 1961. *Triumph News* forecast a potential of 400,000 sales for the industry, and it is fascinating to remember that the vast majority of these were to be from European sources. Although Datsun (later Nissan) and Toyota cars had been arriving from Japan since early 1958, they would not begin their surge to success for several more years. None of us had any idea that homely, slow, but sturdy little four-doors named "Bluebird" and "Toyopet Crown" could have a chance. Triumph dealers had quite a range of cars to compete

The start of the Sebring 12-hour race, March 1963. Charlie Gates, in TR4 Number 38, got an excellent start and is challenging the factory Austin-Healey 3000 driven by Paddy Hopkirk. The Triumph, shared by Ed Diehl and Bob Cole, finished two places ahead of the Healey and second in class.

for their share of that predicted 400,000. The Herald 1200 sedan and convertible, the Sports Six, the Spitfire, and the TR4 were spaced nicely in a price range from $1,699 to $2,849, and there was something for just about everybody except the diehard American car buyer.

"Registrations" are often used as a means of telling how many cars actually went on the road in a given time. Triumphs sold and licensed in June 1963 hit the highest total ever for the United States, with 800 more than the year before. The sales increase at the end of the year was 25 percent and, for several months, Triumph was actually in second place in sales among imports, behind VW. We ended the year in third place. Although sales would go much higher in future years, Triumph would never again be that high in the rankings.

At the end of 1963, Donald Stokes, in addition to his titles as managing director and deputy chairman of the Leyland Motor Corporation, became chairman of

Standard-Triumph International, Ltd. He took over executive control from Stanley Markland, who retired. Since the Leyland takeover in 1960, which rescued a slumping Standard-Triumph from bankruptcy, Markland's good management and a rising automobile market had boosted the corporation back to profitability. The management team was young. Stokes was 49; Chief Engineer Harry Webster was 46; General Sales Manager John Warren was 38; and George Turnbull, titled director and general manager and Stokes' chief deputy, was just 37. All would play important roles in the future of the British car industry.

Donald Stokes' first task in January 1964 was to announce that Standard-Triumph had produced 30 percent more vehicles in 1963 than in 1962. The total of cars and light trucks was 109,200. Still, Standard-Triumph Motor Company was a small producer to be trying to cover the UK and European market with a full range of cars, economy through sports to luxury. Yet, it had established the factory at Malines, in

The full Triumph line for 1963, including the Sports Six, left, Herald sedan, TR4, and an Italia next to the TR4. The nose of a Spitfire is just visible at right. The display was organized by the British Automobile Manufacturers Association.

Belgium, to build cars for Europe and was talking another big production jump in 1964. The company's dependence on exports was obvious when Stokes quoted U.S. sales—more than 20,000 units, nearly 20 percent of total production. In America, we had a lot riding on our shoulders.

There were no new Triumph models for the United States in 1964, unusual given the frequency of new-product launches over the previous three years. The Sports Six was dropped after only two years in the line, a sad disappointment considering how nice a car it was. It was the first Triumph to demonstrate what the GT-6, TR250, TR6, and TR8 of later years all illustrated: the incredible change that a larger, smoother powerplant can make to a car with virtually no other alterations.

The Academy of Model Aeronautics National Model Aircraft Championships, at the Los Alamitos Naval Air Station in California in 1963. The photographer was Bill Dean, an aviation writer whose regular car was a Triumph 1800 roadster! As a lifelong model airplane builder and flyer, I was always amenable to Bill's requests for a press car. Miss Model Aviation was Irma Rahwyler of Anaheim, California.

Sports cars and fashion have always been a perfect combination, and the Spitfire fitted right in with this Fortrel promotion, for which it was a prize in a sales contest.

Nineteen sixty-four would be marked in another major way—it was the year Triumph got well and truly back into international competition. The Competitions Department in England was building new cars for the European rally series, and a team of three fastback Spitfires was entered for Le Mans.

In the United States, given the TR4's success in 1963, it was perhaps surprising that a team was not sent to Sebring. However, there was a major event on the schedule—a three-car TR4 team in the Shell 4000 Rally. This was a trans-Canada event sponsored by Shell Oil, and the usual entry was a heavily reinforced sedan. We ran it with a team of three factory-prepared TR4 rally cars with hardtops, aluminum doors, hoods, and trunk lids and all the basic rally chassis preparation. The cars were shipped to Los Angeles for final prep by our own Competitions Department under Kas Kastner. With one driver/navigator team from Europe, one from the United States, and one from Canada, we had a great international PR operation going. The battered cars achieved second team prize.

Car and Driver magazine, edited by David E. Davis, Jr. (now of *Automobile* magazine) began a series of annual readers' polls on favorite cars in different categories. With a reader group that favored foreign and sports cars (for several years *C&D* readers voted the Corvette "Best All-Round Car"), the results were probably biased, but that didn't prevent us from cheering when the TR4 won "Best GT Sports Car Under $3,000" in the 1963 voting. *Car and Driver* called it a "Slam-bang, hell-for-leather fun car." By April, when David presented Chris Andrews with the award at the International Automobile Show in New York, sales had advanced another 17.4 percent, and Chris had some reason to predict sales as high as 26,000 in 1964. Public interest was back; attendance at the New York show was the highest in its history.

The first of several awards from the readers of *Car and Driver* magazine went to the TR4 in 1964, named "Best Sports/GT Car Under $3,000" in 1963 voting. During the New York auto show, Chris Andrews received the award from David E. Davis, Jr., right, editor of *Car and Driver,* while Triumph Chief Engineer Harry Webster, left, looked on. The central display turntable had a sign featuring the award.

We were still making every effort to promote the Herald. This 1964 publicity shot illustrated the car's best capability—running local errands in style. Today, of course, the picture would probably show her using a cash machine. The Herald convertible was a fine-looking car and deserved a better fate in the market.

In August, Richard Roth announced his retirement and was replaced by Bob Pistor, who had been with Studebaker Corporation. Having merged with Packard and quickly destroyed it, the company had survived for a few years with the economy Lark series, but Studebaker built its last cars in 1964. A lot of senior people, like Bob, ended up with jobs in the imported car field. Their knowledge of the U.S. market helped the importers move more firmly into the mainstream of automotive business.

Donald Stokes announced in August that a $24 million development program covering new models, increased production, and improved quality was being put into operation. The Herald would stay in the line for five more years. With this very positive announcement, we began the round of fall auto shows.

One new item on my travel agenda was the American Road Race of Champions, a first attempt by the Sports Car Club of America to hold national run-off races instead of determining champions by points only. Not yet an official event, it was the first of two experimental run-offs, the first at Riverside Raceway in California and the second to be held in 1965 at Daytona Speedway in Florida. Naturally, I attended the Riverside event, as the various SCCA Regions had produced many Triumph entries, including Bob Tullius, not yet racing under the Group 44 Banner. In the Sunday Production race, Bob prevailed over Jim Adams in an MGB.

The year had been free from the frantic organizational problems of new car introductions. For 1965 we would have two up-rated sports cars to launch in March: the Spitfire Mk II and the TR4A. Making March more complicated, we would also have a team running at Sebring, this time the Le Mans-type fastback Spitfires. Later in the year, there would be yet another Triumph in an entirely new market segment, the 2000 sedan. Sales were still going up, and we were not yet too worried about the onset of government regulations.

Another publicity photo, this time showing trunk space, was shot in the driveway of agency executive Bob Timmerman's home, with Triumph's Al Burns modeling. His passenger was a real model.

TR4s and Heralds being loaded at the Northeast distributor, Genser-Forman, which operated its own trucking company to deliver cars. It was Bud Forman and Les Genser who successfully lobbied Standard-Triumph to produce a low-price 1965 TR4A with straight rear axle, at $150 less than the independent rear suspension model.

Everybody loved the Spitfire. The car had 62 more horsepower than this equine admirer, but it didn't stop the horse from sampling the product.

1965—A Year of Confidence

Late in 1964, Donald Stokes made a 40,000-mile round-the-world odyssey visiting Leyland facilities, ending in the United States for a 10-day cross-country tour to see how the U.S. company operated. Chris Andrews joined him in San Francisco for a press meeting, where they announced anticipated sales of 26,000 cars in the U.S. in 1965.

George Turnbull, director and general manager of Standard-Triumph, dropped in for his own two-week trip in March, including a stop at Sebring to see the Spitfires in action. His visit there was not as pleasant as expected. After only five laps, another car nudged Peter Bolton's Spitfire, causing a rollover. The other two finished second and third in class behind an MG Midget. Distinguished by a rainstorm that dropped up to 5 inches of water on the course, the 1965 race was a good trial for the Le Mans Spitfires

and did prove one thing: in heavy rain, small light cars can run rings around monster prototypes—the Spitfires were lapping Jim Hall's Chevy Chaparrals in the wet.

We could still be certain of the enthusiasm and loyalty of the members of the Triumph Sports Owners Association. The January TSOA Newsletter front page headlined the fact that membership had more than doubled since 1960 and totaled over 13,000. More than 10 percent of new Triumph buyers took advantage of TSOA membership, which was still free. Through all of the mergers to come, U.S. operations never lost sight of the need to encourage Triumph clubs and to support such organizations in whatever way possible.

In March, we presented the Spitfire Mark II and the TR4A to the press at meetings in New York, Fort Lauderdale, and Palm Springs. The Spitfire had a small horsepower boost, much improved seats and better trim, but the TR4A sat on a new chassis with independent rear suspension (IRS). It featured a new, easy-to-erect top, new exterior trim and lights, and did not lose any performance. Using the IRS design, which was already on sale in the UK on the Triumph 2000 four-door, gave a better ride at some cost to the high-speed handling. It was a stunningly effective upgrade.

The public debut of the new models was at the New York Auto Show in April.

The Spitfire Mk II and TR4A were available for several months in 1965 before the late-season announcement of the Triumph 2000. Launched as a 1966 model, the 2000 was a complete departure for the company in North America. Except for the trickle of Triumph Renowns and Standard Vanguards in the late 1940s and early 1950s, there had been no attempt to market a large family car in the United States. In England and the rest of the world, Triumph had built several successful top-of-the-line cars, competing with the Rover 2000 and others.

Dick Fehr submitted a plan for a series of press luncheon meetings and auto show premieres that would be timed to ride the wave of 1966 new-car publicity in October and November. Luncheon presentations started in New York on October 12 and went on to Detroit, Chicago, Los Angeles, San Francisco, and later to all the other sales territories. The Los Angeles gathering was actually a breakfast, timed for the car's first public appearance at the show beginning on October 21.

The 2000 was priced right along with the TR4A and shared the excellent chassis features of all-independent suspension and front disc brakes. It offered the 2-liter version of the wonderfully smooth inline six previously sold here in the Sports Six, and automatic transmission was available. On the face of it, it should have sold very well to people liking the sports car features but needing family transportation.

In 1965, Triumph used the Sebring 12-hour race as a practice event for the 24 Hours of Le Mans. The event was a battle against two elements—torrents of rain and a spectacular MG Midget, which won the class with a five-lap lead over the second- and third-place Spitfires. Bob Tullius, who co-drove for third with Charlie Gates, chats with Randy and Gretchen. There are no numbers on the Spitfire because it's the practice car. The three that ran the race were shipped back to England in a hurry to be prepped for the French Classic.

A *Road & Track* editor takes a Spitfire Mk II down the Pacific Coast in early 1965. These were truly fun cars to drive, especially on the days when there were no other cars in sight—not even parked. *Road & Track*

The TR4A's first New York Show, April 1965, with Chris Andrews driving, George Turnbull as passenger, and models Randy Hague and Gretchen Dahm along for the ride.

A load of new TRs went from the Central Zone Regional Office in Baltimore to new dealer David R. McGeorge in Richmond, Virginia. Although a Studebaker is just visible in the showroom, 1964 had been its last year as a manufacturer. A Mercedes is also visible.

Our primary press kit shot for the TR4A with Randy Hague enjoying herself. Things always seemed to be more fun then!

Despite ads showing the 2000 body being lowered on to a TR4A chassis and heavy publicity aimed at families with sports car desires and family car needs, the 2000 got off to a slow start and never sped up. Like the Rover 2000, which had come on the market a year earlier, the buying public compared it to typical American medium-priced sedans rather than seeing it as a "sports sedan." The base price was $2,875, and you could buy a much larger and faster American sedan for several hundred dollars less. In a

way, Bud Forman and Les Genser were right: Triumph's sedans came too early for the educated buyers of today, who appreciate quality and performance and will pay extra for it.

Press coverage was favorable, but most writers correctly assessed the marketing problem. Bob Taylor, writing in the *Newark Sunday News* for November 14, 1965, called 600 miles in the 2000 "a pleasant experience," but he noted the car was entering a "tremendously competitive price class," the

When we did the TR4A brochure, one requirement was to have a couple of shots of the car demonstrating the handling. Since the shoot was on the West Coast, Kas Kastner was borrowed as driver, and he had a ball throwing the car around on some gravel.

TR4A With and Without

The alterations that created the TR4A added just $150 to the 1964 TR4 suggested list price. Triumph's distributor in the Northeast, Genser-Forman, known for believing that price was the only important factor in car sales, strongly resisted the increase. Warned about it well in advance, Bud Forman and Les Genser pleaded their case for a low-advertised-price TR4A without the IRS. They got it, and so we had both straight-axle and IRS TR4As to sell, which produced an unintended benefit on the racetrack.

The IRS car had two U-joints and a sliding spline on each rear axle, making racing modifications more difficult and expensive because the stock parts couldn't handle racing stresses. Some drivers opted to add TR4A grilles, sidelights, badges, etc., to their straight axle TR4s and continue with the old chassis. Even the Group 44 car, faithfully badged "IRS" for publicity pictures, did a few races with a straight axle underneath until they could engineer modifications to take advantage of the new setup.

The Triumph 2000, posed as we wanted America to see it—a sharp-looking sedan ready for enjoyable driving on a quiet road.

$3,000 range. He praised the handling, the fuel mileage, and the visibility, but said it was "no demon" when it came to acceleration.

During 1965 we also signed an agreement with Hertz Rent-A-Car under which they would have Triumphs for rent in 18 major cities, including Los Angeles, Miami, and New York. The focus of the promotion was the "Hertz Sports Car Club." Renters had to go through a small familiarization session before driving the car away, receiving a membership card in the club after doing so. For a time, we had an exclusive—TR4As were the only make in the Hertz SCC. Later, however, after a year of automatic-oriented renters mangling the TR gearboxes, Hertz added cars like the Mustang GT.

I wrote Chris Andrews a memo entitled "How Do We Fight the Mustang?" It said: "To date, our competition with Mustang and others like Corvair Monza, Barracuda, GTO, etc., has been in our territory. They are nibbling at us. However, we cannot fight the game by our rules alone. If we want to keep our current sales level, let alone increase it, we must

The most-used of our 2000 "performance" photos, this one went into the press kit and also into one of the ads that touted the car as a family sports vehicle.

Hertz Rent-A-Car in midtown Manhattan was one of the locations that offered membership in the "Hertz Sports Car Club," so you could rent a TR4A. The sign on the TR's door says "Join the Hertz Sports Car Club."

have some ammunition to fight back with. The comparison between the TR4A and Mustang shows that only the indefinable combination of size, design, and feel that says 'sports car' is on our side.

"We can overcome their advantage somewhat IF the product will stand the comparison. We need better quality control, immediate adjustment of some glaring faults in all of our models, and an attitude that says the customer should have what he wants."

To their credit, Triumph people at all levels tried to meet our needs with improved products. However, as years passed, market conditions, heavy Japanese competition, and the debilitating UK auto industry mergers combined to negate their efforts.

A Fateful Contract with SAAB

Triumph faced two major problems in expanding U.S. sales: product quality and product suitability. The latter was almost impossible to solve. Triumph made great sports cars that were not duplicated in the American manufacturers' product lines. But any effort to expand offerings to include sedans and economy cars ran up against the Big Three's blanket coverage of

the market. Cars like the Sports Six, which ought to have sold on performance, sat in showrooms. Dealers sold only 679 in three model years, 1962–1964. The 2000 sedan, a good car, and popular in the home market, was lost in the United States. It was in the product line for five model years and sold a dismal total of 1,805 units.

To keep vital revenues flowing, Triumph needed to pursue other opportunities. An article in *Triumph News* in May 1965 alerted dealers to a "Giant Anglo-Swedish Car Deal" announced by Donald Stokes. Triumph and SAAB had agreed to jointly develop a new engine that would go into a new, larger SAAB model in 1970. Although not yet named publicly, this would be the SAAB 99, actually launched in 1969. The engines would be built by Trumph for SAAB, and a possible volume of 50,000 units a year was mentioned. Stokes was enthusiastic about not only cash flow but "the many mutual benefits." It was a fantastic deal, because Triumph was being paid to develop and manufacture an engine for sale to SAAB, and the company was not restricted in using the design for Triumphs. The engine would eventually power the

Tandem champs.
Joyce Hoffman-Triumph Spitfire Mk2

Why did "The Blonde Goddess of the Waves" select the Triumph Spitfire Mk2 as her official beach buggy?

Is it the car's outstanding styling and performance? (Plush, fully-carpeted interior. Smooth 4-speed stick shift.

0 to 50 mph in only 10 seconds.)

Safety features? (Accurate rack-and-pinion steering. Reliable disc brakes. Tight 24-foot turning circle. Bump-smoothing four-wheel independent suspension. And steering column

designed to collapse upon impact.)

Economy? (Only once-every-6,000-miles lubrication. Price: only $2155*.)

To tell the truth, we really don't know. All Joyce said was: "It's so me!" Ah, women!

*Suggested retail price POE plus state and/or local taxes. Slightly higher in the West. SCCA-approved competition equipment available. Look for dealer in Yellow Pages. Available in Canada and for overseas delivery. Standard-Triumph Motor Company, Inc., 111 Galway Place, Teaneck, New Jersey 07666. **TRIUMPH**

Joyce Hoffman, at 19 already the world champ in women's surfing, drove a Spitfire and appeared at auto shows for Triumph in 1965–1966.

Triumph TR7 and other Triumphs, beginning 10 years after the agreement with SAAB.

The second trial run of the Sports Car Club of America national championship races went off at Daytona over Thanksgiving weekend, resulting in Triumphs winning three out of four classes in which they were entered. An MG Midget vanquished the Spitfires, but TR4, TR4A (running in Modified as it could not be approved for Production racing, due to its spring introduction), and good old TR3 all won their classes.

Tied in with his annual statement about the imported car industry, Chris Andrews predicted 25,000 U.S. sales for Triumph in 1966. The company had finished 1965 at around 21,500. Factory production had hit more than 150,000, 40 percent above 1963. Both the Coventry and Liverpool plants were to be expanded in anticipation of continued world market growth. On Madison Avenue, we were already thinking about packing for another move, to Teaneck, New Jersey, where Standard-Triumph Motor Company, Inc., would have its own building and would, we felt, be better able to control its destiny.

While the move to Teaneck transpired in 1966, the projected sales did not. The real news that year was in England, with the start of the mergers that would come to form British Leyland Motors. This was the final period in which individual marques would have the final say in their futures. U.S. Triumph sales were off again in 1967, but turned up the following year.

Once again, we had a year in which no new model would be available to titillate the press and buying public. Meeting Chris Andrews' rosy prediction of 25,000 sales wasn't going to happen, but we would have a good supply of cars and a decent ad budget. Our media selection was still the textbook for the imported car industry—aimed at middle to upper income people with college educations, good jobs, and discriminating taste. The Scotch whisky industry targeted the same group.

The dealers always regarded our selective media policy as inadequate. They wanted mass magazines, big newspaper ads, and above all, Triumph advertising on television. With limited funds, there was only so much we could do.

We had tried television advertising in the early part of the decade, concluding that TV reached too general an audience. However, by 1966, with color television a reality and TV viewing part of everyday life, we reached the conclusion that TV commercials were essential to our media plan. When the 1967 models came out, we had filmed 20- and 60-second spots ready.

Triumph was trying hard to win female customers, especially for the Spitfire. An issue of *Triumph News* had a cover story entitled "Les Girls Turn To Triumph," featuring three women, two with TR4As and one with a

Spitfire. We also arranged an endorsement contract with Joyce Hoffman, world champion woman surfer, who appeared on our behalf at West Coast auto shows in 1965 and was featured in Spitfire advertising.

Triumph's Last Year in New York: The Industry Awaits Federal Regulations

The government was beginning its intrusion into the car business. Following passage of the Traffic Safety Act of 1966 a new organization, the Automobile Importers of America, had been formed to deal with matters in Washington, and Chris Andrews became its first president. AIA was destined to become the primary lobby for import cars in Washington, along with AIADA, the American Imported Automobile Dealers Association. Offices for both were established in Washington, to become involved not just with safety legislation but with emissions control standards as well.

This focus on industry lobbying eliminated the need for fully staffed, one-country organizations like the British Automobile Manufacturers Association. The members voted to close the New York office, reducing BAMA to a trade association administered by the secretary of whichever executive was president, and which met infrequently for lunch and conversation. BAMA Executive Director John Dugdale, out of a job after eight years, landed on his feet back at Jaguar as advertising and PR manager, yet another career man in the British auto industry who would drop into the British Leyland hopper in a couple of years.

As 1966 began, we already had a schedule of major events. First, a return to Sebring with a team of TR4A hardtops prepared by Kas Kastner in our own competition shops in Gardena, California. Next, the Chicago and New York Auto Shows followed very quickly by our epic move from Madison Avenue to Teaneck, New Jersey. Further down the line, we would be introducing the Spitfire-based GT-6 coupe as a 1967 model.

Prior to traveling to Sebring as one of the biggest fans of our team, Chris Andrews visited Los Angeles, where the British-American Chamber of Commerce and BAMA had organized a royal visitor, Prince Philip, to present merit awards to British car dealers. Done with that, Chris joined our group at Sebring, where the cars and drivers did superbly, finishing 1-2-3 in class and winning the Pepsi-Cola Trophy for best performance by a three-car team. A fourth TR4A, running as a prototype, did not finish due to mechanical problems.

One team car had a place of honor in the exhibit at the New York Coliseum with the trophy displayed on the roof. It was not Triumph's only award at the show. David E. Davis Jr. of *Car and Driver* brought another Readers Choice Award, this time honoring the Spitfire as "Best GT/Sports Car under $2,500." Half a million people saw the New York Auto Show.

Triumph's new U.S. headquarters building was in Teaneck, New Jersey, about 15 minutes from the George Washington Bridge to Manhattan. The photo was taken in May 1966, standing in Porsche's driveway across the street.

The 1966 New York Auto Show exhibit featuring the Sebring class-winning TR4A in the foreground, with the Pepsi-Cola Team Trophy on the roof.

Triumph News noted that the admission price was $2.50, "probably the highest admission price to an auto show anywhere."

On press day at the New York show, we made much of the safety features built into Triumph cars. The "Impactoscopic" steering column, first installed in the Herald in 1959, was now a feature on all models and met the new federal standards for columns that would absorb crash impacts. Chris Andrews cautioned, however, that "You can't build a car today that is safe enough to protect the man who falls asleep at the wheel or to safeguard the driver who lacks concentration. Driving will always be a very personal thing, involving each individual's capability, the attention he

gives to the job, and his consideration for the rights of others." These words are still absolutely true.

And then we moved. We left work at 575 Madison on a cool April Friday and reconvened in Teaneck at 111 Galway Place on a rainy Monday. Settled in the Teaneck offices, we found it was an easy 25-minute run into midtown New York for meetings, etc., and it was a great relief to be able to avoid the rush-hour jams at the George Washington Bridge and Lincoln Tunnel.

Sales, while not up to 1965, were good, save for the 2000 sedan. The dealers, having experience only with Triumph sports and economy cars, were unsure of how to sell a Triumph family sedan. Many of them had competing franchises, particularly Volvo, which offered similar cars with established reputations at similar prices. The 2000's superior equipment and finish didn't matter to most of the buying public, who were fully aware that a much larger Ford or Chevrolet could be had for less. The base price of $2,895 was steep for a five-passenger car—I bought a 1966 Ford Fairlane Squire wagon that year for less than $2,700.

As part of the 2000 "sports sedan" marketing effort, we put together a Sports Car Club of America rally team, using white cars with a blue American racing stripe down the center. The team set a schedule of seven SCCA events in hopes of winning the national title. Although it won some and usually scored well, the season ended with Triumph third in team standings. We dropped the project, partly on budget grounds and partly because the usual winners, John and Renee O'Leary, were virtually unbeatable in their sponsored Rover 2000 sedan.

California would put emission control standards into effect in 1967, one year ahead of federal requirements. During 1966, Miles Brubacher, senior engineer of the California Motor Vehicle Pollution Control Board, later called the California Air Resources Board

(CARB), held a meeting with Triumph's entire technical staff to make certain the new regulations were fully understood. California would be ahead of the rest of the nation in pollution standards by at least one year from then on, making it necessary for companies like Triumph to produce cars with different engine specifications for sale in California. Single-carburetor Spitfires in 1970 and one-Stromberg TR7s in 1975 met the standards but didn't meet owners' performance expectations. On the other hand, when the TR8 came, the more efficient California fuel-injected model was preferable for power and drivability.

TV Commercials, the GT-6 and a Lot of Flying

The second American Road Race of Champions at Daytona in 1965 had been successful enough that the Sports Car Club of America had declared its national championship experiment a success and scheduled the first "official" American Road Race of Champions for Riverside Raceway.

The Riverside event did not bring as much success to Triumph as the previous two ARRCs had. TR entries were vanquished by MG, Datsun, and

Making TV commercials in Arizona, 1966. Jerry Barkann, left, from Needham, Harper & Steers; author (third from left); and crew set up a GT-6 for an action shot. The checked cap is from another ad shoot.

Taking a break in a Spitfire Mk II during the advertising photo shoot at Pismo beach in late 1966. A 2000 sedan, another Spitfire, and a GT-6 are visible in the background.

Porsche. Even the party scene was muted. My most lasting memory from the weekend is of a ride in Kas Kastner's personal 2000 sedan. Modified with heavy-duty suspension and a three-quarter race engine with three Weber carburetors, it was a real street racer but still served as his family car.

Christmas and New Years came and went as brief breaks in a schedule of planning the GT-6 introduction. We were doing eight combined dealer and press meetings on a killer two-week schedule beginning in Portland, Oregon, and ending in New York. Supplies of cars were arriving and, at each meeting, every dealer attending would leave in a new GT. We didn't look forward to the traveling, but we did expect positive response to the car. I was a particular fan of the GT-6. It was my size.

Size was actually a marketing problem for the little GT because tall people did not fit in it, any more than they could sit up straight in a Spitfire with the factory hardtop. However, if you were under 6 feet and medium build, it fit snugly, like a well-tailored suit. Once seated, you faced a walnut panel with instruments in front of you and switches ready to hand. It felt quite like the Spitfire until you twisted the key. Instead of the harsh four-cylinder crackle of the Spitfire, the 2-liter six throbbed to life, promising power and performance that was delivered on the road.

A GT-6 pulls out into San Francisco traffic, headed for a Bay Area showroom after the dealer meeting in the Fairmont Hotel, January 1967.

The GT-6 is revealed! At the conclusion of each dealer meeting—this one is in Washington, D.C.—a cover was removed, releasing balloons. Our female spokesperson then popped out of the car to deliver a pitch on the car's features. Getting the balloons off the ceiling was left to the hotel!

On a lunch break during a November meeting with Jerry Barkann from the ad agency, I had driven gently through Teaneck to the on-ramp to Route 4. I floored the GT in first gear and we howled on to the highway in a burst of acceleration that startled both of us. We were both quickly convinced by feel alone that the GT-6 could out-accelerate the TR4A.

In early January we began our saga of meetings beside the Columbia River in Portland. Flying on to San Francisco, we sent dealers out from a garage near the Fairmont Hotel, dodging cable cars. In Los Angeles, we used the old Ambassador Hotel. Very rundown, it still had a grand atmosphere and was centrally located. Getting cars into the ballroom entailed riding up the outside of the back wall of the building on an ancient elevator made of two pieces of channel iron supported by cables and hanging into space over the hotel dumpster. We were pleased to watch 60 dealers leave the meeting smiling.

The Los Angeles meeting was on Saturday, and we had a break until our flights to Dallas late Sunday afternoon. One group left at about noon, but several of us stayed on for a treat provided by Chris Andrews— tickets to the first Super Bowl game, in which Green Bay decisively beat Kansas City in the Los Angeles Coliseum, which was at least one-third empty.

We then flew to Miami, Atlanta, Washington, and finally New York, getting applause every time for the GT-6. We were doubly elated because, in addition to the GT-6, we would be welcoming another new model in the spring—the Spitfire Mk III—which would have more power and the first real styling change since the car was introduced. It looked like a good sales year in 1967, but we were faced with a situation that, at the very least, would influence our concentration on selling. It would not only affect the way our business was run, but for some of us would determine our future as Triumph executives.

The GT-6 is driven into the meeting room in Atlanta. Bob Pistor smokes his ever-present cigarette, while Jerry Barkann and Chris Andrews wait in the wings.

Rover Merges with Leyland

In December 1966, Leyland Motor Corporation and the Rover Motor Company agreed to merge. For Leyland this added a profitable division and control over the Land Rover, the famous, down-to-earth, four-wheel-drive vehicle reputed to be able to go anywhere. Final negotiations were completed and the agreement made official in March 1967. The car side of the business was evidently less important to the Leyland people, but it was of concern to Triumph, as the Rover 2000 sedan was a direct competitor for the Triumph 2000.

Rover's product line in the United States over the years had included the rather dowdy Rover 90 and 105 sedans, the 3-liter sedan, and the Land Rover 75 and 105 four-door. Its 2000 sedan and the 2000TC high-performance version had come into the U.S. market just before our Triumph 2000. None of its cars had sold particularly well, even the 2000TC, which had received raves from the automotive press for its performance and handling. Suffering from the same market resistance as the TR 2000, the Rover was also

higher priced. Rover was best known for the Land Rover, which got extensive publicity for its feats in films and on safari. Unfortunately, the publicity did not translate into sales, once potential buyers looked at and test drove the underpowered, harsh-riding vehicle. While not as rugged, American-built pickups and Jeeps could beat it on price, if not off-road performance—but then truck owners don't spend as much time in the dirt as on the roads.

In the United States, we had been aware of the merger since the beginning. We were making arrangements in Teaneck to accommodate the Rover Motor Company's U.S. staff, which had been working from offices in the Chrysler building in Manhattan. Although Rover was well known, especially for quirky advertising and PR campaigns, its maximum effort had managed only once to produce 3,000 sales in a single year. We tended to view them as a minor issue in our higher-volume Triumph world, but the tenacity and attitude of Rover's American management had an immediate and lasting effect on Triumph marketing, beginning even before they arrived in Teaneck.

Rover's U.S. operation had been run since 1962 by a team unique in the car business—Bruce and Gertrude (known universally as "Jimmy") McWilliams. After a time at the United Nations, Bruce had been with SAAB in the United States for three years and then was sales vice president for Mercedes-Benz when Studebaker Corporation was the U.S. distributor. Jimmy had been with the Office of British Information and then went into developing sales promotion and advertising material. Bruce's experience was in sales and business management and Jimmy's was in writing, but their talents overlapped. President of the company, Bruce had a creative flair that helped him in everything from styling new models to setting up sales promotions. Jimmy's talents had led her to success in selling insurance before she became director of advertising and public relations for Rover. She looked for the unusual, sourcing Rover advertising from leading-edge ad agencies like Freeman and Gossage of San Francisco.

The McWilliams team ran Rover North America like a family hardware store. Everyone had a job description and established duties, but everyone pitched in to help out in crisis situations. A last-minute mailing would be prepared, assembled, and mailed by staff members on overtime, sometimes working at home, rather than by a professional mailing house. Staff members doubled as models for photo sessions. One year, some wore animal suits for a "Safari to Lime Rock" that started in Times Square and finished at the BAMA Press Trials.

At Standard-Triumph, our lines of command and our office behavior were much more formalized. We were used to having meetings, making plans, and carrying them out. A large percentage of our decisions were made by committees or by individual managers relying on input from subordinates and other departments. We had a boss, but he was seldom dictatorial. Bruce and Jimmy were used to conceiving a project over the weekend and handing it to their staff to carry out on Monday, the new inspiration overriding whatever else was on people's desks. Sometimes it worked and sometimes not, but it created an atmosphere of upheaval. Trying to mix the two systems was like trying to sweeten a cake with half sugar and half salt.

The Leyland people called the new North American company Leyland Motor Corporation, Inc. George Turnbull spoke to the press in New York to announce the new company, claiming, "The new company will have many advantages. Rover, which has received tremendous acceptance of its '2000' in the United States, will benefit from the much larger Triumph organization and facilities, which have been firmly established in the market for the past 15 years." He claimed new efficiencies and economies in operation through the merger which were true but, in the case of marketing, Rover's tail would wag the dog.

Having created the new company, Leyland waffled on who would run it, Chris Andrews or Bruce McWilliams. These two strong personalities offered nonconflicting management experience, Chris in exports and administration, Bruce in sales and North American marketing. It might have been better in the long run to name a single chief executive but Leyland took the easy way out. Stokes, now Sir Donald, was named president. Chris became vice president, administration and finance, and Bruce got the title of vice president, marketing. Their authority was virtually equal, and both were board members. Their different approaches to management created numerous conflicts of Bruce and Jimmy vs. Chris. It was clear from the start that Stokes would not be taking part in day-to-day management, so the warring parties were fortunate to have the steady head and hand of Ed McCauley as mediator.

Previously vice president and treasurer of Standard-Triumph Motor Company, Inc., Ed received the same title with the new company and also was appointed a director. The other board members were George Turnbull, director and general manager of Standard-Triumph International, and William Martin-Hurst, managing director of the Rover Company, Ltd.

As the two groups elbowed their way into jobs in the new company, there were some redundancies but few basic conflicts over positions. Sales Vice President Bob Pistor was an early casualty, his job absorbed by Bruce McWilliams. Rover had a small staff and some of its specialists, like Richard Scullin, who handled auto shows, were welcome additions. I kept my title as advertising manager, but Jimmy McWilliams was given overall command of Rover and Triumph advertising. I would report to her on Triumph and she hired Angus Laidlaw, an imported car writer and magazine editor, as her deputy on Rover advertising.

The new organization actually took effect on March 30, only a few days before the New York International Auto Show, but the McWilliams group had already started work. Leaving the sports cars alone, the group had concentrated on our biggest sales problem, the 2000 sedan. The immediate need was to sell our aging stock before the cars started to deteriorate. The solution was the "2000 SEm," which created the illusion of a different new model while using cars already on hand. SEm stood for "Special Equipment model," and the special equipment was all off-the-shelf stuff or paint.

The retail price of the dressed-up 2000 was only slightly higher. It came with a wood steering wheel, wood shift knob, pin-striping, the Michelotti crossed flags as previously applied to the Herald, wheel covers similar to those installed on the Herald and Spitfire, and a vinyl roof. Roofs covered in vinyl fabric were just coming in on domestic cars and an after-market industry had sprung up, offering less expensive spray-on roof

Triumph Sports Cars, the New York dealer, believed in placing cars wherever it could. This GT-6 is in the lobby of the Manhattan Savings Bank in midtown Manhattan, near Grand Central Station.

coatings for a trendy look. The 2000 SEm used this technique, even using three-dimensional tape under the paint to simulate seams. It looked pretty good. All 2000s in dealer or company stock were to get the package. Instructions went out to the zone and regional offices to start exchanging SEm modified cars with cars in dealer stock and to have the roof treatment applied locally. The accessory items were installed by the zones, and the promotion was advertised beginning in April, with the first car on display at the New York show.

Call it smoke and mirrors or badges and stripes (or both), it was a classic McWilliams package. The same technique would be used over and over on future Triumphs and other models under British Leyland. Helped by extra company advertising and a special dealer advertising allowance per car sold, SEm created enough activity to clear out the stock of 2000 sedans during 1967 and 1968. The model was then dropped from the United States in favor of the Rover 2000, not much of a victory, as the Rover faded from the scene after 1971.

The launch of the new Spitfire Mk III was my last major event at Triumph. Having just visited with the automotive writers during the GT-6 launch a few months earlier, we felt we could publicize the new Spitfire through the mail without the usual high-dollar press send-off and operate a good-sized press fleet. The method worked. This was an important car on the import scene and the press recognized it instantly.

With 1,296 cc instead of 1,147, the increase in horsepower and torque was enough to make 100 miles per hour just possible, but that wasn't the most important part of the Mk III. Inside, there were even better seats and carpeting and no more painted metal on dash and door frames. They were covered with vinyl and the central instruments were mounted in a walnut panel. Outside, there was a new front-end treatment with the chrome bumper across the center of the grille, giving a "bone-in-the-teeth" look. The convertible top was now a one-hand operation affair like the TR4A, requiring only four snaps and two latches to make the occupants snug and secure. *Road & Track* matched the Mk III against the latest MG Midget and found that, while acceleration and top speed were similar, the Spitfire was way ahead in comfort and handling, altogether a more modern package. It was

Late in the spring of 1967, we announced the face-lifted Spitfire Mark III. Brought up to federal standard height, the front bumper was directly in front of the grille and had rubber-faced guards. The rear bumper moved up to match. The other major change was the convertible top, which went from two-piece stow-in-the-trunk to a snug, fully attached affair that could be operated with one hand.

the third new Spitfire in four years, but there would not be another until 1971.

I kept busy at work scheduling Spitfire road test cars and busy at home sending out letters and resumes. Jimmy McWilliams was calling the advertising shots now, and her style and mine were too different. Rather than change a marketing approach nearly a decade in the making, I decided to change employers. Tapping some connections, I ended up at Mobil Oil in its Special Promotions Group. The job paid considerably more than Triumph had, which I put to good use preparing my TR3 for amateur racing—a bug that finally bit after years of covering Triumph motorsports. Before leaving I pitched Jimmy McWilliams on letting me take over the *TSOA Newsletter* as a freelance project. She agreed, leaving me with good ties to the Triumph scene. I was given a great luncheon send-off on my last day at Triumph, but the more important

occasion was after work. Remembering Alan Bethell's personal farewell party six years before, I had invited the entire company to stop by the house for a drink after work. To my delight, nearly everyone came! The house hummed until long after midnight, as we both reminisced and talked of new opportunities.

Triumph Goes On

I was away from Triumph for only 16 months. During that time, Leyland Motor Corporation introduced two new TRs. One, the TR250, was a transition model that had a brief, one-year lifespan. The second was the glorious TR6 which, even after it went out of production, defined the company in its final years. Announced as a 1969 model, it was built through 1976 and could have gone on much longer.

When I left the company, I was aware that a new TR5 was on the way, powered by the six-cylinder

A 1960s Insight on the Future of Sports Cars

Ron Wakefield was the respected technical editor and editor of *Road & Track* magazine for a number of years in the 1960s and 1970s. Fully aware of what the auto industry was doing worldwide, Ron was deeply interested in trends and developments. After his first drive in the TR250, he made some insightful notes—still on file at the magazine's offices. His reflections accurately described the sports car's state at that time and its fate for years to come.

"You know, as I was driving home in that thing last night, it suddenly came to me what's wrong with the sports car field today. (Spring 1968.) The best cars from Europe today are sedans. They've kept them up-to-date, really have some good ones. But the sports cars are neglected. How many sports cars below $3,500 can you think of that you'd have at all? Perhaps the Fiat 124S, because it's the exception."

Ron then listed how he felt about the British sports cars then available: GT-6—"pretty decent but still a cobble job"; MGB—"cart springs and crash first gear"; Healey—"dead, and it costs as much as a Corvette"; Sunbeam Tiger—"no value for money." Then he took on the TR: "This TR250 is a real relic of the past, with its cobbled-up rear suspension, rattles and squeaks, noisy top. I wouldn't pay $3,000-plus for anything less than the latest state-of-the-art. If this keeps up, the sports car may be on its way out!"

Ron liked the smoothness and quiet of the TR250 engine, but called it "almost mousey" for its lack of power. He thought the springing was overly soft, a frequent comment from editors, but he praised the handling on the Michelin X tires. He addressed the car's compliance with the new federal emissions standards in great detail and noted that Triumph people were very proud of not using an air pump in their system. He concluded: "The total result is that the car meets the emissions standards. Performance isn't quite what it might have been, but Triumph people feel that they attacked the problem in the right way and that "they can restore performance later." I agree, and think they should be given credit for this."

Ron Wakefield had his crystal ball perfectly tuned. Far from becoming more modern over the following two decades, only the very expensive open

Ron Wakefield of *Road & Track* magazine scorching down a favorite test road in the TR250 in the late 1957. He praised some details on the car, but thought it was "a relic of the past." *Road & Track*

two-seaters stayed anywhere near the leading edge in automotive engineering. The popular British brands stuck with their 1960s engineering until, sales dropping and profits dwindling, they simply disappeared. Alfa Romeo launched the Duetto in 1966 and was still marketing the same basic car here in the 1990s, before leaving the market altogether! Porsche kept introducing new models, but all played second fiddle to the 911 concept until the launch of the Boxster in 1996. Regardless of Ron's opinion, Fiat could not sell enough 124s, and they left the U.S. market too.

Meanwhile, tidy, attractive, high-performance sedans and coupes became the trend of the 1970s and 1980s. The BMW 2002, the Datsun 510, the Toyota Celica, the Datsun/Nissan 240-260-280-300 Z-cars, the Camaro, the Firebird, and all the rest supplied the sports car enthusiasts' needs until the Mazda Miata started the new go-round of sports cars.

Whoever thought Triumph could "restore performance later" was doing some wishful thinking. TR performance never came back to 1966 levels. Starting in 1968, it went steadily down. There was a momentary spike, when the Spitfire 1500 came in, but even the all-new TR7 was no quicker than the TR6. Only the 1980 TR8, not in showrooms until 12 years after Wakefield's comments, had performance to match its contemporaries and, by then, the financially devastated Jaguar Rover Triumph, Ltd., could not afford to build them.

This is the TR250, as announced. Cosmetic changes to the basic TR4A body include special hood badge, hood stripes, full wheel covers, 185x15 Goodyear red-band tires, wider chrome strip, new rear-view mirror, badge above rear sidelight, etc.

On the way to the TR250. This is a TR4A used to study suggested McWilliams cosmetic changes for the 250. Waiting for review in the parking lot of the Teaneck building, it has a Rover 2000 wheel on the left front, stripes on the forward edge of the hood, simulated louvers and a Michelotti flag emblem on the fender, and stripes at the rear. In the background is one of the 2000 rally team cars.

The dealer drive-away ready to depart the Thunderbolt. About 20 TR250s went to showrooms that day. Only about 8,000 of this one-year model were built before it was supplanted by the TR6.

engine in fuel-injected, 2.5-liter form. I did not know that the Lucas mechanical fuel injection used on the engine to give 150 horsepower had two problems. First, it was expensive, adding between $400 and $600 to the cost of the car. Second, it would be difficult to make it pass the rather basic emissions standards in effect in 1968.

In 1967, behind the scenes, some very quick decisions were made. It was decided to launch the TR5 in North America with twin Zenith-Stromberg carburetors, which would readily pass the emissions standards. The horsepower figure with this setup would be about the same as the four-cylinder TR4A, but the torque of the six would give better performance. It was already established that the TR6 would be launched in 1969, but the company had to sell cars in 1968 and the TR5 still used the dated TR4A body. Again working with little budget, the McWilliams team set to work. With their tape and paint technique, they achieved a new and distinctive identity for the car which, after much trans-Atlantic discussion, was called the TR250, based on the new engine displacement.

At the front, the 250 grille was like the TR4A but blacked out between the horizontal bars and without the central vertical bar. Across the forward end of the hood ran three reflective tape stripes that extended down the fenders. They were in dark or light colors, contrasting with the paint. New hood and trunk badges in chrome with cream background identified the car. Both TR5 and TR250 had a broader side chrome strip running back from the sidelights. The 250 also had full, stainless-steel wheel covers in a simulated mag wheel pattern and red-band 185x15 tires that gave the car its muscular look. On the standard 4-1/2-inch rim wheels, the big tires tended to squirm, not helping the handling. The optional wire wheels had 5-1/2-inch rims, which took care of the problem and became the standard width on all TR6 wheels. One can always quibble about styling. The 185x15 tires were much bigger than the 250 and TR6 needed, being the same size specified for the Jaguar E-type, which was capable of over 140 miles per hour!

The McWilliams touch was also applied under the TR250 hood, where the hoses were black with yellow stripes, a restorer's nightmare to obtain 30 years later.

Triumph TR-4A is a two-fisted sports car that has features for 98-pound weaklings.

Like the new easy-up, easy down convertible top.

Triumph

The interior, with new ventilated seats and a steering wheel with both rim and spokes padded and leather-covered, was much more luxurious. The final touch was reflective material strategically applied to the convertible top. A silver-gray by day, in the dark the top detail stripes stood out under lights, a safety feature.

The year ended with Triumph announcing a 7 percent price cut, attributed to an advantageous exchange rate. Inside sources suggested that the staff in Teaneck had settled down to good working relationships, and business for 1968 looked promising. Into this relatively calm atmosphere dropped another corporate bombshell. On January 17, 1968, the Leyland Motor Corporation, Ltd. and British Motor Holdings Ltd. merged to form the British Leyland Motor Corporation Ltd. This is the text of the announcement as published in the January 1968 *TSOA Newsletter*:

A merger agreement between the Leyland Motor Corporation, Ltd. and British Motor Holdings was concluded in England on January 17, 1968, in order to form a new company called British Leyland Motor Corporation.

Sir George Harriman, Chairman of BMH, will be chairman of the board and Sir Donald Stokes, chairman of Leyland, will be deputy chairman, managing director and chief executive officer.

BMH, which recently merged Jaguar into its organization, markets MG, Austin-Healey, Austin, Morris and Jaguar in the United States and Canada.

Leyland, which owns both Triumph and the recently acquired Rover, markets the Triumph, Rover and four-wheel drive Land Rover lines in the United States and Canada.

In England and among BAMA members in America, it was as though Ford and Chevrolet had merged, alarming company people and owners alike. Trained for years to consider MG and Austin-Healey as arch-rivals, Triumph people had a hard time dealing with being part of the same corporation. Hackles were raised at the suggestion that the U.S. subsidiaries might join forces. Not only were personal tastes and loyalties involved, rivalry between brands was a built-in part of marketing and was seen to be essential, whether the paychecks came from the same place or not.

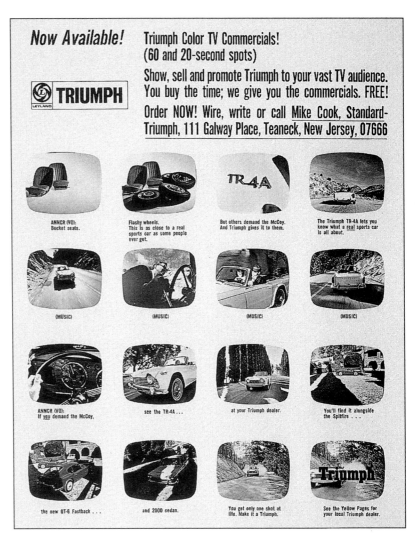
Storyboard for the TR4A commercial shot on Mount Lemmon. The closing frames showed the other Triumph models.

And that is how it was at the beginning of 1968. After the initial announcement about British Leyland, all went quiet until later in the spring when the *Newsletter* published some scanty information about the new corporation being second in size only to VW, outside the United States. Behind the scenes, discussions were under way between Leyland and BMH people in New Jersey regarding a British Leyland corporate headquarters. The Teaneck facility was too small, but BMH had a new building actually under construction nearby, in Leonia, New Jersey, which might be able to accommodate Triumph, Rover, and the multiple BMH makes, including Jaguar, which still had offices on 57th Street in Manhattan.

8 Back to the British

As spring came in and I got ready for my second season of sports car racing in my TR3, I began to miss the car business even more than I had expected to, especially because work on Mobil projects had prevented my visiting the 1968 New York International Auto Show. I was thus quite pleased to bump into Chris Andrews at a luncheon and have him tell me that, when British Leyland moved into its new building in the fall, there might be a slot open in Public Relations.

I tried hard to keep up with Triumph activities. I was editing the *TSOA Newsletter* but that emphasized racing and product matters almost exclusively, and I was also interested in the business side. Sales were good—the company began 1968 by selling 1,817 cars in January, 78.4 percent better than January 1967. Much of the marketing focused around racing performance, and the *Newsletter* reported the TR250 being classified in Sports Car Club of America Class C

Production. After years of Spitfires and TRs being near-certain winners in most classes, Triumph enthusiasts would now have to deal with a classification in which the Triumph was marginal in performance.

Also in Class C were the Porsche 911, Lotus Elan, Toyota 2000 GT, and Datsun 2000. All of these had overhead camshaft engines with greater performance potential than the pushrod six in the TR. Among all of British Leyland's products, only the Jaguars had overhead cam engines and really sophisticated chassis. Failure to meet the competition in technology and equipment would soon be a major obstacle to our sales.

In the Sebring 12-Hour race in March of 1968 there was no official factory entry, but there was a very exciting Triumph in the race. Called the "TR250K" it had been designed by Pete Brock, famed then as designer of the Shelby Cobra coupes that ran at Le Mans. The chassis was basically a TR4A IRS

Kas Kastner got Cobra designer Pete Brock to style this spectacular sports car on a TR250 chassis. Built as a racer, the car ran only once, at Sebring in 1968, and was retired. *Plain English Archive*

updated to TR250 specs with the 2.5-liter engine moved back 9.75 inches to aid weight distribution. The body, intended as a "dream car" design for possible production, was up-to-the-minute contemporary, with aerodynamic wedge shape, sharply raked windshield, and clear plastic covers over the headlights for streamlining. The project had been conceived and ram-rodded by Kas Kastner, who wanted to maintain Triumph's performance reputation and was also an advocate of more modern styling. It was built as a race car because that was Kastner's area and because it was the simplest way to build a complete vehicle.

The TR250K ran less than three hours at Sebring, retiring after a broken wheel caused an excursion off course and serious suspension damage. As an exercise to inspire the engineers, stylists, and marketing people at Triumph in the UK, it didn't last much longer. It got tremendous press coverage, appearing on the covers of *Car and Driver* and *Autoweek* and much press comment on whether it would be the next TR. However, although approved as a project by Bruce McWilliams, the car was regarded by the factory only as an interesting special, not as something to be seriously considered for possible production. Bruce firmly states that the car could not have been built as a production vehicle. To make the design meet the Federal standards for bumper height and impact would have ruined the appearance just for openers. Despite its great appeal to enthusiasts, the design was not practical.

Very disappointed, Kastner still maintains that the car could have been produced and that the resistance came from the "NIH (not-invented-here) syndrome" common to car company executives when viewing outside design submissions. Certainly, none of the TR250-K design features were ever used on production cars. A wedge-shaped Triumph eventually appeared but the TR7 was not in the same styling or performance league as the TR250-K. After some years in obscurity, the car, now painted red, was brought back to public view by ex-Sebring team driver Bob Cole, who showed it at the Pebble Beach Concours, in the Dream Car section, in 1992. The car is now restored to its original metallic silver blue and lives in the collection of Patrick Hart in the Pacific Northwest, near another dream that had only one brief flight, Howard Hughes' *Spruce Goose*.

In the 1990s, multiscreen audiovisual displays have become the norm at auto shows, but in 1968, a display featuring rear projection via eight slide projectors, 640 different slides, timed lighting, and music was unique. A Jimmy McWilliams inspiration, the TR250 psychedelic light display debuted at the San Francisco show in late 1967 and went on to wow the crowds in Chicago and New York. Inside a booth with standing room for an audience of about 30 people, a TR250 was canted over at a 45-degree angle toward the audience. For 90 seconds, the audience joined a couple on the screen in a sports car adventure showing scenes from several parts of the country. While the action slides flashed on the screen behind it, spotlights on the car changed color and others blinked on the wheels, simulating motion. Tijuana Brass music completed the experience, which was recognized in *The New York Times* and other papers.

In addition to excellent sales, Triumph observed some milestones during 1968. First was the completion of the 100,000th Spitfire, which was built at the Canley assembly plant in February. Forty-five thousand Spitfires had been shipped to the United States since the car came out in 1963. Another 31,000 had gone to Europe and other markets, indicating just how important exports were to the health of the company. Later in the year, SAAB announced its new 99 sedan, which had the Triumph-designed and built overhead cam, 2-liter, slant-four engine.

Although the British Leyland Motor Corporation became a reality in England in April of 1968, in the United States the various components of the company would not be brought together, even on paper, until October. This did not prevent Graham Whitehead, president of British Motor Holdings USA and nominated president of British Leyland Motors Inc., from getting his executive group together. I had met Graham once or twice at British Automobile Manufacturers Association functions but did not know him at all. From my acquaintants at BMH, I learned that he was a businesslike individual, demanding to work for, but fair. Although I had a future with

One of the very first multiscreen audiovisual displays introduced the TR250 to crowds at 1968 auto shows. *Plain English Archive*

Mobil, it did not appeal to me. After discussions with both Chris Andrews and Ed McCauley, I submitted an application to Graham for the position of Corporate Public Relations Manager with British Leyland Motors, Inc.

While the business of selling cars proceeded, behind the scenes a great deal of organizational activity was going on to get British Leyland in shape to do business in the United States. Consolidation of warehouse facilities, customs services, legal counsel, office supplies and printing, and many other items had to be considered. Consolidation of personnel was not yet a priority. The full staffs from the British Motor Holdings offices in Ridgefield, New Jersey; Leyland Motor Corporation in Teaneck; and Jaguar Cars, part of BMH, in New York would all be housed in one building in Leonia, New Jersey, which had originally been designed to hold only BMH and Jaguar. With a hasty redesign, part of the warehouse space was converted for second-floor offices, and construction proceeded with a December target occupation date.

In July 1968, Triumph announced the "second highest July wholesale sales in the history of Triumph in the U.S." Announcing wholesale sales figures rather than retail, using the highest figure to get the best publicity, was sometimes quite misleading, because cars could remain in distributor or dealer stock for months after the press release was issued. In this case, however, the more than 12,000 units wholesaled seemed to be going right through the showroom and out to customers. The TR250 was selling well and the Spitfire Mk III was a runaway success. Triumph had the 1969 versions of the Spitfire Mk III and the GT-6 to announce in the early fall. On the horizon for launch at the start of the year was another new TR. The TR5/250 was gone after a one-year run and the TR6, last in the original TR series, was about to begin eight years in the limelight. Until the end, Triumph would be the British Leyland sports car marque with the most new models, a conscious management decision in the UK.

I had preliminary telephone conversations with Graham Whitehead and, finally, an interview in his office at BMH in Ridgefield Park, New Jersey. We chatted about what British Leyland would mean to the American car buying public, that nobody would recognize the name and that it would be hard to educate people that their treasured TRs and MGs and Jaguars were now all built by a sort of British General Motors. We shared the opinion that it would be better if people continued to think that these were separate companies and that promoting British Leyland would only confuse the issue. However, this was not an option—the assignment of the corporate PR manager would be to establish British Leyland Motor Corporation in the minds of the buying public as the second largest auto manufacturing conglomerate outside the United States.

Another problem with the formation of the new company would be functions duplicated for the various marques. There would be four advertising agencies, each pursuing a different theme and media philosophy, and each with a different budget and target audience. Three advertising managers would compete for budgets to advertise the various cars, some of which were going after the same market segment—TR vs. MGB, Spitfire vs. MG Midget, etc. Graham wanted someone to attempt to monitor, if not control, the advertising for the individual products so that there would not be too many clashes and fractures of corporate policy. So, part of the corporate PR job was to be chair of the BL Advertising Committee.

Graham offered me the job and I quickly accepted. British Leyland Motors Inc. would take over from British Motor Holdings and Leyland Motor Sales on October 1, but I would start my new job in December when the new building was completed.

The 1968 American Road Race of Champions at Riverside came before I started at British Leyland Motors, but I had arranged to be out there to cover it for the *TSOA Newsletter*. It was a memorable weekend. Over 40 Triumph drivers competed in five classes coming up with three National Championships. The TR250, Bob Tullius driving, was third behind a pair of Porsche 911s—the best the low-tech Triumph could do, even with Bob's talent at the wheel. However, Brian Fuerstenau won F Production in the Group 44 Spitfire Mk III, ensuring good advertising headlines for the year to come.

This was the last SCCA Championships at the historic Riverside track. Racing would continue there until the mid-1980s but the SCCA, after one more event at Daytona in 1969, would move the Run-Offs to Road Atlanta for a long stand. I would return to Riverside again to see Group 44 in professional events, the last one with the amazing Jaguar V-12 GTP car, but the raceway finally closed and is now fully developed with houses and shops where the road course once twisted and turned.

Back from California, I had three days to tidy up my desk and all my affairs at Mobil before Thanksgiving weekend. There were only a few goodbyes. I took one last long look out of my 18th floor window from which, on a clear day, I could see all the way to the Verrazzano Narrows Bridge at the entrance to New York harbor. Then, I picked up my briefcase and left with no regrets.

All in the Same Barrel

The British Leyland Motors Inc. building in Leonia, New Jersey, and a similar facility in Burlington, Ontario, were the first two places in the world where operations for all of the British Leyland marques actually came together under one roof on Monday, December 2, 1968. Each group arrived,

The author started amateur sports car racing in this TR3, purchased from a fellow Triumph employee who had put over 70,000 miles on the car. Here the race TR3 has a new paint job, Minilite wheels, and other items like a fully race-prepared engine. Shown here at Cumberland, Maryland, in 1969, next to Group 44's truck—always a good source of parts. *Mike Cook*

sleeves rolled up, ready to scuffle for their share of the turf. All shipping, parts, sales, marketing, and executive functions for the United States were now controlled from the rather unimpressive "warehouse with office block" on Willow Tree Road.

Leonia is a quiet residential community with little commercial or industrial activity and no real restaurants, due to a local ordinance against selling liquor by the drink. The advantage of the town for British Leyland was easy access to both the George Washington Bridge and the Lincoln Tunnel into New York City and to the New Jersey Turnpike and other major highways including Interstate 80, at that time still under construction. Willow Tree Road is paralleled by railroad tracks and a creek at the north end of the New Jersey "Meadowlands," a long tidal swamp stretching several miles, much of which has since been filled and used for construction of office buildings, Giants Stadium, etc. At the corner of Fort Lee Road, where Willow Tree began, was a small junk yard where activity was so light that families of pheasants had moved into the junk cars and sometimes flew across the road in front of us as we drove to the office.

Graham Whitehead had appointed a primary executive group of six vice presidents for the new British Leyland Motors Inc. From Leyland Motor Corporation, there were Chris Andrews, who had been executive vice president, administration; Ed McCauley, who had been treasurer; and Bruce McWilliams, who as executive vice president of marketing,

had shared the management of the company with Chris. From British Motor Holdings came Michael H. Dale, who had been sales manager of BMH; Anthony Thompson, formerly general sales and marketing manager of Jaguar Cars Inc.; and R. Graham (Jock) Reid, who had been vice president, parts and service. Chris Andrews and Ed McCauley were named directors of BLMI.

Jaguar's long-time chief executive in the United States, Johannes (Jo) Eerdmans, was also named a director. As Graham Whitehead was now CEO for all British Leyland makes, Jo gave up his title of president of Jaguar Cars but remained involved in management and occupied an office next to Graham's. Every other executive who stayed with BL sooner or later became involved with all of the company's products, but Jo remained exclusively a Jaguar man until his retirement in the spring of 1970.

With a set of executives for each marque, all of the offices in the new building were filled and space was already tight. My office was not quite completed when we moved in so I had a desk out in the general office for a few days. There was the impression of a lot of people milling around, not quite sure where things were or who had authority over whom. Management guidelines were lacking, so the staff was forced to cope. This was actually beneficial, because few had arrived ready to cooperate in business with fellow employees who had been archrivals the previous Friday.

The Austin America, a 1971 model shown here, was a terrific little car carrying the original mini theory to a new size. Comfortable for four adults, it lacked highway performance and was not able to make a dent in the VW Beetle's small-car domination. *Plain English Archive*

My office was convenient to Graham's office. As corporate PR manager, I had a distinct advantage in that I reported directly to the president. He and I were among the very few British Leyland employees who were focused on the corporation, without having some product ax to grind. The advertising managers, Bob Burden for Austin/MG; John Dugdale for Jaguar; and Jimmy McWilliams for Triumph, Rover, and Land Rover, were not interested in taking time away from their product responsibilities to consider the welfare of British Leyland. The marketing executives were Mike Dale on Austin/MG; Bruce McWilliams on Triumph, Rover and Land Rover; and Tony Thompson on Jaguar; they fought for competitive secrets but openly discussed product strategies at lunch in the executive dining room. Jaguar had no in-house competitors but it would take a while to get used to MG and Triumph competing vigorously in the marketplace while contributing profits to the same bottom line!

With 17 different models of 7 different makes, the parking lot at Leonia looked like a gathering of British products for the old British Press trials. British Leyland products for 1969 included the Austin America; Austin-Healey Sprite; Jaguar XJ6; Jaguar E-type Roadster, Coupe and 2+2; Land Rover 88; MGB; MGB GT; MG Midget; MGC; MGC GT; Rover 2000 and 2000 TC; Triumph TR6; Triumph GT-6; and Triumph Spitfire. Parked in the executive area were a couple of Jaguar 420G sedans for Graham Whitehead and Jo Eerdmans. John Dugdale still drove a Jaguar 420. Fortunately, at first, we did not have to stock parts for all of these cars. The Leonia warehouse held only Austin, Austin-Healey, MG, and related BMC parts. Jaguar spares were still warehoused in Long Island

City and Triumph parts were at the Genser-Forman distributorship in Union, New Jersey.

I ordered a GT-6+ as a company car, but was first issued an Austin America until the Triumph could be prepped. Within a week, the car was seriously rear-ended by a Pontiac on an icy overpass. The tough little America protected four of us from injury and kept running but was totaled out by the insurance company, and the GT-6+ was ready just in time. I had always been fond of the GT-6. The Plus, with its new, quite sophisticated independent rear suspension, handled amazingly well and had the power the Austin lacked. The Triumph Herald had been dropped at the end of 1967 so the America was BL's only low-end family car, selling for less than $2,000 complete with automatic transmission. Unfortunately, the little 1,275-cc two-door didn't have enough highway performance and the automatic, the car's biggest selling point, was particularly prone to failure! Like other small British sedans, it had great promise, but it flunked out of the market at the end of 1971.

December 1968 was a month of settling in. People got to know each other, systems began to work and the kinks were worked out of the new corporation. The Triumph people were putting the finishing touches on the launch of the TR6, and samples of the car were seen in the service shop and parking lot. It was easy to tell when one went by—no other Triumph, not even the TR250 with the same engine, had that distinctive, throaty sound. It was *the* new British Leyland product for 1969 and so received a lot of attention.

The Rowland Company had been doing product and corporate PR work for BMH for some time, and now was also handed the BL corporate assignment. This supposedly meant only the news about business affairs, sales, and corporate actions, but it was impossible to separate product from corporate. The three advertising managers also claimed PR responsibilities, so my biggest conflicts in those early days were with them, over Graham's requirement that I check product news copy against corporate policy.

Working on the BL account from Rowland were Peter Smith, formerly the Dunlop Tire representative in the United States, and my friend, Lyman Gaylord.

Products and Directions

January 10, 1969, was the official announcement date for the TR6. A press meeting was held in England, hosted by George Turnbull, A. C. (Cliff) Swindle, and C. Spencer King. This was a major product launch for Triumph and British Leyland, but the executive lineup was also important, for it illustrated what was already happening within the organization in terms of personnel as well as products.

George Turnbull had been chief executive of Standard-Triumph but had been named a deputy managing director of British Leyland by Sir Donald Stokes, with the responsibility of running the Austin-Morris division. Representing BL at the TR6 meeting, he apologized for Stokes' absence with the flu. He also announced that on that day the Queen had bestowed a life peerage on Stokes who would be known, from then on, as Lord Stokes of Leyland.

Speaking about the TR6, Turnbull apologized for not being able to provide press test cars. He explained that all initial production had been left-hand-drive cars for export to the United States and Europe, which would get the car immediately, while British buyers would have to wait until April. He then began to introduce Cliff Swindle, now managing director of Standard-Triumph, as "his right-hand man" for several years but, before completing the introduction, got in a PR plug for the Austin-Morris 1100/1300 and the forthcoming Austin 1500. It might be considered bad manners to inject news about another division into Triumph's news conference, but it was a perfect example of the British Leyland philosophy, which always emphasized the parent corporation over the manufacturing divisions.

Cliff Swindle had nothing but good news. Standard-Triumph had built 139,000 vehicles in 1968, 14 percent more than 1967. He reported shipments to the United States up 70 percent to 19,000 units and to Europe up 27 percent to 25,000. Twelve thousand of these had been assembled at the plant in Malines, Belgium, which would now also build TR6s. He noted that demand for the Triumph 1300 had grown beyond their capacity to supply, and the front-wheel-drive four-door was one of Britain's 10 top cars. He said the 2000 sedan and new 2.5 P.I. (Petrol Injection, using the same engine as the TR6) were dominating the British 2-liter market "in company with their friendly rival, the Rover 2000." Corporate-speak again.

He then said, "We are currently producing for the SAAB Company, in Sweden, 400 per week of the new Triumph 1,700-cc overhead camshaft engine. What I am not prepared to tell you is when you will see this in a Triumph car!" In England, it came only three years later, in the 1972 Dolomite sedan but, in America, it would not come until 1975 in the TR7.

Swindle then introduced C. Spencer "Spen" King, the new engineering director of Standard-Triumph, "whom many of you may have known at Rover." King, well known for his involvement with the Rover gas turbine-powered Le Mans cars and the Rover 2000 sedan, had also done a corporate shuffle to a larger assignment. He introduced the TR6 in terms of the changes and improvements made over the TR5/TR250 that preceded it. He said: "The body has been extensively restyled by Karmann-Ghia and this has been done while still using a number of panels common to the TR5. The overall effect achieved is more modern and elegant. Some of you may wonder why we went to Karmann-Ghia—in fact the initial approach was made by them, at a time when we were overloaded in our Engineering Department. Furthermore, they were able to offer us an attractive package deal, whereby they could design and manufacture the dies to produce the modified body panels in the time required by us." It has been reported since that Triumph first went to Michelotti to do the restyling but he had been too busy to take the assignment.

Not mentioned at the conference was the input of Triumph styling people to Karmann's efforts and especially the contribution from the United States. Bruce McWilliams and his team had strongly influenced major elements of the TR6 including the grille and the new rear panel design.

King praised the Lucas fuel injection system used on the TR6, saying it has "a bright future." In fact, the system was troublesome from the start. In the United States, although we would have liked the performance, considering the potential warranty costs we were generally happy not to have it, except on the racing cars. He also discussed safety and emissions standards, calling them "on the whole, sensible and justified," but expressing disappointment that standards set by different nations so lacked uniformity, creating great expense for manufacturers who had to carry out testing on all specifications.

The U.S. announcement of the TR6 was carried out by the Triumph advertising and marketing team with little help from the corporate side. Media reaction to the car was very positive. The chassis was virtually identical to the TR250, save for wider steel wheels, but the restyled body was so well done that it was treated by most editors as a new car instead of a face-lift. There was one major difference in our message. In the UK, Triumph people spoke openly of the fact that Karmann of Germany did the restyling and convertible top design, but it was kept very quiet in North America. None of the sales training or press kit materials even mentioned it. While UK and European road tests usually covered Karmann's involvement, tests in U.S. magazines did not. It seemed to be all right to publicize the use of Italian stylists like Michelotti but not to let it be known that a German firm had reworked a British car.

The McWilliams touch was evident at the TR6 dealer meetings, where each attending dealer received a merchandising kit including printed material on the features and equipment; a brochure; a day-glo sticker to place in the license plate area of the car when in the showroom; a salesman's test on the TR6; a TR6 lapel pin for salespeople who passed the test; and a comparison chart detailing TR6 advantages over competing sports cars. This was all tucked into a plastic briefcase with a Velcro seal. Bruce's memo to company staff included this comment: "The Velcro

The prototype TR6 (note wipers parked on UK side) and a TR250, side-by-side on the McWilliams' lawn. The center section of the cars, including windshield and doors, is identical, but what a difference Karmann made in the front and rear!
Plain English Archive

seal on the briefcase can be used in the showroom to illustrate how the Velcro fastening on the cantrails of the TR6 top provides a wind-tight seal, a unique feature of this car." These Velcro strips, which held the top tight against the rail above the door, were a great idea but, after a few months of use, the convertible tops shrank enough to prevent the strips from joining, a problem that was never solved.

At the first meeting in Chicago in January, the car received raves from the dealers. It premiered to the public at the Chicago Automobile Show in March, where an improved version of the "Magic Box" created for the TR250 entertained the crowd. The psychedelic sound and light show, for reasons unrecorded, did not appear at the April show in New York. Instead, Jimmy McWilliams staged the Great Triumph Car Painting Contest, in which show visitors who had applied in advance were given the chance to paint their own designs on a Spitfire, GT-6, or TR6, right there in the New York Coliseum.

Three white cars sat on drop cloths in a fenced-off area with large containers of water-based paint at hand, offering the would-be artists a variety of colors. Each entrant had a certain amount of time to complete his or her design, which would then be inspected and photographed for judging. That done, the car was washed off and readied for the next contestant. As inspiration, sample cars stood nearby, painted with unique designs created by Triumph's advertising agency. My company GT-6+ had been summarily taken from me because its dark blue paint

was perfect as the background for a multihued cloud design. The design part of the contest was extended nationwide with thousands of applications received over the next few months and a winner selected the following spring.

During the New York Show, the Spitfire again received the *Car and Driver* magazine People's Choice Award for Best Sports/GT under $2,900. The magazine called the Spitfire "an ideal first sports car" with a "virtually indestructible" powerplant.

I didn't get my GT-6+ back—with the special paint, it was sold at a handsome profit. So were the decorated Spitfire Mk III and the TR6 with a fanciful scheme of stars and stripes. I have often wondered if these three cars still exist with their psychedelic 1960s paint schemes.

There was no question about the TR6 being the most important car in the Triumph line, but it was hard for me to understand why there wasn't more interest in the GT-6+. It had a new, very sophisticated independent rear suspension that replaced the swing-axle type with its erratic handling characteristics. The interior and dashboard had been redesigned, and the car was attractive, comfortable, functional, and *fast.* It had been launched, along with an improved Spitfire Mk III, in the early fall, and I thought it was a wonderful car. However, despite selling over 4,000 units in each of its first three years, the little GT would fade away after only six years in the market, proving again that sports car buyers wanted roadsters. In my opinion, if the GT-6 power train and rear suspension had

On Press Day at the 1969 New York Auto Show, journalists donned smocks and got to work painting designs on three white TRs. Water-based paint allowed quick cleanup after each design was photographed. This was the start of a year-long design contest in which the public was invited to submit designs for paint schemes, with a Spitfire to be given to the winner. Three cars were painted as examples, of which the GT-6 at top left and Spitfire, top right, can be seen. Viewing their idea in action are Bruce McWilliams, standing next to the Spitfire, and Jimmy McWilliams in the group at bottom left. *Road & Track*

been installed in the open Spitfire body, the sales potential would have beaten the GT-6 and four-cylinder Spitfire totals put together. The marketing staff did not agree. They pointed out that the $2,295 price of the Spitfire was one of its major selling points. A six-cylinder model would have to cost considerably more and, due to production line limitations, it appeared the company could not build both versions. Another issue was that the hot Spitfire would quite likely take sales away from the more expensive and more profitable TR6.

In the ensuing years, a number of enthusiasts, including my son, Tim, and long-time BMC/BL/Jaguar service and competition adviser Mike Barratt, built their own six-cylinder Spitfires in 2- or 2.5-liter form. The performance of their creations reinforces my opinion.

The Spitfire Mk III for 1969 had its own set of improvements, including new bucket seats with headrests, a new dash panel which, for the first time, placed the instruments in front of the driver, easy-to-use heater controls, and a leather-rimmed steering wheel. Externally, there were new full wheel covers. The car still had twin SU carburetors but it was the last year. The 1970 U.S. models would make do with one Stromberg. With one virtually new model and two with extensive new technical and comfort features, the Triumph line for 1969 in the United States was far ahead of MG, which had nothing new to offer.

Triumph was back to selling nothing but sports cars, and it would remain that way for the rest of its

With very little change, the Mark III Spitfire for 1969 offered a lot more in appearance and features. The instruments moved in front of the driver for the first time, and bumpers, front and rear, were raised to the height required for impact standards. High-back seats were fitted, and unique wheel covers. It was the last year for twin carburetors. *Plain English Archive*

run in North America, despite having some very good sedans in the home market in the 1970s. The Herald had run its course in the United States. The 2000 sedan, good as it was, simply did not sell, but through a couple of facelifts and engine changes, the car survived as the 2500 in England through the 1977 model

The first Group 44 TR6 racing car was being built when a top-level delegation from Leonia made a visit to the Group 44 shop, then in Falls Church, Virginia. Ed McCauley, vice president and treasurer of British Leyland Motors, Inc., and Graham Whitehead, president, spent a morning with the team prior to more serious government meetings at the Department of Transportation. Having set up the TR250 for the previous season, the Group simply substituted a TR6 body and were ready to go racing! From left, Ed McCauley, Brian Fuerstenau, Bob Tullius, John Kelly, Graham Whitehead, Mike Downs. *Mike Cook*

year. The Rover 2000 and 2000TC did not move out of showrooms much faster but they were retained in 1969 as much as anything, I suspect, to give Rover more presence in the market. Under the stated philosophy that British Leyland would have a car in each market segment, the Rover filled the gap between the MG/Triumph sports cars and the Jaguars.

To get a feeling for what the other half of British Leyland had grown up with, I tried both the new MGC with the 3-liter, six-cylinder engine and the MGB with the 1,800-cc four. I found them comfortable, bland in performance, and pretty archaic in cockpit and control design. With unit body construction, they were undeniably more rigid and had fewer rattles than a typical TR. However, I still could not fathom the MG mania that seemed to characterize not only the customers but the dealers and the company people who marketed the bearers of the octagon. Besides, the MGC put me off. It was an ill-conceived, nose-heavy beast with every fault in the lexicon of British car unreliability, and I was glad to be rid of it after about three months. The MGB proved reliable and even fun, but, having done my product research, I switched to a TR6 in 1970 and stayed with it.

Like the original Spitfire in 1963, the TR6 introduction was hampered by an East Coast dock strike, so deliveries east of the Mississippi did not start until March. The car had been accepted by SCCA for racing in 1969 and the Western racing team had one on the track starting in February. Driver Jim Dittemore, playing tag with a Porsche for the entire race, finished second but beat his best TR250 lap time on the old Las Vegas track by four seconds. They won at the

next event in March. Meanwhile, in northern Virginia, Bob Tullius was supervising preparation of the Eastern team car.

On a trip to Washington, Graham Whitehead and Ed McCauley joined me on a visit to the Group 44 facility in Falls Church, Virginia. Graham was struck by the spotless shop and crisp uniforms of the crew and listened with interest to Bob's pitch about the team's capabilities. Ed and I were more used to Bob's passion for neatness and carefully kept Graham away from the green-lidded trash cans, which were still wet, Bob having sprayed the green paint himself about five minutes before Ed and Graham arrived. Tullius started 1969 with a win in the TR6 first time out.

Profits Early On

British Leyland in the United States in 1969 had a sales increase of 22 percent going for the first seven months, selling more than 41,000 cars. In August, interviewed in London by the *Los Angeles Times*, Lord Stokes talked enthusiastically about the profit made by BLMC in its first 12 months, ended September 1968, and the shakeups being carried out to reduce management staff to a minimum. The article reported on Stokes' close working relationship with leaders and shop stewards of the many labor unions involved in BL factories and his appreciation that workers needed to earn satisfaction from their jobs as well as money.

That was the right attitude, but the *LA Times* article also quoted a London stockbroker as saying that labor troubles were the direct cause of the drop in the price of Leyland shares from 18 shillings to 12 in the time after the corporation was formed. The example given was the Jaguar XJ6 sedan. Announced in late 1968, it was still virtually unavailable 10 months later in its most important market, the United States.

All parts of British Leyland were dealing with a dozen or more different unions in the factories. The relationship between management and labor was generally confrontational. Strikes happened without notice. Groups of workers would simply drop their tools and walk out over some grievance and most, if not all, of the other unions would honor their picket lines, stopping production.

The old British class system was exploited by the unions, making hourly paid workers suspicious and jealous of management. Management seemed unable to understand how to communicate with the men who built its products and acted as though the labor force wasn't bright enough to understand business problems. In any case, management directives had to be communicated to the workers through the shop stewards. Involving the workers in the planning and development process wasn't considered.

Fortune magazine in the 1970s called it "The British Disease." Design and engineering could be inadequate, especially for export markets, resulting in cars or components that did not stand up to the stress of American weather and driving conditions. While the TR6 and MGB were sturdy enough, turnpike driving was stressful for Heralds and early Spitfires and the little Minis and Austins simply weren't up to it. Although Joseph Lucas, Ltd., was labeled "The Prince of Darkness" on account of British cars' electrical problems, many electrical and other items were built to meet a cost specified by British Leyland, and Lucas and other suppliers could not build a decent part for that price.

In practical terms, the labor and specification problems left British cars with a reputation for unreliability that stayed with U.S. buyers to the end of the twentieth century, when only Jaguar and Land Rover were left as "volume" sellers in North America. In the 1950s and 1960s, Triumph could continue selling sports cars because they were the primary source. When the Japanese competitors came on strong, starting with the 240Z in 1970, the aging designs and simple mechanical components of British Leyland cars could not compete. Just keeping up with federal safety and emissions regulations drained money intended for new product development. The U.S. marketing effort faced erratic supplies of cars with indifferent quality and high warranty costs. U.S. management battled constantly for improvements on existing models and faster development of new ones. The corporation first would not, and later could not, make the investment.

In the United States, with hundreds of dealers looking to us for products they could sell at a profit, we had a tremendous responsibility. To sell cars with dated styling, slumping performance, and a bad rap on quality, British Leyland in North America came up with some of the best and most creative advertising and publicity campaigns in the auto industry. But, eventually, we fell behind.

It is telling that, in the 1969 British Leyland Annual Report, Lord Stokes spent three lines reporting an increase of 21 million pounds sterling in gross North American sales, and six paragraphs describing industrial relations. He used the phrase "plagued by industrial disputes." After noting that 100,000 cars and 2,000 trucks had *not* been built due to strikes, he reported a 12 percent increase in profits over 1968 but noted that, in the first three months of 1970, profits were down.

Stokes visited Leonia for the first time in June 1969, during one of his round-the-world inspection trips of the extensive British Leyland facilities. He toured the building, met with the board, and gave a half-hour address to the employees assembled in the service school. Then he left for JFK airport and took off for Madrid. His up-beat speech detailed the BL share of market in the UK, touted the solid investment base in overseas markets, talked in terms of competitive products, predicted a profitable year, and generally reinforced our own enthusiasm. In the early days of British Leyland, we were all hopeful that the new corporation would work and keep its status as the second-largest vehicle producer outside the United States. (VW was first.) They were exciting times, and even though there were a few cynics, we all wanted to believe that the future was bright.

In October 1969, we launched the new U.S. employee journal, *High Gear*, with myself as editor. A message to employees from Graham Whitehead mentioned progress in creating a U.S. public image for British Leyland, and praised the consolidation of BMH and Leyland Motor Corp. as having given the U.S. company "a solid base on which to build a coordinated marketing plan that will improve the sales of all of our vehicles." He announced a 16 percent increase in unit sales for 1969 over 1968 with primary credit going to the Austin America. Perhaps most important, he pointed out that the U.S. market for imports was growing, even in the face of a decline in sales of domestic makes, proving that imports were now firmly established. He said that the British Leyland dealer body was now "strong, well-financed, and knowledgeable about selling our cars," fully capable of meeting the competition from Detroit.

The dealer body was being reduced in size, as the company tried to eliminate overlapping MG and Triumph dealers and consolidate to a British Leyland franchise. J. S. Inskip, Inc., the long-time distributor of Austin, MG, and Austin-Healey, was taken over at the end of September and became the Eastern Zone of Leyland Motor Sales, with the same staff and using the same facilities in Carlstadt, New Jersey. Eliminating independent distributors and initiating other economies were priorities in the campaign to streamline the new British Leyland financially. Thirty years later, remembering these efforts, Ed McCauley and I agreed that few people in Leonia had any idea of the dire financial problems of our parent corporation. Good profits produced by our enthusiastic North American subsidiary simply disappeared into the mounting UK deficit.

At the end of September 1969, Mike Dale was named vice president, sales, for Jaguar as well as Austin-MG. Tony Thompson left to join a Toyota distributor in Chicago, a company owned by the Chicago-based group that distributed Jaguar and Triumph in the Midwest. Bruce McWilliams retained his title as vice president, sales, for Triumph, Rover, and Land Rover, but his wife, Jimmy, departed the firm to take a job for Chevrolet in Detroit, working on the yet-to-be-announced Chevrolet Vega. John Dugdale was made advertising manager for Triumph, Rover, and Land Rover, retaining his Jaguar responsibilities only for a short time. Bob Burden was given the Jaguar advertising brief a few months later, establishing the division in responsibilities that would be in effect until John Dugdale's retirement.

Although he had spent most of his career with Jaguar, John Dugdale had plenty of experience with other British makes from his tenure at the British Automobile Manufacturers Association. He would guide Triumph advertising and promotional activities through a very interesting time, presiding over campaigns such as "From The Land of British Racing Green" and the TR7 "Shape of Things To Come" campaign, with TV commercials featuring wedge-shaped garages, trucks, etc.

An Olympic Petition

The 1969 American Road Race of Champions was at Daytona International Speedway again, over Thanksgiving weekend. British Leyland cars had qualified in force. All participants and spectators were asked to sign a petition to make motor racing an Olympic sport! Conceived by Lyman Gaylord and the Rowland Company as a publicity exercise, the project earned exceptional press coverage and was accepted seriously and enthusiastically by many competitors. The petition suggested the competition be in road racing, hill climbs, and rallies on the Monte Carlo format. It noted that the International Olympic Committee required that a sport be "widely practiced in at least 25 countries" and that motor sport met that requirement at least as well as events such as tobogganing, fencing, and water polo.

In a letter to the I.O.C., Graham Whitehead said, "Events such as the Monte Carlo Rally go through several countries with little regard for national borders. A forthcoming rally sponsored by a London newspaper will take competitors halfway around the world from London to Mexico. A list of the sport's best-known figures, amateur or professional, is an international roll call. The cars themselves are lessons in international cooperation. It is time that motor sport, one of the true international popular favorites, be recognized and included in the Olympic Games, which have the advancement of international brotherhood and understanding as one of their goals."

The application with the required number of signatures was filed with the I.O.C. and rejected. We had anticipated this but we were still disappointed at the brief response from the committee. Still, it was a great publicity idea for British Leyland and accomplished that purpose. Who knows, had it passed, what impact Olympic racing might have had for the manufacturers of competitive cars.

The London-Mexico Rally, sponsored by the London Daily Mirror, which was mentioned in Graham Whitehead's letter, was run in the spring of 1970 and turned out to be a great success for Triumph. Triumph 2.5 PI sedans, driven by Brian Culcheth/Johnstone Syer and Paddy Hopkirk/Tony Nash/R. Johnson took second and fourth places. The 16,000-mile race took 38 days from April 19 through May 27.

A large group of British Leyland people attended the ARRC at Daytona, watching GT-6s finish 1-2-3 in E Production, the TR6 take Third in CP, and the Triumph Competition Department Spitfire Mk III, Lee Mueller driving, hold off Jon Woodner's MG Midget to win FP. The close race, in which Mueller won by two car lengths, earned him the "Outstanding Triumph Competitor" award. I had a special interest in the Spitfire, having arranged with Kas Kastner to buy it after the ARRC.

The company ended the decade and its first full year as British Leyland Motors Inc. with excellent sales and good public acceptance of the newest Triumph, the TR6. Also launched that year was the Rover 3500S, a V-8-powered version of the 2000 four-door sedan. The four-cylinder 2000 and 2000TC were dropped from the U.S. line, leaving only the 3500 and the Land Rover 88 representing Solihull in the British Leyland lineup.

Investment to Support the Market

A photo in the January 1970 issue of *High Gear* shows the new Rover in front of the new office and warehouse under construction for Leyland Motor Sales, Central Zone, Mt. Clemens, Michigan. Our new company was expanding and had already completed construction of a new Northwestern Zone headquarters in Brisbane, California, south of San Francisco. Like Brisbane, the Central Zone facility

Leyland Motor Sales Northwest Zone office in Brisbane, California. Only Triumph and Rover products were handled at that time, but the Zone eventually became full-line and still exists as the Jaguar Cars Western Zone office. *Plain English Archive*

had its own parts warehouse, service and sales training area, etc. Other zones were the Southeast, in New Orleans, Southwest, in Gardena, California, and the Northeast Zone in New Jersey, close to our Leonia headquarters. The financial condition of British Leyland may have been shaky, but it was still willing to invest in the U.S., knowing that this market had the best potential for both volume and profit for years to come.

In the early days of selling imported cars in America, when cash-poor British manufacturers needed quick access to the lucrative U.S. market, it made sense to depend on independent distributors. The distributor's investment eased the financial load on the importing company and reduced the number of employees needed to run the import operation. The distributor's knowledge of the market helped in setting up a dealer network and organizing distribution. But, the extra markup in the price structure for the distributor both raised retail prices and reduced manufacturer/importer profits. Some of the distributors were taking their profits without providing adequate customer service. Poor dealer back-up reflected negatively on the importing company's reputation.

The two remaining Triumph distributors, Genser-Forman in the Northeast and Midwest Triumph in Chicago, theoretically maintained facilities equal to the zone offices, but their methods varied from the corporate standards. We had service people assigned to keep an eye on their territories and assist them in running training programs, regular sales training guid-

In the early 1970s, *Time* magazine did a series of posters featuring its key advertisers. British Leyland products were heavily advertised in *Time,* so we were asked to provide a selection of cars for a shoot. Left to right are a Triumph GT-6+, Rover 3500S, Austin America, MGB, and Jaguar E-type, all 1970 models. For these posters, the "I" in *Time* was always made into a representation of the advertiser, in this case a huge ignition key. *Plain English Archive*

ance, and parts people keeping a close eye on their inventories. Maintaining control over distributors was a headache, and company policy was to eliminate them as quickly as possible.

The 1970 Triumphs looked a great deal like the 1969s but federal regulations had dictated a large number of changes under the bonnet. The Spitfire, with new wheel covers, new badges, plusher interior,

Graham Whitehead, right, and Keith Hopkins, publicity director of British Leyland Motor Corporation, with the latest Spitfire at the 1970 New York Show. The 1970 Spitfire was a one-year car with special RAF style badges, unique wheel covers, some unusual paint colors, and a single-carb engine. It bridged the gap between the original Mark III and the 1971 Mk IV. Hopkins, world PR chief and reporting directly to Stokes, built one of the largest communications staffs on record in the UK motor industry. *Plain English Archive*

and better convertible top lost its twin SU carburetors to one Stromberg. The engine was rated at the same horsepower but performance was down, the start of a trend. Evaporative loss systems, ignition warning buzzers, and other mandated items increased the cost and complication of building all three Triumph models for the United States.

However, the Spitfire once again copped the *Car and Driver* Readers' Choice award with 40 percent of the vote, over the Fiat 850, Datsun 1600, MG Midget, and VW Karmann Ghia. The award was presented at the New York International Auto show where British Leyland, for the first time, had a unified exhibit area with the various marques set apart by different design themes. Triumph's exhibit, designed by Ivan Chermayeff, featured red, white, and blue bull's-eye logos, very like the British aircraft wing markings and echoing the new Spitfire hood and trunk badge designs.

Visiting the show, Lord Stokes addressed a meeting of the Society of Automotive Engineers and called for uniform international safety and emissions standards. He volunteered to get together with American car manufacturers and others worldwide to discuss developing and implementing such standards. He also said that once they have given the industry guidelines, governments "must allow the businessman or industrialist to get on with the job." Good idea, but, given the nature of politicians, unlikely ever to be accomplished.

Befitting a company whose products often made up nearly one-third of the entries at the Sports Car Club of America championships, we were concerned when the club announced that future America Road Race of Champions events, "Run-offs"

The overall view of the 1970 New York Show exhibit. This was the last year that the component parts of British Leyland had separate exhibits. Triumph is in the foreground, Austin/MG, across the aisle, Jaguar next to Austin/MG and Rover far to the left against the back wall. In following years, all the makes were grouped under a British Leyland banner. *Plain English Archive*

The "Sonic Spitfire" was the winning entry in the car-painting contest held nationwide following the 1969 New York Show. In pale blue on a white car, it was actually rather attractive, but never adopted for one of Bruce McWilliams' tape stripe schemes. That's Bruce at left with Bob Tullius, who attended the show with the 1969 SCCA Champion GT-6+ that Mike Downs had driven to victory at Daytona the previous November. *Plain English Archive*

Lord Stokes, left, examined the winning Group 44 GT-6 with Bruce McWilliams, Graham Whitehead, and Mike Dale. These last three were, essentially, British Leyland's marketing team for the United States. Mike Dale was still vice president, sales, for only Austin/MG and Jaguar but, at the end of the year, would take the sales responsibility for Triumph and Land Rover away from Bruce. Bruce would become vice president, product planning, a job that suited him perfectly. Dale, a "natural" as a marketing executive, went on to be president of Jaguar in North America following Graham's retirement. *Plain English Archive*

as they were known, would be held at Road Atlanta, a brand-new racing facility in Gainesville, Georgia, north of Atlanta. The track was not even completed and with the Run-offs slated for Thanksgiving week, the first race was not held until September. Mike Barratt, the eastern competitions manager, and I traveled to Atlanta to get together with Bob Tullius and the Group 44 team to learn about the new track. It turned out to be one of the most spectacular road courses any of us had seen, with a modern three-story tower sited to see the cars race down a hill and along the pit straight, and climb out of sight again through Turns 1 and 2. That trip, the first of many, began a long relationship with Road Atlanta through several owners.

As 1970 came to a close, Graham Whitehead announced that Bruce McWilliams would become vice president, product planning. This new post was a significant one with responsibility for planning U.S. models plus supervision of environmental testing and matters relating to federal safety and emissions standards for all British Leyland cars sold in the United

States. Triumph and Rover marketing responsibilities were given to Mike Dale, making him chief sales executive for all BL makes.

There were other consolidations. In September, the Roosevelt Automobile Company, headed by Franklin D. Roosevelt Jr., ceased to be a Jaguar distributor and the territory was taken over by the Southeast Zone of Leyland Motor Sales. After 12 years, Needham, Harper and Steers Advertising lost the Triumph account. Along with Rover advertising, the business went to Papert, Koenig, Lois of New York. At the same time, Jaguar advertising moved from Cunningham & Walsh to Reach McClinton & Co., which also had the Austin-MG account.

The new agency and the new sales vice president had three new Triumph models to market for 1971. Two were new incarnations of familiar models: the Spitfire Mk IV and the GT-6 Mk III. The third one was perhaps the most ambitious Triumph since Donald Healey's 1935 Dolomite—the V-8-powered Stag, which created great excitement but even greater disappointment.

New Shapes Before the Shape of Things to Come

Following the lead of the TR6, the new Spitfire and GT-6 were restyled front and rear while using the same chassis and center section. Michelotti did the job, using a rear shape styled like the Triumph 2.5 PI sedan of 1969 and reshaping the front to better accommodate the "bone-in-the-teeth" high-mounted bumper. It was such a successful face-lift that, like the TR6, people often thought of the cars as new, rather than reworked. The Spitfire proportions were exceptionally sleek, while the GT-6 gave a good imitation in looks, performance, and appointments of a scaled-down Jaguar E-type.

Mechanically, the GT-6 Mk III was a clone of the GT-6+ except for engine tune. Still rated at 95 horse-power, it did not perform as well because the compression ratio was lower and the ignition timing was retarded as part of the emissions control package. The Spitfire still had a four-cylinder, 1,296-cc engine, but it was not the same unit as the Mk III. It had a heftier crankshaft and beefy connecting rods that made the engine much less willing to rev. A package of tuning changes for reduced emissions cost the car 17 horse-power! Down from 75 horsepower to 58, the car was a dull performer, but sold well on its looks.

This was the era when engine design had not caught up to Federal regulations and all manufacturers were meeting emissions standards by any means that allowed the car to be reasonably drivable. Vacuum controlled distributor advance *and* retard meant that Triumph engines did not always return to idle speed during shifts, making smooth shifting difficult. The retarded timing caused very sluggish response when accelerating from rest. Until fuel injection became common and computerized engine management was developed, the old-style carbureted cars with emission controls and standard distributors with points could not match the performance of Triumphs from the early 1960s.

These negatives aside, 1971 sales of all three car-ryover models were brisk, and we looked forward to announcing the Stag at the New York show. On sale in England since July 1970, the unusual new Triumph was aimed at an upscale market and was priced only about $1,200 below the Jaguar E-type V-12, with which it had shared a Palm Springs, California, press introduction in March. Styled by Michelotti, the Stag looked very much like a convertible version of the Triumph 2.5 sedan, not sold in North America. The Stag was a fast, comfortable, reasonably roomy,

A later Stag with mag wheels, top down, showing the unusual rollbar with forward T-member attached to the windshield. Although it was a convertible, the chrome window frames stayed in place. *Plain English Archive*

A 1971 Stag doing duty as official pace car at Road Atlanta. British Leyland often supplied cars to racetracks on a promotional basis, gaining quite a bit of publicity. This Stag is pacing Class D Production. Brian Fuerstenau, in the Group 44 GT-6 Mk III, is behind the Stag and Carl Swanson, in the Kastner-Brophy Number 6, is a little farther back. *Plain English Archive*

attractive, and modern luxury 2+2 GT/sports car. It was available with automatic and air conditioning, and it had power-assisted steering and brakes, and power windows, as standard equipment. The upholstery was vinyl but luxurious in feel and appearance.

The manual convertible top presented no real problems. When it was down, a padded roll bar was visible, a three-point unit that anchored behind the front seats and extended forward to the windshield frame. It was essential to the rigidity of the car. The Stag could be ordered with a removable hardtop which made it into a snug, silent coupe. It was a good-sized car, close to 2 feet longer than a TR6 but only 5 inches wider. It was a true 2+2, but the rear seat kneeroom and headroom (especially with the hardtop installed) were comfortable only for children—despite the car's wheelbase, a foot longer than on the TR6.

At $5,773 with the hardtop, the Stag was in a new market segment for Triumph. The price, more than $2,000 higher than a TR6, seemed astronomical and the car itself was an unknown quantity. Everything about it was new, including the overhead cam, 3-liter V-8. As Stags went out to customers and we started to learn about reliability, the news was not good.

Over the years, Triumph had tried to sell certain cars that were unsuited to the United States. The Triumph 10s and the original 948-cc Heralds were

really short on power. Heralds, and the 2000 sedan, had reliability problems. But prior to the Stag, purchasers and dealers had never been presented with a car that could not be fixed! The Stag had more electrical systems than other Triumphs and had problems with all of them. The 1971 Stags all had wire wheels with attendant truing and balancing problems. Poorly assembled Stag V-8s overheated, warped cylinder heads, and leaked coolant. The first item on the dealer predelivery check list was pouring a can of Bar's Leaks® into the radiator! The list of recalls included the possibility of the throttle jamming wide open, the fuel filler hose splitting, and failure of the upper U-joint in the steering column.

We all loved driving the Stag. It had pep, it was comfortable, it handled well, and it had eye-catching looks. But even if it had been a well-built and reliable car, the price would have killed it. It survived in the line for three years. By halfway through 1972, most of the cooling problems had been solved, and wire wheels had given way to attractive, easily balanced alloy rims. Unfortunately, the price did not come down, and there were no advertising dollars to spend on a loser. The Stag was gone from the United States at the end of the 1973 model year, even though Triumph built it through 1977. It has since gained a following as an unusual collector car when

R. W. "Kas" Kastner had been Triumph competition manager in the United States since 1962. He resigned at the end of 1970 to become a partner with John Brophy to run racing teams in amateur and professional events. Kastner-Brophy contracted to run a Spitfire, GT-6, and TR6 for British Leyland but also ran an Indianapolis entry. *Plain English Archive*

original, but many owners gave up on the Triumph V-8 and installed Ford V-6 or Buick/Rover aluminum V-8 power.

Although not a racer, the Stag immediately joined the Triumph competition program as a rally car. Renee and Jack O'Leary, nationally ranked in Sports Car Club of America rallying, stepped out of their Rover 3500S sedan and into a Stag. They won a shelf full of trophies with both cars.

Rallying was still a major activity for sports car clubs at the time. SCCA had a two-level National/Regional program. The Triumph club of Ventura County, California, was a leading organizer of professional-caliber rallies and its Mission Trail Rally was in its fourth year in 1971. In addition to the usual time-speed-distance rallies, Monte Carlo–style events were popular, especially in the West. These rallies are based strictly on achieving the correct time from checkpoint to checkpoint without enforcing average speeds or exact routes.

In the racing area, Triumph lost its Western Competitions Manager and long-time Triumph racing expert, Kas Kastner. At the beginning of 1971, he left

British Leyland to join with a friend, John Brophy, in a new racing enterprise titled Kastner-Brophy, Inc. The new team contracted with British Leyland to run a TR6 and GT-6 in SCCA events. Including Huffaker Engineering from northern California, that meant British Leyland had three independent teams racing against each other for SCCA titles, as well as the hundreds of private entrants still running everything from Minis to E-types. It made sense. Each team did its best to outdo the others. Triumph and British Leyland won more races and had more guaranteed headlines. Winning races with modified production cars gave the company more ammunition to sell more cars. It was a philosophy that worked for British Leyland, its predecessors, its successors, and for Jaguar Cars for over 40 years.

By June, sales were up 38 percent for the year and May retail volume was an all-time record for the month. Press coverage quoted Graham Whitehead stating that Triumph sales had been limited in the past due to shortages of cars. He said, "We have now turned the corner on supply, thanks to improved labor relations and additional plant capacity and are looking forward to 1971 being a record-breaking year for Triumph."

Sales did go up sharply in 1971. Imported cars in general sold very well and the U.S. government, urged on by the Detroit car manufacturers, responded by applying a duty surcharge on all imported cars. This temporarily raised Triumph prices by 3.5 percent but, before long, the surcharge was dropped and free market competition was ensured. However, prices continued to rise in part due to more federal safety and emissions legislation.

Triumph sales were 20,250 in 1971, beating all previous TR sports car marks and coming close to the all-time high set back in 1959. They were 39 percent better than 1970, an excellent indication that the feds had not yet killed the market. However, drivability was becoming a problem, due to emissions standards that first restricted performance.

Performance Drops and Sensitivity Rises

For 1972, Spitfires had to make do with an 8.0:1 compression ratio and a miserable 55 horsepower. Returning to a 4.1:1 rear-end ratio helped the low-speed acceleration but raised the noise level when cruising. The GT-6 was down to 85 horsepower but the TR6 hung in with 112. The problem with all of them was the retarded timing and lean fuel mixture, which combined to make them sluggish on the road. New colors and accessories couldn't help them keep up with traffic.

There was great sensitivity within British Leyland about declining performance. The Japanese were coming into the market with new engine designs

TR6s and other British Leyland models being unloaded at the Port of Halifax in late 1974. A good, year-round port, despite the snow, Halifax became one of British Leyland's main eastern entry points, the cars going by rail across Canada and down to the United States. *Plain English Archive*

Alan Alda in his Leonia, New Jersey, driveway with his 1974 TR6. The company sponsored the TV series M*A*S*H, starring Alda, for several years. He was an occasional visitor to British Leyland's corporate service shop. *Plain English Archive*

in modern chassis that could meet regulations without such severe losses in power. Datsun's 240Z approached Jaguar E-type standards of acceleration and speed. While TR sports cars could usually hold their own on the racetrack, the TR6 was usually unable to beat the hot Z.

British Leyland was doing the majority of its business in convertible sports cars, so it was chilling news to hear that federal safety standards for automotive structural strength in rollovers were being proposed. The standards would have required convertible rollover protection to equal that of a steel-roofed car, virtually eliminating convertibles. In Detroit, industry observers were saying the convertible was finished.

"Wrong!" retorted Graham Whitehead. "The convertible is alive and well, only nowadays it is

almost exclusively an imported product." British Leyland, heavily dependent on open sports car sales for U.S. profits, was selling around 60,000 convertibles per year. While Whitehead conceded that some structural changes might have to be made to make Triumphs and other British sports cars conform, he assured dealers and potential buyers that the company could handle the problem.

With limited development funds available, BL product planners had to be practical. TR7 development was well under way and a convertible was part of the plan, but caution dictated putting the convertible on the shelf until the legislators made up their minds. The same thing happened to the Jaguar XJS with the result that, when the anticonvertible legislation was thrown out by a federal district court judge in Cincinnati in the fall of 1973, both convertibles were years behind schedule.

In 1972, Triumph became the first imported car to be a participating sponsor of a major, prime-time TV series. The company got in at the start of a new TV classic, M*A*S*H, starring Alan Alda, McLean Stevenson, and Loretta Swit. The original M*A*S*H film had been an incredible success and the CBS-TV series was eagerly awaited. Even the sponsors shared the press coverage.

One benefit of the M*A*S*H involvement was the occasional appearance of Alan Alda at British Leyland's Leonia, New Jersey, headquarters. Coincidentally, Alda was a resident of Leonia and spent much of the year there when not filming in Hollywood. In 1974 he acquired a TR6 in exchange for some advertising work, including a poster, and would sometimes bring it in for service in person.

The TR series passed a milestone in October. It was 20 years since the first TR, the so-called "TR1," was exhibited at the London Motor Show. That 1952 prototype was first the subject of unmerciful criticism from Ken Richardson and then served as the base for the first successful TR2. Although Triumph expected to sell a reasonable number of TRs, it's doubtful that Sir John Black and his crew could have imagined that, two decades later, Triumph would be selling close to 20,000 sports cars per year in the United States alone!

Recognizing the importance of the U.S. market, Triumph brought Bob Tullius and his Group 44 TR6 racer to London for the Motor Show in October of 1972. In England, where production racing rules were very different, a factory-supported, 160-mile-per-hour Triumph TR6 racing car was unheard of and was a sensation. Once the show was over, a press conference was held at the Silverstone circuit where the lap record for the equivalent class, 2,000–3,000-cc "Modsports," was held by an Austin-Healey 3000. Bob, in his first time on the historic track, lapped regularly at five seconds under the class record while carrying reporters as passengers!

Bob Tullius with show models at the Earls Court Motor Show in 1972. The TR6 was part of a display honoring "Twenty Years of TRs." Following the show, Bob and the car went to a press exhibition at the Silverstone circuit, where he broke the class record. *Plain English Archive*

1973: A Golden Anniversary and an Important Year

Nineteen seventy-three was a big year for Triumph and British Leyland. The company had a revitalized and exciting range of cars to sell. Jaguar introduced the XJ12 sedan at the high end of the range, the Austin Marina sedan and coupe at the bottom, and the Spitfire 1500 to spark up the sports car range. The TR6 got a variety of updates. Even the GT-6 and Stag, in their final year in North America, got cosmetic changes.

The Spitfire 1500 solved the car's power problem with an American solution. "There's no substitute for cubic inches!" the saying goes and the Spitfire's new engine jumped 20 percent, from 1,296 to 1,493 cc, creating a healthy torque increase and producing an exhaust note more worthy of a British sports car. Underneath, at the rear, was the new "swing-spring"

arrangement, introduced on the Mark IV, that got rid of the pernicious swing axle "tuck-under." A further aid to handling, praised by *Road & Track*, was a 2-inch-wider rear track. The GT-6 got this rear-end treatment as well, losing the more sophisticated system installed since the 1969 GT-6+.

Among many TR6 changes was the availability of dealer-installed air conditioning. The factory-tested and approved kit was made by ARA in Texas (now out of business) and worked extremely well. British Leyland had tried A/C installations on all of the sports cars but only the TR6 and Jaguar had the power to handle it. In the TR6, especially with the hardtop, the unit was reliable and made the car into a luxury GT. It helped sell thousands of cars in the hot parts of the United States.

Another 1973 Triumph feature was the installation of "vehicle-sensitive" three-point seat-belt/shoulder harness, which allowed vehicle occupants freedom

Spitfire Number 200,000, a 1973 1500, was delivered through San Jose British Motors. The name of the lucky buyer is unknown. *Plain English Archive*

to move without loss of protection. Now ubiquitous, these belts were very new in 1973 and Triumph was among the first to have them.

The British Leyland exhibit at New York and other auto shows once again put all of the products on one stand, each with its own area. Jaguar featured the XJ12 sedan, the Austin/MG display had the new Austin Marina, and Triumph showcased the Spitfire with a little help from an old competitor. In the TR area was a 1935 Triumph Southern Cross two-seater, a car engineered and tested by Donald Healey, who was Triumph's chief engineer in the 1930s. Actually at New York to announce his own new car, the Jensen-Healey, he obligingly posed for photos with the Southern Cross. Seventy-five years old in 1973, Healey was in great shape, full of stories and industry gossip, and thoroughly enjoying life.

In 1973, once again, the Spitfire and GT-6 received the *Car and Driver* readers award for "Best Low-Priced Sports/GT." This was a perfect lead-in to Triumph's 50th Anniversary celebration, which began in May. A special press kit with a company history

and photos of significant Triumph cars was widely distributed. Fittingly, in what seemed to be a Spitfire year, the 200,000th Spitfire was built in July, driven off the line by Sales Director John Carpenter. A U.S. model, it was sold, eventually, to a young woman in San Jose, California.

Our news release stated that over 150,000 Spitfires had been exported, 57 percent to the United States alone. Some 33,000 had been built at the plant in Malines, Belgium. In its 11th year, the Spitfire was far and away Triumph's largest-selling sports car and it still had eight years to go. In Spitfire marketing, the company finally took advantage of the car's historic name and produced both print ads and a TV commercial featuring a real Spitfire fighter piloted by Ginger Lacey, one of the World War II Battle of Britain aces. Opening to the sounds of pilots scrambling to their aircraft, ready for combat, the commercial shows a brilliant yellow Spitfire 1500 accelerating down a grass airstrip beside the airplane, in World War II camouflage. The car has an attractive blonde passenger. As they race down the runway and

On Press Day at the New York Show, we often had film stars or actors as visitors and, in 1973, we enjoyed the presence of Diana Rigg. She was then starring in *The Avengers* on television but would end up as a leading interpreter of Shakespeare.

the airplane eventually lifts off, the voiceover says "Like your first love, you never forget your first Spitfire. You not only get a car and a girl, but a piece of history."

On a less romantic level, at that year's American Road Race of Champions at Road Atlanta, Triumph staged the Great Spitfire Challenge Race for the Male Chauvinist Pig Trophy. Conceived by the fertile minds of Max Wickens, British Leyland's Canadian PR man, and Lyman Gaylord of our U.S. public relations agency, the race pitted Bob Tullius against Canadian challenger Stephanie Ruys de Perez, a racing champ who normally drove a Mini north of the border. They drove matched "showroom stock" Spitfire 1500s. The cars were prepared in Group 44's shop and were virtually stock except for roll bars and safety harness.

In November 1973, I stood on the start-finish line at Road Atlanta in the midst of reporters, TV newscasters, cameras, and eager fans, savoring a true "media event." Bob and Stephanie, whose lap times in practice had been virtually identical, signed autographs and traded quips while a coin was tossed to determine who would choose the green or blue car. Tullius won the toss and elected green. Both cars were numbered 44. Mike Barratt, BL's eastern competition

manager, and I stepped forward and installed "class letters," gender signs, the circles with the arrow for male and cross for female.

The five-lap race saw several lead changes but Tullius won it by a couple of lengths and took home the trophy with the sterling silver pig on top. We made the network news and a good time was had by all!

In the October 1973 *TSOA Newsletter* came the announcement that a new editor would take over, ending my 15-year association with the publication. John Dugdale, already in charge of Triumph advertising and PR, would become editor, giving me more time to pursue corporate and racing PR activities. Club administration, which had been under Dugdale, went to Fred Horner, a former BMC employee who now had the task of managing all British Leyland marque clubs, the TSOA, MG Car Club, Austin-Healey Club, and Jaguar Clubs of North America. John continued as editor, even after his retirement at the end of 1977, until the final issue in 1981, when the *Newsletter* and the TSOA administration was formally handed over to the Vintage Triumph Register.

The third round of changes in Triumph's U.S. distribution system also came in 1973. Round two had taken place the previous year when the territories of Genser-Forman Distributors in the Northeast and

The Spitfire takes off. Featuring an operational World War II Spitfire and the new 1500, this ad ran in many magazines in 1973. A TV commercial, showing car and airplane racing side-by-side down the runway, was shown extensively. The pilot is Ginger Lacey, Battle of Britain ace. *Plain English Archive*

Midwest Triumph Distributors, operating out of Chicago, were consolidated in Leyland Motor Sales. The Northeast Zone, based in Carlstadt, New Jersey, near British Leyland headquarters, took over the Genser-Forman territory and now handled Triumph, MG, Jaguar, and Land Rover. The Central Zone, in its brand-new building in Mt. Clemens, Michigan, took over from Midwest Triumph in 1972 and added MG and Jaguar in 1973.

At the end of 1973 Triumphs were distributed through Leyland Motor Sales in the Northeast, Central, Northwest, and Southeast Regions. British Motor Car Distributors of Los Angeles for southern California; Continental Cars of St. Louis, with four

states for TR; Royston Distributors of Philadelphia; and Overseas Motors of Fort Worth all now became full-line British Leyland distributors.

It was a great disappointment for many on the Triumph side when George Turnbull resigned from his position as one of two deputy managing directors of British Leyland in the UK. The other was John Barber. Following the resignation of Sir George Farmer, former head of Rover and BLMC deputy chairman, John Barber had been promoted to be not just deputy chairman but managing director.

George Turnbull knew the car business from the manufacturing side, knowledge badly needed in British Leyland management, while Barber was a financial man from Ford. George went on to become a consultant to the automotive industry worldwide. Operating from a home office in Switzerland, he was a major force behind the development of Korean auto manufacturing and other activities until his death.

Worldwide British Leyland sales were up, but labor problems made the supply of vehicles erratic. Product quality was poor, leading to high warranty costs. Worse, there was little money for development of really new cars, and competitors were nibbling away at British Leyland's share of market in every category from Minis to Jaguars.

The year closed out with the on-time announcement of the 1974 Triumphs and passed into what many would remember as the final year of the "old times" for Triumph and British Leyland.

A Bridge to an Uncertain Future

The British Leyland Annual Report for 1973 (year ending September 30) was issued in December and, on the face of it, was extremely encouraging. Sales were up nearly 20 percent over 1972 and profit after tax was 27.9 million pounds, more than 30 percent better than 1972. The trouble is that by the time these figures reached the shareholders, the world situation and the potential for car sales in 1974 had been drastically affected by the fuel crisis that began in October 1973.

Precipitated by the Yom Kippur War between Israel and Egypt, artificial restrictions by the Arab states on fuel shipments to Western countries created an energy crisis. Overnight, the simple act of buying gasoline became a matter of lining up, sometimes for hours. Stations posted signs like "Three dollar limit" or "Five gallons per car" and it became a habit to automatically join any line of cars waiting for gas if it wasn't very long. Gas had been less than 50 cents a gallon, now the price was 75 cents or more. People with oil heat worried about the coming winter and the federal government called on businesses to reduce building temperatures to 65 degrees.

In Britain, heavily dependent on imported oil, the crisis was much worse. By the beginning of 1974,

the fuel shortage, coupled with a strike by coal miners, forced the country to save energy by allowing only a three-day work week for industrial plants. The loss of production thus created, together with a worldwide disinclination to buy new cars, turned British Leyland's profit picture upside down.

Fuel economy became everyone's concern. The *TSOA Newsletter* had feature articles on fuel economy in three out of the first four issues of 1974. An argument erupted between British Leyland and the Environmental Protection Agency over Spitfire and TR6 fuel mileage. The EPA figures were 22.7 and 16.4 while Triumph, over a 50,000- the end of the year, the EPA had revised its testing methods, described in the *Newsletter* by John Dugdale as "strange and arbitrary," to something fairer.

Minissima was the perfect city car, according to British Leyland press material. It was intended to park straight in to the curb and had only one door, at the rear. In the gas crisis of 1973–1974, it was touted as doing 40 miles per gallon. At the 1974 Chicago Auto Show, the model is about to get in. Watching to see how she fares are, from left, the author; Lyman Gaylord from the Rowland Company, BL's PR agency; and Richard Scullin, the corporate exhibit manager. *Plain English Archive*

Instead of touting horsepower and speed, at several auto shows, the British Leyland exhibit featured an "idea car" called Minissima. Designed as a city runabout seating four, Minissima could do 40 miles per gallon and had only one door, at the rear. Less than 8 feet long, it was short enough to be parked nose-in to the curb anywhere.

The GT-6 and the Stag were gone from the Triumph lineup. Although the little coupe seemed to have potential when introduced, it had never sold as

many as 5,000 units in a year and 1973 sales had been only 2,198. The styling changes that had made the Spitfire Mk IV and 1500 so appealing to buyers had not helped the GT.

More than one auto writer and some company people have said that, by 1973, the Stag's basic mechanical and quality problems had been solved. That may have been true, and the car continued to sell in England, staying in production until 1977. Better or not, the U.S. dealer body had no confidence in the car and that is something that cannot be overcome by advertising. In three years of trying, U.S. dealers had moved only 2,500 Stags and more than 400 leftovers were still sitting in showrooms. The company decided to go with just the Spitfire and TR6, knowing that a new model, the TR7, would arrive at the beginning of 1975.

British Leyland continued to promote product performance by going racing. A convenient study by the Automobile Competition Committee of the U.S. showed that all forms of auto racing added together totaled just 1/10th of 1 percent of leisure-time gasoline consumption. Following government guidelines, however, the Sports Car Club of America reduced the length of its sprint races by about 20 percent and did not sanction any endurance events.

Tennis stars Jimmy Connors and Chris Evert won their singles events at Wimbledon and were presented with new Triumph 2500 TC sedans, which they used while in the UK. Since the TR sedans could not be brought into the United States, both Chris and Jimmy picked up TR6s when they returned. John Dugdale succeeded in getting both of them to pose for showroom posters.

After battling the three-day week for three months and then watching the British inflation rate top 17 percent, British Leyland management watched vehicle sales drop by 141,000 units for the year, creating a loss of 6.7 million pounds after tax. More and more bank loans were needed just to pay wages. After allowing for "extraordinary items"—mainly the cost of closing down local assembly of BL cars in Australia— the company was in the red by nearly 24 million pounds. In the Annual Report, Donald Stokes stated that additional financing could not be obtained, "making the corporation more vulnerable in the immediate future to erosion of cash by inflation and strikes." The liquid assets would not cover the debt. The corporation was broke. Stokes said that the choice was to cut back on investments "to an unacceptable extent" or seek financing from other than normal commercial sources. He appealed to the government.

The government suggested a third choice, in the form of loan guarantees, on the condition that a government-appointed team would look into and advise on the company's situation and prospects. Support for long-term financing "would involve a measure of public ownership." We would now learn a new acronym, "NEB," standing for National Enterprise Board. With approval of Parliament, this new British Labor Government agency would oversee future British Leyland operations and be involved in other industries as well.

It was inconceivable that the corporation could be allowed to go under. British Leyland employed more than 50,000 people and still had a one-third share of the British car market. Exports, especially to North America, brought in generous amounts of foreign currency, a big help to the British economy. Watching from Leonia, we assumed the situation would be worked out and thought only of production dates to be met, vehicle volumes needed for 1975, and the all-new Triumph that we would be showing to the world automotive press for the first time in January. Moreover, the first two years' production were all to be exported. Home market sales would not begin until 1977.

A TR7 test car was left in Leonia in early fall for a couple of days so management could test-drive it. Approaching the car for the first time, my reaction was that it was short, high off the ground, and dull-looking, with no bright metal trim except wheel trim rings. I got in and faced an interior that was all black from upholstery to dashboard. There was no chrome or bright trim, and only the instrument markings and the lettering on the switches and knobs provided contrast. Starting it up and hearing the flat, dead sound of the highly touted (but detuned for the U.S. market) overhead-cam engine, many of us were glad that the TR6 would be built for at last two more years.

Limited to local streets and 40 miles per hour, we managed to get a feel for the car's capabilities by running it through a section of landfill next to the beginning of Interstate 80. There, on pathways usually used by kids on dirt bikes and off-road Honda three-wheelers, we did broadslides through turns and vaulted ditches and did hands-off braking tests. The little car was willing enough and took the punishment without breaking. It was comfortable despite the short wheelbase and had to be the widest sports car any of us had ever seen. The power was just okay, and we were all disturbed that it had an Austin Marina gearbox and rear axle. Worse, it was a coupe and there was no convertible on the horizon.

Whatever our collective opinion, we were scheduled to announce the car in Boca Raton, Florida, in January. About 75 journalists and several hundred dealership owners and employees would be expecting a good show and an exciting new car. With scant attention paid to Christmas and the New Year, we got busy.

CHAPTER

9 More Than Just Racing

The story of Triumph in competition has never been fully told in one volume. There is so much: European and North American rallying, Le Mans, SCCA championship competition in the United States, and the IMSA pro series. But Triumph's racing success can't just be chronicled by listing victories, trophies won, or championships.

Winning on the racetrack helped Triumph to sell cars to people who wanted performance and liked to drive a winner. Even when federal regulations drained power and performance, the cars' race track exploits kept buyer interest high. It was always a marketing program—if the Triumph entries had won and not sold any cars, the racing budget would have been spent on magazine pages or TV time in a hurry.

It wasn't all just cars and parts. The British Leyland racing support extended to items like corporate sponsorship of the SCCA convention and helping the Nelson Ledges track build an infield access bridge. We also provided pace cars at various times to

several circuits including Road Atlanta, Pocono International, and Laguna Seca. The company's awards program won the hearts of competitors, not only through checks but with parts discounts and technical advice from East and West Coast competition managers. Even more, we kept our following of loyal racers, because the factory team people were always ready to give advice or lend a hand in the paddock at the races . . . helping fellow Triumph drivers who might, that day, beat them in the race!

Corporate ego might have demanded that factory cars always be the quickest and have the very latest components, but marketing sense said that if a Triumph was first it didn't really matter which car it was . . . a win was a win and could be advertised. So the factory-backed teams did the development work, but the technology was quickly passed on and the new parts made available to other Triumph competitors when needed. Such was the enthusiasm of private competitors that they often pursued their own paths

The presentation made by Group 44 at racetracks was always tidy and professional. Under British Leyland, an MGB had joined the team, along with the Spitfire 1500, GT-6 Mk III, and TR6. Taken in 1973 or 1974.

to performance, frequently coming up with solutions which, in the hands of a good driver, could beat the factory teams. It was a friendly rivalry, but deadly serious, and it went on for 20 years, ending only when Jaguar Rover Triumph had to eliminate racing from its budget at the end of 1982. Several important teams and personalities marked the racing years.

Group 44

Group 44 came to life in the Fuji bar in 1962. Bob Tullius turned it into an actual company in 1965 with Brian Fuerstenau and Dick Gilmartin as cofounders. The team workshop was a cinderblock lean-to on the end of a garden apartment building in Fairfax, Virginia. Built by Ed Mernone, who owned the apartment complex, the shop had low rent as long as the group would service a Morgan 4/4 raced by Ed's daughter, Pat.

In those early days there was no monster transporter with Quaker State Oil sponsorship. Bob's TR4, his old TR3, and Dick's Spitfire traveled to races in the Northeast on individual trailers behind sometimes battered tow vehicles.

By 1966, Bob had secured Quaker State sponsorship and the cars went to events in style. However, Quaker State didn't pay for parts or other vehicles. Bob's well-used Ford Galaxy was prone to breaking things like tie rods in the midst of a desperate dash downhill from Watkins Glen, going for parts. In 1966, I arrived at the Glen for a spring

Lawton "Lanky" Foushee came out of stock car racing to boss the Group 44 crew at amateur and professional races for close to 20 years, applying his engineering talent as needed. He was a pillar of the organization.

The fastest Triumph ever was the TR8 GTO coupe, raced with distinction in 1979 and 1980 by both Bob Tullius and Brian Fuerstenau. Here it is exiting Turn One at Watkins Glen in the 1969 Six-Hour Manufacturers' Championship race. *Mike Cook*

Kas Kastner is serious about racing but not always. At this race at Riverside he's demonstrating "Kas' Porsche Stop" spray while Richie Ginther, left, manager of the Porsche team, and Triumph driver Jim Dittemore enjoy a chuckle. *Courtesy R. W. Kastner*

SCCA national race driving a new TR4A, and parked by the truck. Bob greeted me with unusual warmth. He led me around the trunk, talking a blue streak. In 15 minutes or so, we walked back, and the first thing I saw was my TR4A, back end up on jack stands,

wheels off, and brakes removed. The race car needed rear shoes, and the team was out of parts, time, and, most importantly, money.

I once asked Lanky Foushee, famous in his own right as Group 44 crew chief beginning in the early 1970s, what it was like to work for Bob, when the hours were "until it's done" and the pay was far less than he could earn in NASCAR. "Well," he said, "we eat good and we always stay in a decent place." Even in the tight-budget days, Bob saw to it that the crew had a good breakfast, fed them wholesome sandwiches at lunch (often made by long-time girl-friend Pam Compton), and got them back to the motel in time for dinner. That and clean uniforms and the prestige of working for the team made up for the low pay. Bob had a talent for business and an eye for competent people whether drivers or technicians. His ex-crew members are still working on top teams today or running their own businesses and trading on the self-respect he gave them. But he was a tough boss.

When we moved into our new offices in Teaneck, New Jersey, I was sending Bob a check for $350 per race weekend for advertising services, hardly enough for food. Bob was supposed to pay dealer price for race cars and parts but, according to Ed McCauley and unknown to me at the time, an

The Kastner-Brophy rig in the paddock at Road Atlanta for the 1972 championships. Color scheme on the cars was two-tone blue and white.

The TR7 convertible came out in 1979 and won the DP championship, courtesy of Huffaker Engineering and driver Lee Mueller. The classy black/blue/silver car had a roll cage designed to look like the convertible top. Joe Huffaker Jr., in glasses, took a victory lap with the crew.

upper management decision had been made to keep the team account open. The value of the team's promotional services was obvious to other manufacturers as well and we didn't want to lose them. The team qualified for racing support payments, and Bob still has the very first Standard-Triumph check he received for a win. He told me the $100 check never arrived, so we cut him another one and he framed the original. Tight by nature, he made every penny count on his team. Drivers got expenses and glory. He paid himself, Brian, and the crew like Scrooge, but he did not stint on what was needed to make the cars win races.

Bob's concept of a "professional amateur" racing team worked. Every race weekend, he contacted the local Triumph dealer and tried to set up a promotion for which he charged a fee. The team cars and drivers would appear in the showroom for a couple of days prior to the race to meet the public and local media. The dealer could advertise the event and would have his name on the cars for the race. In some cases, after a win, the team would be back at the dealership on Monday but usually the truck was on the road before the trophies were handed out, trying to make it home in time for a night's sleep for the crew, saving motel costs.

Mild-mannered Californian Charlie Gates started racing in his 40s. Tenacious on the track, he drove for Kas Kastner, winning several regional championships and the SCCA 1965 D Modified crown in a very special TR4A. Charlie, left, and Kas are shown with the "Macao" Spitfire, an open version of the Le Mans cars, built to run in the Grand Prix of Portuguese Macao.

Dick Gilmartin (center) and Brian Fuerstenau, right, share a laugh with Bob Tullius during practice for the 1965 American Road Race of Champions at Daytona. An advertising executive, Dick was one of the original partners in Group 44 with Bob and Brian. His relaxed approach did not match Bob's intensity and he left the Group but continued to race his GP Spitfire.

Bruce Kellner shadowed Bob Tullius at race after race in the early 1960s. Tullius takes the checker from Tex Hopkins at Marlboro, Maryland, in 1962, with Kellner second by a few feet.

After the cinder block shop, the team was head-quartered for about 10 years in a steel building in Falls Church, Virginia, where it had more room to work and space to park the truck. Quite a few championship cars came out of the little building. It was the place where British Leyland people like Mike Dale and Graham Whitehead were first introduced to Group 44 operations and began the association that took them to Le Mans with Jaguar 15 years later.

In 1975, Bob leased space in an industrial complex in Herndon, Virginia, near Dulles International Airport, and built a modern race-preparation facility. This was the shop where the first TR7 racers were built. The E-type V-12 and the first Trans-Am XJS also came out of Herndon where, for the first time, the team had its own dyno and a "clean room" where engines were built. The last and most exciting

Ed Barker won the SCCA GP championship in this Spitfire at Riverside Raceway in 1964. His crew was son Jerry, left, who later won both GP and FP titles in Spitfires with Dad as his crew.

Don Devendorf had been a Spitfire racing champion, but became a terror on the track in the Kastner-Brophy GT-6 Mark 3.

Triumph racers from Group 44, the two IMSA GTO TR8s, were built and dynoed in Herndon. Bob had made his racing concept work and made money doing it. The team had an airplane now, flown by both Brian and Bob. Later, Bob invested in an oil distributorship, Skyline Oil, in Winchester, Virginia. Alongside the oil warehouse he built a racing facility complete with dyno room, machine shop, clean room, paint/body shop, and every necessity to handle the demands of professional racing.

Group 44 is out of business now. The last racing shop, in Winchester, Virginia, is still there next to Bob's Skyline Oil Co. headquarters but is occupied by other businesses. Now a vintage aircraft enthusiast, Bob lives in Sebring, Florida. He has a hangar at the airport filled with his own air force, including a Beech King Air, a Stearman biplane, and a P-51 Mustang. Crew chief Lanky Foushee, who ran Group 44 as a vintage racing and restoration shop for several years, is semiretired in South Carolina. But the concept of a squeaky-clean, pro-am racing team lives on.

Lee "Mother" Mueller on the victory stand at Road Atlanta after winning the DP championship in a TR7 convertible. He drove for both Kastner and Huffaker in Spitfire, TR6, TR7, and TR8. Later he raced a Jaguar V-12 E-type for Huffaker. He loved to uncork the champagne and have a good time, but was a fast, no-nonsense competitor.

Ken Slagle raced Triumphs exclusively, starting with a TR3 and going on to a TR8. He built his racers primarily on his own, at home. The essence of a tenacious SCCA competitor, he attracted sponsorship from British Leyland becoming, in effect, the eastern factory TR8 driver in SCCA after Group 44 went pro. Ken won national championships with an FP Spitfire and the C Production TR8.

R. W. Kastner

Born in Batavia, New York, not far from Bob Tullius' birthplace of Rochester, Kas Kastner (what "R. W." stands for is a well-kept secret) went into the army after high school and was stationed in Colorado. He fell in love with the Rocky Mountains and moved there, becoming a service manager at a dealership in Salt Lake City. He got into sports car racing, driving an MG TD, and built two MG-based specials. In 1954, Alan Bethell and Joe Richards, Triumph's western sales and service reps, came to the dealership to set up a Triumph franchise. Kas found the TR2 had the performance and room he needed and bought one.

Over the next four years, Kas raced the TR2 and then a TR3, winning a raft of races and, in 1959, three separate championships. Eager to move to Los Angeles, he had lucked into the service manager's job at Cal Sales, via his connection with Joe Richards. When Standard-Triumph bought Cal Sales, he was told that, as an executive, he couldn't race any more. Now in management, he was still the only person employed by Standard-Triumph who really knew about racing and racing politics. When Fred Gamble started the discussion on how to support Triumph owners in racing, Kas came up with the "expenses for next race" concept. Soon he was developing parts—cams, sway bars, magnesium wheels.

Quiet, reserved Carl Swanson drove for Kas Kastner in several Triumphs including the TR6 during the Kastner-Brophy racing years.

The idea of sending a team of TR4s to Sebring may have been mine, or Kas'. Wherever it came from, late in 1962, three hardtop TR4s were delivered to the service shop at the Western Zone in Gardena, California, and Kas started building cars. To gain maximum publicity, we made a PR decision to invite

Rick Cline is a race preparation specialist from Gainesville, Florida, who did his own development work, entirely separate from the official Triumph racing program. He raced GP and FP Spitfires and a GT-6 in EP, winning national championships with all three. In 1973 he qualified all three cars, winning GP and taking second in FP. Friendly and accessible, he shared his secrets and prepared cars for competitors.

the top TR4 SCCA drivers to drive at Sebring, rather than using international drivers more familiar with endurance racing. In the end, we invited Bob Tullius; Charlie Gates, the Pacific Coast champion; Jim Spencer, who had won in the Midwest; Bob Cole, from northern California; Bruce Kellner, who had his own TR4 on the track in the Northeast about the time Tullius started racing his; and Ed Diehl, Bob's partner and car builder, who was a first class driver in his own right. For insurance, management (UK and U.S.) said we should include a more experienced crew. The UK suggested Peter Bolton, a Triumph dealer from Leeds, England. We paired him with Mike Rothschild of New Jersey, who had driven for us at Sebring in 1957 in a TR3. Both men had driven for the factory at Le Mans in the TRS. Bolton and Rothschild got one car and the other six shared two, an arrangement that didn't please very many people, including Kas.

When the checker dropped, the problems were over—the TR4s finished first, second and fourth in class. Later that spring, Kas was named competitions manager for the United States. Kas has said more than once that, to get and keep credibility, all you have to do is "do what you said you would do." He carried that philosophy through prepping TR4s for the Shell 4000 Rally in 1964; co-managing the factory Spitfire team at Sebring 1965, returning in 1966 with a TR4A team; developing and racing the TR250K in 1968; and, from 1964, preparing and running

official competition department team cars. He also authored several handbooks on Triumph racing preparations. Quite a plateful.

At the end of 1970, Kas became a partner in a new company formed with a well-to-do racing enthusiast friend, John Brophy. Kastner-Brophy Racing built Triumph racers for SCCA racing, and also ran a Triumph Vitesse 2-liter in the professional Trans-Am series, competed at Indianapolis, and won the 1971 USAC road racing division with a Lola 192 driven by Jim Dittemore. After a three-year run, the team was dissolved, and Kas started his own business, designing and marketing items as diverse as turbo-charging kits and hardware for racing sailboats, one of his hobbies.

In 1986, finding that Nissan was looking for a senior manager to run its overall racing operations in North America, Kas applied for the job. As head of Nissan Motorsports, he managed teams to championships in everything from SCCA to off-road trucks. Later, in charge of Nissan Performance Technology Inc., he managed the company's highly successful International Motor Sports Association GTP team, winning at Sebring, winning the championship, and competing at Le Mans.

Now retired but still doing consulting, Kas frequently gets calls and letters about Triumph racing and is active on the internet, always prepared to give useful, hard-hitting advice. Triumph enthusiasts have enjoyed seeing him at major club events.

Hardy Prentice in his former "daily driver." His first and only car for many years, the TR3 was driven from Michigan to California and then to and from the races. Always doing his own preparation on a tight budget, Hardy finally won a national championship with the TR3 after owning it for nearly 25 years. He and his car demonstrate what amateur racing is all about.

Huffaker Engineering

Joe Huffaker's record includes preparing the most successful Jaguar E-type racer in history, building countless racing MG Midgets and Austin-Healey Sprites, running the West Coast factory Jaguar E-type V-12, and even building an Indianapolis car called the "MG Liquid Suspension Special."

It seems unlikely that Triumphs would appear anywhere in Joe's list of credits, but his San Francisco Bay–area shop constructed several of the fastest TR7 and TR8 race cars in the 1970s. Already established as British Leyland's western MG team, running an MG Midget and MGB, Huffaker was given the TR7 assignment in 1975, because the factory West Coast Triumph effort had ended with the dissolution of Kastner-Brophy. In 1976, the team's first year, its TR7 coupe, driven by Lee Mueller, ran an epic contest against Paul Newman in a TR6, finishing second to the actor by inches.

Huffaker's new TR7 convertible won the SCCA DP championship in 1979 with Mueller driving. Huffaker also built TR8s for JRT, winning the West Coast CP championship but losing to the Nissan effort at Road Atlanta in 1980.

Joe Huffaker is happily retired, but Huffaker Engineering lives on, managed by Joe Jr. Winning racers still pour out of the shop, although these days they are exotics like the new DeTomaso Mangusta for the Trans-Am series.

Dick Stockton, a mild-mannered, all-makes mechanic from Pennsylvania, had talent both as a driver and race car engineer. Shown competing at Vineland, New Jersey, in 1965, his black TR4 was frequently in the lead. Stockton's shop was a mecca for TR racers who wanted high-quality car preparation; they became known as "The 71 Crowd."

Against the Odds–
The Last, Brave Years

The Final Strategy

On April 23, 1971, a group of 15 to 20 men had gathered in Coventry to discuss the sports car policy of British Leyland Motor Corporation. Called and chaired by Lord Stokes, chairman of BLMC, the meeting included engineers and sales executives from Triumph, Austin-Morris, Rover, and Jaguar, all parts of the corporation. Even Sir William Lyons, the legendary chief of Jaguar, was asked to play a part, and the meeting was held in the styling showroom at Jaguar. Attending from the United States were Graham Whitehead, president of British Leyland Motors Inc., and Bruce McWilliams, vice president, product planning.

The purpose of the meeting was to discuss existing BL sports cars, study their competitors and the potential of various export markets, and make decisions that would commit the corporation to certain policies. As it turned out, these commitments were to last through the rest of the company's life. Most important of the market segments considered was the midrange area, where the MGB and TR6 were the corporation's major products. The large sports car market, according to the outline for the meeting, would be covered by code-name "XJ27," the future XJS, already being developed at Jaguar. A new small sports car, code-named Calypso, was recommended to replace the Triumph Spitfire and MG Midget.

The Lynx concept in clay form. Several prototypes were built and survive. The car was close enough to being produced that environmental testing was done in the United States. *Courtesy J. Bruce McWilliams*

Triumph Styling had produced two midrange designs for the meeting to consider. Both were running prototypes. One, a 2+2 fastback, was code-named Lynx. The other, a two-seater with removable Targa roof, wore the code-name Bullet. Both were to have a variety of engine possibilities. Lynx, as a midrange, luxury sports model, would offer a 2.5-liter six and the Rover aluminum V-8. Bullet, a lower-priced car, was to offer a small 1-500-cc four, Triumph's 2-liter slant four, and, possibly, the V-8.

Although the design presented that day was not accepted, Bullet remained the name of the project that resulted in the TR7 and, ultimately, the TR8. The concept of offering the more powerful V-8 version was established from the beginning. Whatever it was, Calypso was hardly discussed at the meeting and simply disappeared. Bruce McWilliams doesn't even remember it.

Lynx survived the 1971 meeting. It had been conceived first and was eventually developed far enough that six prototypes were built and extensive testing was done in the United States and elsewhere. A fastback with "love it or hate it" styling, it got some positive comments from people at clinics set up to test consumer reaction, but North American management and dealer reaction was strongly negative.

The concept of a "family sports car" with a back seat had never attracted buyers in export markets, which preferred the sportier two-seaters. The final rejection of Lynx, which was now based on the TR7, took place during a later meeting at Longbridge about 1978, in which Bruce says it was brought up at the start of the meeting and "was gone in 10 minutes."

Bullet quickly became a serious project, in line to replace the TR6 and possibly the MGB as well. The documents prepared for the meeting clearly state that there would be just one future midrange sports model from British Leyland, to be built by Triumph. The ingredients of performance success were certainly part of the original plan.

Once the two styling submissions had been reviewed, the meeting reconvened and things began to get complicated. The Triumph design for Bullet was rejected as "unsuitable." Bruce

Harris Mann's original sketch for the TR7 shows that the design was stubby from the beginning, but had more sculpture details on bumpers, etc.
Plain English Archive

In clay form, this is the TR7 that was approved by management. Done in the styling studio at Austin-Morris in Longbridge, it clearly has MG badges in the wheel centers, a little marque chauvinism showing through. *Plain English Archive*

McWilliams felt it was ugly and not capable of being improved. The stylists were sent back for another try, but their second attempt never made it to the evaluation process. George Turnbull and Harry Webster, both ex-Triumph men but now top executives of British Leyland, attended the meeting carrying a large case that evidently held styling drawings, but it was not opened or mentioned. Turnbull was deputy managing director of BL and Webster was chief engineer for Austin-Morris. It turned out that they had asked Harris Mann, styling director of Austin-Morris, to do some drawings of a midrange sports car. Mann's drawings were in the case.

After the rejection of the Triumph design, the meeting broke up, with Stokes asking Lyons, among others, to work on some styling ideas. However, the Harris Mann drawings were evidently shown privately to Stokes and other top BL executives, who gave the go-ahead without benefit of another group meeting. The next time Bruce McWilliams saw the Bullet project, it was in clay form at the Austin-Morris styling studio in Longbridge, and was the now-familiar TR7 wedge shape. By then it was too late for Bruce or anyone from the United States to influence the shape of the car.

The decisions had been made by Stokes, Turnbull, and Harry Webster, who, according to Bruce McWilliams, were not "strong car people." They were businessmen—Turnbull was a respected factory boss; Stokes, a truck company boss; and Webster, a practical engineer. Bruce's success with the TR250 had given him entree into styling matters in the corporation but too often after the fact.

Despite British Leyland's attempts to erase strong product identity and marque loyalty, people who had worked under one company banner all of their lives still had deep feelings for the product. Thus, it is perhaps not surprising that the Longbridge stylists presented the new Triumph styling buck wearing MG badges! Photos show octagons quite clearly present in the center of the various wheel choices.

While discussions on the future sports car plan proceeded, management in the United States had been asking over and over for more TR6s. There was such a shortage that dealers thought we were holding back. Triumph was capable of building around 10,000 units per year, of which 9, 000 were exported, mainly to North America. The TR6 was a sound, reliable, proven vehicle, and dealer gross profit on the car was about five times what could be made on a Buick! It was so popular that Bruce calculated we could sell 18,000 per year. Keeping the TR6 in the line alongside the TR7 was proposed, but was felt not to be feasible because it would take sales away from the TR7.

Triumph sports car supply was seldom adequate. The problem was too many other Triumph models, most of which were sold only in the UK. For a small manufacturer, the company had a huge range, starting with the Herald and proceeding through Toledo, 1500, and Dolomite sedans to the 2000 and 2.5, which were midrange cars. Add the sports cars, and it was easy to see why Triumph engineers, production people, and marketers could not focus like people at MG, who only had three or four models to consider. Bruce McWilliams says Triumph people were splendid to work with and tremendously receptive to new ideas. They worked incredible hours but were often overwhelmed by the volume of work.

Turning the TR7 Concept into a Car

The process of developing a new car had always been achingly slow in the British industry, and British Leyland made the process even more agonizing. Corporate committees poked into every aspect of the individual operating units and made seemingly arbitrary decisions on everything from production rates to final styling. Although the Bullet project was styled in the old British Motor Corporation studios at Longbridge, Triumph people, bitterly unhappy at being shut out of the design selection, were charged with the engineering and development and would build the car. Chief Engineer John Lloyd was put in charge.

Development of four-cylinder and V-8 models of Bullet proceeded in parallel. A photo in William Kimberley's book on TR7 and TR8 shows a V-8-powered TR in company with a four-cylinder on test in Wales in 1973, two years before the TR7 was introduced and seven years before the TR8 went on sale. In a 16-millimeter film made for the U.S. TR7 press introduction in 1975, an overhead shot of the experimental area at the Triumph factory in Liverpool clearly showed a car with the hood removed, revealing a V-8.

Even in 1971, when Bullet was only a project on paper, there were barriers to use of the V-8. Production of the aluminum engines was low and was dedicated to Rover, which used it in the exciting new Range Rover and had just brought out the 3500S, a V-8 version of the four-cylinder TC sedan. Also, although Triumph was developing a five-speed gearbox, it was not ready and a four-speed was considered

The cover of the original 1975 TR7 brochure began the "wedge" theme and the phrase "The shape of things to come" used to market the car for several years.

inadequate for the V-8. So TR8 development slowed and TR7 went ahead.

British Leyland bean counters dictated using the four-speed, "single rail" gearbox and light-duty differential assembly from the Austin Marina sedan in the TR7, a money-saving ploy that seriously hurt the car's marketing potential. This was the same gearbox introduced in the Spitfire for 1975. At least the Spitfire could be ordered with overdrive, but the TR7 was stuck with just four speeds. In one of the first road tests, a British car magazine commented that droning across Europe using 4,000 revs to attain only 70 miles per hour was not their idea of sports car performance!

British sports cars had always been roadsters first with coupes an afterthought. As mentioned in chapter 8, however, federal roll-over regulations proposed in 1971 would have virtually eliminated convertibles, and European sports car manufacturers began concentrating on designing coupes. A Cincinnati federal district court threw out the proposed regulations in 1973, but the TR7 appeared in 1975 as a coupe and it took four more long years before the convertible was ready for market.

Desperate to get more profitable sales volume in North America, British Leyland executives dedicated the first year's TR7 production to the United States and Canada. Then began a big push to get production started and cars into showrooms. The timetable was so tight that we were having to plan an introduction for January 1975, with cars going on sale April 1. There were no early cars for press testing or even for dealer service training! As the host for the world announcement, we were being badgered by the automotive magazines to at least provide cars for photography.

Faced with demands from *Road & Track* and *Motor Trend* in California, we decided to make a California emissions test TR7 available, for photography only. We were very nervous about journalists driving a California car because, to meet that state's stricter emissions standards, they had only one carburetor, which severely reduced performance. I went out to Los Angeles just before Christmas, collected the car from the garage of our California manager, Al Fetta, and set off to meet photographer John Lamm high in the Hollywood hills. We spent a pleasant morning with me driving the car back and forth through curves and John snapping action shots for *Road & Track*.

During the driving, I had discovered that quite a few things on the TR7 didn't work . . . like the turn signals and horn! When I tried the headlights, one popped up, but the other was obstinate. When John was finished, I headed down to Sunset Boulevard so Bob D'Olivo of Petersen Publishing could shoot for *Motor Trend*. Arriving at their garage, I discovered that the up headlight now refused to join its twin in the down position. Cranking the obstinate device down with the small knob attached to the motor, I was surrounded by amused *Motor Trend* editors who promised not to reveal the problem in print. This was a preproduction test car, so I should not have been too worried, but there were butterflies in my stomach all the same as my plane lifted off on its way back to New Jersey.

At Speke, outside Liverpool, the TR7 assembly line was modern and well equipped, but the workforce was the same old chip-on-the-shoulder crew. In Leonia, we had seen only well-used test cars, but reports from our executives traveling to England were not encouraging. When TR7s started coming off the assembly line, they did not look like the styling buck that management had approved. Although its short wheelbase tended to make it look stubby, the original design had a low, racy silhouette, and attractive four-spoke alloy wheels were fitted. Production cars were high off the ground with dull 13-inch steel wheels and narrow tires. The panel below the front bumper looked unfinished. Pretty obviously, the original design had been laid down with no thought to meeting U.S. federal bumper height requirements. When it came to production, due to the integrated wedge design, the bumpers could not be raised, so the whole body had to go up a couple of inches, more at the back than the front.

Finally, what was this new Triumph to be called? There was a lot of support for "Bullet," the code name. It gave the impression of speed and power, and it suited the sports car image. On the down side, did the company really want to name a new car after a projectile fired from a gun that could kill people? Product identity was a major point. Since 1953, the premium Triumph sports car series had all been "TRs." Marketing won. Although unrelated to any previous Triumph, the new car became the TR7.

The TR7 Meets the World

For those of us charged with organizing and running the press meeting, the biggest concern was that this was the *world* introduction for the squatty little coupe. Stokes and other British Leyland directors would be there. John Lloyd, chief engineer of Triumph, would be on hand to make a presentation on the engineering of the car. There would be a full complement of British journalists, plus 50 or so U.S. and Canadian writers, all eager to see Britain's first all-new sports car in years, and ready to smear British Leyland if it wasn't right. Lyman Gaylord and I set out to put the meeting together, working with Roy Gordon, who was master-minding the national dealer meeting at the same venue.

We had chosen the plush Boca Raton Hotel and Club, located a few miles south of Palm Beach on Florida's Atlantic coast. January in Florida sounded pretty good, even for another press introduction with hard hours of work, little sleep, and a bunch of critical journalists to deal with. That was the least of our problems. A strike in the factory in Liverpool meant that our world launch would be using preproduction TR7s, cars unlikely to be finished to final production standards.

TR7 bodies were stamped out and assembled in Triumph Plant Number 1 at Liverpool, then transferred to Plant Number 2 where the cars were built. It was Plant Number 2 that was eventually closed. *Plain English Archive*

David Bate, from British Leyland's service division, was in charge of getting the test cars ready. Arriving two weeks ahead of the meeting, his first job was to oversee getting the cars off the ship and transported from the port to a big tent on the grounds of the Boca Raton Hotel and Club, where they were to get final adjustments, wash, polish, etc. One look at the cars and he was on a pay phone from the port to me, panic in his voice.

The factory had sent 35 cars to select from, supposedly giving us a cushion against poor initial build quality. In his brief survey, David had seen ill-fitting bodies, shipping damage, bad paint, broken windows, and missing parts.

Test driving all the cars proved only that none were ready for any serious road work. David didn't have the manpower resources to

get them ready in a couple of weeks. The word went out and, 24 hours later, the Group 44 racing team crew arrived to help out. The flurry of activity from then on made the walls of the tent bulge. The roads around Boca Raton were sprinkled with undisguised new Triumphs, still wearing their shipboard Cosmoline coating, going through their paces with sweating drivers trying to decide if the amount of repair work required disqualified that car from the start. Mechanical woes went all the way from broken switches to leaking head gaskets.

They got 17 cars nailed together well enough to show to the press and dealers. With fingers crossed, we reported to Graham Whitehead and Mike Dale that the fleet was ready. It was Thursday, January 16, the day before the start of the press meeting.

John Humphreys of BBC-TV gave his review of the new TR7 from the driver's seat. *Plain English Archive*

A Three-Ring Circus

The official schedule of events listed the press introduction for the Great Hall, located in the hotel's new convention center. On arrival, only 24 hours before the press were due to start checking in, our PR group went to set the stage and were told we couldn't have it—the Sales and Marketing people were setting up for the dealer presentation, and the show for the news media would have to go elsewhere. After frantic negotiations, we had our gathering of journalists at 9:30 A.M. on Saturday in the ornate banquet hall of the Boca Raton Club's original building, a second-rate, 1920s vintage facility.

A short 16-millimeter film showing TR7 testing and early production was well received. John Lloyd, Triumph chief engineer, reviewed at length the engineering and development work that went into the TR7. Then, Mike Dale and Graham Whitehead went through the marketing plan and a quick roundup of the state of British Leyland. The exhibit area of the Great Hall was opened and the media were able to look at displays of TR7 components and familiarize themselves with display cars before going on the road. There weren't enough test cars, even with two in each car, so some journalists made use of time by interviewing any BL person they could catch. All of us from the company were reluctant to voice any opinion at all until we had spent enough time with the new coupe to know more about it.

As part of the presentation, a local Triumph club member had brought his 1956 TR3 for comparison with the new model. Mike Dale was persuaded to drive it, about the only time I saw a smile on his face during the meeting. The TR3 certainly looked vintage beside a TR7 but its throaty sound put the wedge's wheezy exhaust note to shame. Yet, coming back for lunch, the first test-drive group seemed to be having a good time and were talking animatedly about the car's handling. One of my personal opinions was confirmed—if you could get past the styling and into the car, the TR7 offered a comfortable driving position and a good drive . . . it may have needed more gears, but there was nothing wrong with the handling.

The BBC-TV crew set up and started taping reporter John Humphreys in the car. Others of the UK press group, having much earlier deadlines than the North American corps, finished lunch and started composing leads for their stories. Dermot Purgavie, representing the *Daily Mail* of London, was inspired. His story began "It has the profile of half a pound of Cheddar and is, they say, the shape of things to come."

The line, "The Shape of Things to Come" was our whole presentation. We would sell MGs based on tradition but the new Triumph would be our marketing path to the future. The auto writers at Boca Raton, most of them good friends and all familiar with the troubles of our parent company, gave the TR7 the benefit of the doubt when they could and most of them actually seemed to like it.

Pat Bedard of *Car and Driver* called it "very predictable and easy to drive fast." John Dinkel of *Road & Track* called it up-to-date in comfort and ergonomics, modern and refined. Others called it rakish, functional, civilized, responsive. We had plenty of positive comments on which to base our ad campaign.

Several of the U.S. magazines had requested test cars to drive back to their home cities. These included John Christy of *Motor Trend*, Leon Mandel of *Car and Driver*, and John Dinkel of *Road & Track*. By the time the press meeting started, we had to face the truth—only two of the test car fleet met any sort of criteria for a journalist to take on a long trip. We tossed coins, compared notes on which publications might take the most offense, and finally told John Dinkel that unspecified components had failed on the car assigned to them, and parts were not yet on hand due to the strike in England.

On the morning after the dinner concluding the meeting, Leon Mandel and John Christy left the hotel early, Leon headed for Michigan and John on his way west. Leon made it partway across Tennessee before the engine blew. Unbelievably, in the midst of a parts shortage, a complete spare engine was available. A plane was chartered and the engine, with a district service manager to supervise installation, were flown to him to get the car together to continue the trip.

Christy was forced against a curb by a truck during a snowstorm in El Paso and rolled his TR. The structural rigidity being one of the things about the car that really was top quality, there was surprisingly little damage to the car and none to John, who was very savvy about seat belts. The police report noted a broken side window, caused by the exit of his briefcase weighted down by the police .45 he always carried. Later, he wrote in *Motor Trend* that "If he had to roll a sports car, he'd rather do it in a TR7"!

The Dealers Have Their Doubts

Showing the TR7 to the dealer body was a more difficult job than presenting to the press. Triumph dealers were used to the traditional shape, feel, and sound of the six-cylinder TR6 roadster. A wheezy four-cylinder two-seater coupe shaped like a door-stop was hard to swallow as a replacement. There were rumblings of discontent because the dealers suspected that TR7 profits would not equal the grosses they were earning on the TR6. The TR7 base price was a couple of hundred dollars below the TR6, but the dealers feared the lack of a convertible would make the new TR a tough sell. They were right. Before the year was out, we would be looking for any possible way to move TR7s out of showrooms.

It was not only the Triumph people who were worried. Jaguar dealers on hand got a sneak preview of the new "sports car" that would arrive in their showrooms in the fall of 1975. It was the XJS coupe, not a real sports car but a grand tourer. Touted as a replacement for the E-type, which had ended production in 1974, the XJS was not the same sort of car at all. Then there was the price. The last E-types were stickered at $9,200. The 1976 model XJS started at $19,000.

The yellow coupe originally assigned to *Road & Track* carried me and my wife home, rear end howling all the way but causing no trouble. We were confirmed TR6 fans but the TR7 did a great job. Even so, I kept my last TR6 until it had over 150,000 miles on it.

Nearing the end of their spectacular run, the TR6 and Spitfire underwent various updates for 1975. Both had transmission changes, heavier bumpers with large black rubber guards, and chromed license plate mounts that made them appear quite different. For the first time, air pumps were added to the antipollution gear, sucking more power from the engines. Ads showed the two cars posed in verdant British fields with the headline "From the Land of

A major shipment of TR7s, with some MGBs at left, waiting on the dock at Liverpool. Roll-on, roll-off shipment was standard by the mid-1970s. *Plain English Archive*

British Racing Green." It was a neat comparison of tradition to the "Shape of Things to Come" campaign for the TR7.

In the middle of the decade, despite doubts concerning our new sports car, life was rather good at British Leyland in Leonia. We were well staffed. We had a broad range of products to sell, although both the Austin Marina and the Land Rover were dropped during the year. MGBs were in demand, every TR6 that arrived had a customer, Spitfires sold well, and the TR7, supported by merchandising programs, was selling in quantity, if not very profitably. Jaguar, despite more than 5,000 units moving through dealerships, was almost an afterthought, something that could be sold IF any arrived and IF they ran reasonably well, and most of their systems functioned most of the time. Nobody knew how well or how long British Leyland would last, so we got on with the business of selling cars.

The Enthusiast Fire Burns Strong

It seemed unbelievable, but Group 44 celebrated its 10th anniversary in 1975, marking the occasion by opening a new race preparation shop in Herndon, Virginia, near Dulles International Airport. Now the team had three marques on the Quaker State transporter. Besides the TR6 and Spitfire, there were an MGB, MG Midget 1500 (new in 1975 with Triumph engine and gearbox), and the Jaguar V-12 E-type. We chartered a Beechcraft 99 and flew a group of auto editors to Herndon for a tour. Although the TR7, under SCCA rules, would not be eligible for production class racing until 1976, the Group was already working on development.

Although founded and operated by the manufacturer, the Triumph Sports Owners Association had been the only international organization catering to Triumph enthusiasts regardless of model, our only equivalent to the

MG Car Club. The TR Register, based in England, was, at that time, for TR2 and TR3 lovers only. Late in 1974, the situation changed dramatically with the formation of the Vintage Triumph Register and establishment of a national publication, *The Vintage Triumph*. A founder and first president of VTR was Randy Mason, then automotive curator of the Ford Museum in Dearborn, Michigan. Also involved from the start was Dick Langworth, co-author of the definitive history of Triumph cars, who became editor of the magazine.

Over 400 people joined up in the first few months of VTR's existence. The club held its first national convention in July 1975, with speed runs at the old Packard Proving Grounds and a concours at Greenfield Village in Dearborn. A TR-S Le Mans roadster was on hand, along with the one-off, TR-S twin-cam-powered, Michelotti-bodied Conrero coupe. VTR is still a robust organization in the twenty-first century, with 3,500 members, an established circuit of events, and a national convention every year.

Despite the desperate financial situation in England, the corporation was still wisely investing in facilities in the profitable U.S. market. In September 1975, the company vacated the Civil War–era Southeast Zone office/warehouse in New Orleans and opened new zone headquarters in the Baymeadows area of Jacksonville, Florida. Managed by Zone Chief Gary E. Cooper, the modern offices and warehouse were located in a parklike setting next to a pond. Employees enjoying picnics next to the water soon discovered the pond had a resident alligator, which bothered no one as long as it got a share of their lunch.

We were enthusiastic at Leonia as 1975 ended with British Leyland sales in the United States hitting 70,839, best since the company was formed in 1968. Overall TR sales were 22,803, and August was Triumph's highest monthly total ever in the United States at 2,869 units. However, there were only 6,211 TR7 sales in the total. In 1976, sports cars would have to make up the 20,000 sales lost with the departure of the discount-priced Austin Marina. TR7s

The photo of the TR7 on test in Morocco was intended to enhance the styling but may have been too successful. Most people don't even see the car! *Plain English Archive*

The Vintage Triumph Register, formed in 1975, held its 1977 national meet at the Ford test track, where a Mayflower led a parade of Spitfires and TRs. *Bill Smith photo*

weren't moving that fast. Something would have to be done.

Jazzing Up the TR7

America's bicentennial year, 1976, began with one of the biggest marketing meetings ever held by the company in the United States. For two days at the luxo Eden Roc hotel in Miami and Miami Beach, the home office and zone sales, marketing, communications, and technical people joined the principals from the independent distributors for a series of seminars. We learned about a new computerized vehicle reporting system, new distribution methods, advanced sales training programs, and revised dealer development policies. Advertising and marketing plans emphasizing the TR7 were presented. Every one of these programs was aimed at improving the quality of the marketing organization from headquarters to dealer showroom.

The Eden Roc meeting was followed by a series of seven regional meetings for district sales/service personnel and dealers. Bob Burden, national ad manager, and Mike Jackling, national sales manager, were on the road for weeks. This type of road show became our annual way of selling new marketing programs to our own people and the dealer body.

Among the new items for the TR7 was a sunroof option, sourced in the United States and installed at dealer level. It was expected to take care of some of the sales lost by the lack of a convertible. Decorative striping kits were all the rage in the 1970s, and buyers would now have a choice of several, all created under supervision of Bruce McWilliams' product development crew. There were even regional special editions—the six states in the Southeast Zone sold the TR7 "Southern Skies," with sunroof, unique side stripe, and special badges. These items, together with the changes in the Spitfire and TR6, propelled Triumph sales to record levels by spring. There were 2,960 Triumph sales in June, including 1,537 TR7s, also a record.

The TR7 factory in Liverpool was cranking out pointy little coupes at a great rate, finally pressuring sales forces with too many, rather than too few, cars. We needed a way to draw more people into the showroom and, once again, the racing program came to the rescue. Now eligible to run in SCCA Class D Production, the TR7 was part of the Group 44 racing fleet, driven by Bob Tullius himself. Another TR7 was being run by Huffaker Engineering in California, Lee Mueller driving. Tullius took his new mount to victory in its first five races, providing the inspiration for the Triumph Victory Edition, a TR7 with stripes, special wheels, and a "textured vinyl roof" (sprayed on), all included in the normal retail price. The "spoker" wheels, sourced in California, were called "competition type" but looked more like Conestoga wagon equipment than racing rims. The kit helped make the car look lower, and the overall effect was eye-catching if not very racy.

The optional, U.S.-installed sunroof was a feature of the TR7 Southern Skies, a special edition with unique stripes and badges sold only in the Southeastern Zone of British Leyland. Round motif on front fender is a sun/moon decal. *Plain English Archive*

Paul Newman on the victory stand at Road Atlanta after winning the D Production race ahead of Lee Mueller's TR7. Joanne Woodward is congratulating Paul. Lee is occupied with Miss Road Atlanta. *Plain English Archive*

British Leyland Reorganized—
Stokes Leaves

As predicted, Lord Stokes was gone from the corporation after seven turbulent years. He had resigned from the board in November 1975 and was made honorary president through 1976. A new chief executive, Alexander Park, had been named. This was the direct result of a document known as The Ryder Report. Commissioned by the Department of Industry, Lord Ryder and a group of businessmen had reviewed British Leyland operations during 1975 and recommended changes in management and a different organizational structure. Stokes and John Barber were out, and the corporation was now divided into only four units: Leyland Cars, Leyland Truck and Bus, Leyland Special Products, and Leyland International.

We dealt primarily with International, which was in charge of world marketing, but we also maintained direct contact with the individual manufacturing companies. They were having trouble maintaining their identity. Part of the new philosophy was to reduce the importance of the individual marque companies. Big "Leyland Cars" signs went up at all factories. Jaguar, MG, and Triumph factories were identified by size as "Large Car" or "Small Car Plant Number so-and-so." Management was centralized and the people running the factories, used to making business decisions on the spot every day, had to submit many of them for review at corporate level in London.

Individual car units within British Leyland still had their successes. Rover, having introduced the world's first luxury SUV, the Range Rover, in 1970, came out in 1976 with the Rover 3500, an all-new sedan that won Car of the Year in Europe. The car's styling was leading-edge, with a Ferrari-like front and a practical hatchback. Not destined to be sold in the United States for several years, the new Rover would soon contribute to our welfare by donating its five-speed gearbox and heavy-duty rear axle to the TR7, eliminating several of the main criticisms of the car.

Alex Park's first official visit to the United States came shortly after we announced a 5 percent increase in July sales, a good base for a press conference high above San Francisco in the Bankers Club. Park steered clear of questions about the state of British Leyland—we had excluded British press from the luncheon for that reason—noting that he had been chief executive for only a few months. He did say, "We've adopted the approach of not tampering with the allocation of overseas vehicles to meet the demands of the home market . . . we're dedicated to having consistent overseas supply." Park confidently predicted further sales increases for Triumph and MG in the United States.

Park and our BL group next went to Monterey, where Jaguar was being honored at the Historic Vehicle Races. For a long weekend, we were immersed in Jaguar history, products, and enthusiasm from the club members gathered at the event. Even Group 44 was now running Jaguars, winning the SCCA BP championship in 1975 with an E-type and starting development of the XJS. It was a taste of things to come.

At the SCCA Championship Run-Offs, the big year-end news for Triumph was made by film star Paul Newman. Racing as "PLN," he had been a hot competitor in SCCA amateur events for several years. He turned out to be very quick in a Datsun 510 B Sedan. At the end of 1975, he purchased the Group 44 TR6 that John McComb had just driven to the D Production national championship. Group 44 had switched to the TR7, and all season long Newman was there in the old car, making Bob Tullius work for his money. At the championships, Newman qualified on the pole and won, barely ahead of the Huffaker Engineering TR7 driven by Lee Mueller. He had robbed us of the advertising headline we needed, but it was a great drive! A film, *Success By Design*, includes a segment on his championship run.

The battle between Paul Newman's TR6 and Lee Mueller's TR7 looked like this for most of the race, with one or the other in front. *Plain English Archive*

163

The last TR6, owned by Bob Tullius, had this silver plaque on the dashboard.

Writing in the November–December 1976 *TSOA Newsletter*, John Dugdale noted that 22,000 TR7s were now on the road. Of those, 16,000 had been sold during 1976, helping Triumph sales to a record 28,238. This was far more than the best we ever did with the TR6 but we had always been chronically short of TR6s. With the TR7, as soon as we had sold one batch, another shipload would appear on the horizon. Without referring to marketing ploys like the Victory Edition, John credited the TR7 sales rate of close to 2,000 per month to the car's amenities, like air conditioning and spacious seating. It was the company line—the dealers kept saying that selling the cars was like pulling teeth, but with sales so good, we all felt rather optimistic as 1977 began.

A Record Year and Farewell to My TR6

The TR7 was offered with automatic at the end of 1976. Creating excitement and interest in the wedge was our most important marketing task, and automatic was another selling tool. At wholesale or retail level, the TR7 did not make the profit that the TR6 had, and sales promotions like the Victory Edition ate up what margin we had.

Graham Whitehead used the Chicago Auto Show in February as a platform to announce that British Leyland in North America would avoid the economy car market in future, pointing out that 1976 sales had been 11 percent higher than 1975 despite dropping the Marina sedans. He credited the TR7 and Jaguar XJS for the increase and said, "The decision was to concentrate on the sports and luxury car fields, in which our products enjoy a well-deserved reputation for quality and performance. British Leyland sells more convertibles in the United States than any other manufacturer and we feel strongly that the buyer should have a choice of an open car which has both modern design and convenience and the traditional performance of a genuine sports car."

Some of us thought that the last "genuine sports car" had ceased production shortly before. The TR6 was gone. Back in February of 1976 I had tried to buy the last one only to be told that it had already been ordered—by Bob Tullius! He has it to this day, a memento of what he has sometimes said was his favorite race car, even though he never won the championship in it. On the dash is a silver plaque confirming that the car is indeed the last of the "Big Mutha" sixes and, for my money, the last of the real TRs.

The TR7 Is a Pro Rally Champion

With such a strong emphasis on sports cars, racing and rallying were interwoven into our marketing program. The excitement factor was high, and our sales executives were highly competitive themselves.

British Leyland jumped into professional rallying with both feet in 1977, on both sides of the Atlantic. There had been an active UK pro rally program for some time, first using the Triumph Dolomite Sprint and switching to TR7s in selected events in 1976. Well-known drivers Tony Pond and Brian Culcheth would drive. In North America, where rallying was thought of in terms of club time-speed-distance events on ho-hum routes through the suburbs, both the Sports Car Club of America and the new North American Rally Racing Association were working to establish a bigger and better image for the sport. Like Formula One, pro rallying had developed in Europe to serve big money corporate sponsors, and this would be the direction taken here as well.

The North American Rally Racing Association was the creation of David Ash. He had been advertising manager for J. S. Inskip, the old MG distributor; a racing driver; and a successful writer and publisher. Having just left a stint as editor/publisher of *Sports Car*, the SCCA magazine, he was trying his hand as a promoter and agent. And he was representing John Buffum.

Buffum had started his rally career while stationed in Europe with the U.S. Army. Placing 12th overall as a private entry in the 1969 Monte Carlo founded his reputation. On his return to the United States, he and his Porsche simply took over pro rallying, winning eight events in 1975 and nine in 1976. Now he was ready to make a sponsorship deal. Dave Ash called longtime friend John Dugdale, and the three of us met at Leonia. David's pitch was simple: Pro rallying is just beginning in North America, and the first manufacturer to get involved in a big way will get the publicity benefits. Winning is the way to get publicity and hiring John Buffum's Libra International team is a guarantee of winning. NARRA offers the best series.

This was the most self-confident sales pitch I had heard since Bob Tullius gave me his "I will win" spiel from an adjacent barstool 15 years

In 1977, John Buffum and co-driver Vicki Gauntlett won Triumph's first U.S. rally championship. *Plain English Archive*

earlier. I found myself thinking that Buffum would have to be superman to equal his past Porsche and BMW performance driving a humble four-cylinder Triumph. I said so. Ash remained confident. Buffum came to a second meeting and gave the same impression. The two convinced John Dugdale, me, Mike Dale, and Graham Whitehead, and we had ourselves a pro rally program. In the general mood of confidence, it hardly seemed unusual that John's navigator was a woman, his ex-wife, Vicki, otherwise Victoria Upjohn of the pharmaceutical family.

The quickest way to get John a competitive car for 1977 was to order one from the competitions department in England. Actually, two were ordered, the second for the Canadian team of driver Walter Boyce. Identical to the European cars except for left-hand drive, the cars had Dolomite Sprint engines with the unique single-cam, 16-valve head. They developed nearly 200 horsepower. The cars would not be shipped until April. John and Vicki went ahead and earned some points in the Porsche while we nibbled fingernails.

In April, I found myself at 2 A.M., standing in pitch darkness at the edge of a dirt logging

British Leyland's European rally program used TR7s in this livery. Prepared to FIA rules, they were heavier than the U.S. cars but had more heavily modified engines, developing over 200 horsepower—pretty good for 2 liters!

Prior to the TR7, the UK rally team depended on the Triumph Dolomite Sprint with the special 16-valve version of the single-cam slant four. A real competitor for the BMW 2002 in performance, the car was a delight to drive. *Plain English Archive*

road in a forest somewhere near Tacoma, Washington, waiting for cars to come down the "stage," as the various sections of a rally are called. It was my first taste of rally competition. Often run at night to get clear use of the roads, to spectators pro rallies were a series of brilliant action vignettes. Out of the blackness came a blaze of headlights, a glimpse of a white coupe slewed sideways across the road, the scream of an engine wound tight, and then only the glow of taillights receding quickly toward the next bend. There was no way to tell who was ahead or even, as you brushed dirt out of your hair and shook pebbles out of your shoes, which car had just gone by. All you could do was proceed to the end of the stage and get the results there.

I did, only to find that the TR7 had broken down on the stage and the crew were out picking it up. The car appeared shortly, under its own power but subject to unpredictable engine failure—either electrical or fuel system problems. Buffum handed me the key and I drove it back to the motel. The next day I flew out of Seattle on

British Airways, headed for a public relations conference in England, where I had hoped to boast to my colleagues of a victory. Instead, a few hours later, as the 747 flew over Winnipeg, Canada, where I was born, I tossed down a brandy, said to myself, "This was the shakedown. He'll win the next one." I went to sleep.

Those who have seen *Buffum & Company*, the excellent film of the 1977 rally season made under John Dugdale's supervision, enjoyed exciting footage from the Rim of the World rally in California, the Susquehannock Trail in Pennsylvania, the 20 Stages in Michigan, and the Criterium du Quebec, the only FIA international points rally on the schedule. John and Vicki finished only the Criterium! Actually, they DNFed the first four rallies, then won six out of the next seven, but we had a tight budget allowing the film crew to attend only four events!

The Buffum team finished the season first in the SCCA Pro Rally Championship and first in Canadian Auto Sports Club North American Rally Cup. Dave Ash was vindicated, but the NARRA title went to someone else. Having

John and Vicki in the Criterium du Quebec, an FIA event in 1977. The daring photographer is about to get showered with dirt and pebbles. *Mike Cook*

done so poorly in NARRA events at the start of the season, John had dropped out to concentrate on the other two series.

A Real Car at Last

The big Triumph product news of 1977 was the TR7 five-speed. Designed and built at Standard-Triumph, the new gearbox had first gone into Rover's successful new 3500 sedan. Now, the TR7 would become much more of an enthusiast's car, using the five-speed and the heavy-duty rear-end assembly. The car's appearance was improved by lowering the rear and fitting 185/70x13 tires, rather than 175. Attractive full plastic wheel covers disguised the steel wheels. Loud red or green plaid inserts in the seats and door panels were a questionable addition, but the car was vastly more fun to drive, handled even better, and was less tinny. I gave up my green TR6 for a blue TR7 five-speed.

The Spitfire got new seats as well, with houndstooth check inserts, new wheels, smaller

steering wheel, and gizmos like new controls and a map light. None of these could mask the car's achingly slow performance from an engine optimistically listed at 52 horsepower. The only "performance" modification for 1977 was an automatic choke. The price was $4,500.

Our launch pad for the revised TR7 was the New York International Auto Show, and the new cars went on sale at the end of April. In Queen Elizabeth's Silver Jubilee year, the company created a Jubilee Jaguar XJS with champagne and purple ultrasuede upholstery and gold wheels. British Leyland people wore royal purple buttons with a silver royal coat of arms. While the Jaguar made a splash in the press, the new TR7 was a real seller and would help Triumph sales reach yet another record by the end of the year—29,258 cars, of which 18,068 were TR7s.

Such was the scope of British Leyland's business that we were included in *Advertising Age*'s list of 100 Top Advertisers for 1977. Our $18.3 million put us fifth in the list of imported car ad

John Buffum with the TR7 in downtown Montreal before the start of the Criterium du Quebec. *Plain English Archive*

In the Queen's Jubilee year, 1976, Triumph sent out this shot contrasting the TR3 and TR7, illustrating sports car progress during Queen Elizabeth's reign. *Plain English Archive*

When the five-speed TR7 was announced, it also carried this rather loud plaid interior in tan or green with color-coordinated carpeting. *Plain English Archive*

expenditures, behind VW, Toyota, Datsun, and Honda. On another list, Graham Whitehead received the OBE (Order of the British Empire) in Queen Elizabeth's Birthday Honors List, for his services to British commercial interests and to the British community in New York.

A New Parent Corporation and a New and Different Leader

Our management changes paled against the announcement from England in October that British Leyland would again have a new chairman, who would this time, also be chief executive. Michael Owen Edwardes, of Chloride Group, which were battery manufacturers, had been selected by the National Enterprise Board as someone with the background, experience, and personal strength to make the drastic moves needed to save our ailing corporation. Edwardes, who was South African, took control in November 1977, presiding over a new and smaller Board of Directors, on which David Andrews was the only carry-over member. Andrews was promoted to

executive vice chairman, responsible for financial and legal functions.

Alex Park, who had served well and was respected in the corporation, was offered a post as executive vice chairman, responsible for Leyland Special Products, but he elected to resign at the end of December. He was one BL chief who was a real car man, despite coming from outside the industry. It was his inspiration that resulted in the establishment of the British Leyland Heritage Trust, now the Motor Industry Heritage Trust. The trust first acted to preserve British Leyland historic vehicles and now performs the same task for most of the British auto industry, with a museum and archives at Gaydon in Warwickshire.

Edwardes took action immediately to improve efficiency and boost morale. Recognizing that centralized management had sapped the strength of the various car companies by taking away their identity, he decentralized Leyland Cars into Austin-Morris, Jaguar Rover Triumph (JRT), and BL Components. As part of a campaign to restore identity and commitment

A very successful promotion at auto shows was this skateboard stunt, here performed at the Atlanta show in December 1977. The jumper is Mike Russell, son of John Russell, sales manager at the dealer, Andy's Sportcar Center. Owner Andy Anderson is the man with the moustache and striped tie standing behind the Spitfire. *Plain English Archive*

in the minds of management and employees, responsibility for export sales, shipping, etc., was taken from Leyland International and given back to the individual manufacturing units. Once again, we could talk to Abingdon about MGs, Browns Lane about Jaguars, and Canley about Triumphs.

Our new boss, head of JRT, was W. Pratt Thompson, an American born in New Jersey, who had spent his business career primarily overseas with American Machine and Foundry Company, becoming vice president, international business development. He came to BL from Bowthorpe Holdings, where he was deputy managing director. Like Michael Edwardes, he had no experience in the automobile industry but was brought in for his management expertise.

New Sales, Old Designs

Road Test magazine for July 1976 had an article by Steve Thompson entitled "Flashback Specials." Thompson and two others took an MGB, MG Midget, and Spitfire 1500 through the streets of southern California and out to Riverside Raceway for performance tests. They found the MGB a big disappointment, calling it awkward and ungainly with an unkind interior and heavy, dead steering. They called the Midget "a pleasant, amusing little car" but warned that it only gave the illusion of being a sports car. The car's differential disintegrated during the track tests!

Road Test concluded that "in many ways, the Triumph Spitfire was everything the other cars weren't." They liked the suspension and interior the best, said the styling would still turn heads, and found the engine would pull much harder than the same unit in the MG Midget and even better than the 1,800-cc MGB. They praised the finish, the ease of using the convertible top, and the driving position, calling it a "real" car as well as a sports car. Yet it and its cousins were dated

In 1978, John Buffum and navigator Doug Shepherd competed in snowy Missouri in the 100-Acre Wood Rally, which they won by over 11 minutes.
Plain English Archive

cars, selling at high prices because of the strong British pound in the world economy.

The 1978 Spitfire had a price of $5,150, what a TR7 had cost three years earlier. The TR7 was up to $6,750.

TR7 Supplies—Good News and Bad News

Michael Edwardes brought disturbing news to his meeting in Leonia. As part of the new policy to trim costs, reduce the labor force, and improve efficiency, the Speke Number 2 factory at Liverpool was to be closed at the end of April, and TR7 production transferred to Triumph's home plant at Canley in Coventry. As Graham Whitehead said in our official news release, the Speke factory, with its dreadful quality record, was a logical candidate for closure and we could expect better cars to sell. The bad news was that the transfer would take five months, and Canley production would not begin until October. Our stock of 1978 TR7s would be whatever was built at Speke. Getting more Spitfires and MGs to compensate was unlikely, so we would suffer an unavoidable loss of sales and profits. The impact would be strongest on our dealers.

Showing a good public face, we launched a new ad campaign featuring a skateboarder leaping over an MG Midget. This became an auto show press preview gimmick in which skateboarders leaped over Spitfires.

Driving fun and the performance image generated by racing were still the heart of our advertising program. Although we were still supporting the Huffaker Engineering team in SCCA racing with a TR7 and TR8, Group 44 had become strictly Jaguar in 1976, running an XJS in the SCCA professional Trans-Am series. Despite budget cuts, the company continued to recognize the advertising value of race victories through the racing support program for amateur drivers. The 1978 Rally program got off to a great start with a victory for John Buffum and new navigator, Doug Shepherd, winning two out of the first three events. The rally film *Buffum & Company* was previewed on East and West Coasts to good reviews.

V-8 Rumors

It was now pretty common knowledge that a V-8 version of the TR7 would be built. The first public exposure came in the Leyland Motorsports team cars during 1978 when they began running the "TR7 V-8." John Buffum had been invited several times to drive on the factory team and did four events during 1978, returning to North America with fierce enthusiasm for the extra power and performance available with

The TR7 convertible finally arrived in July 1979, the first new open TR since the TR6 came out 10 years before. *Plain English Archive*

3.5 liters instead of 2. His hopes were fulfilled by the arrival of a UK-built V-8 car in time for the Criterium du Quebec in September. Unfortunately, it had to go back to the UK but, finishing the season in the TR7, he and Doug Shepherd won the rally hat trick—championships in the SCCA, NARRA, and Canadian Auto Sports Club series.

It had been a year of hope, for the future of BL, for improvements in the TR7, for success in our marketing. There was much upbeat news. Club activity was more and more prevalent with new Triumph organizations forming all the time. The Vintage Triumph Register, now with more than 40 member clubs and the Triumph Register of America were both growing and held well-attended national events.

TR7 production had resumed at Canley on October 2, right on schedule. The first Coventry-built TR7s would not get to us until the beginning of 1979, but BL had made a promise and kept it. It was a big step forward. Coincidental with the start of production was a corporation-wide change in logos. TR7s made at Canley wore the new Triumph laurel wreath in the form of a large decal on the front of the hood. The 1979 Spitfires, unchanged from 1978, were pictured in the *TSOA Newsletter*, but these were interim cars and there would be some major modifications during the production run.

Most exciting on the racing front was the news that Group 44 would switch back to

This is a 1978 TR8, the car that was never sold. Much photography was done and expensive brochures were printed, but the car did not go on sale until 1980. This and the other 1978s went into service as company cars. *Plain English Archive*

Triumph for 1979, preparing two TR8s for the Sports Car Club of America Trans-Am and/or the International Motor Sports Association GTO category. The team had done a terrific job for Jaguar in 1977–1978. Bob Tullius had won the driver's championship both years and they had clinched the Manufacturer's Title in 1978. Now it was time to apply the racing machine to boosting Triumph sales again. As before, we would have two teams running

Triumphs. Huffaker Engineering in California would prepare two TR8s as well as an MGB for SCCA competition.

Wedge Developments

With the closing of Speke, just about everyone with a company car in the United States was given a TR8 to drive. These cars, about 145 of which had been built at Speke, were preproduction models built when TR8 introduction was planned for as early as 1977 (I had already done some preliminary search for a suitable venue). The TR8 kept getting pushed back but development had continued. When the factory closed, the 145 coupes were shipped to the United States, where they could be used in extensive testing. Many of us who worked for JRT put thousands of miles on Liverpool-built TR8s, recording our impressions weekly on special forms. I put over 26,000 miles on a five-speed coupe and never had a bit of trouble. Others were not so lucky, but my wife and I loved that red car and drove it all over the eastern half of the country including trips to Florida.

It was fun driving an incognito TR8. Undisguised, the test cars had no badges on them at all, not even Triumph ID. The cars could not be told from TR7s except by their alloy wheels and dual exhausts. And, of course, a glance at the rev limit and top speed indication on the speedo would clue you in. The cars tested in United States were mostly automatic but still quite fast. Even the automatics, held in low range, had startling acceleration. Adding a V-8 would broaden the TR's appeal, as would another change, long awaited—removing the top.

We did not have the usual expensive press introduction for the TR7 convertible, counting on a good-sized fleet of road test cars to get publicity. This worked fine, and the reviews were almost over the top. *Car and Driver*: ". . . a roomy and striking interior . . . tracks straight as a laser . . . a happy proposition for a long trip . . ." *Road & Track*: " . . . a pleasure to extend to its limits . . . well-constructed convertible top . . ." *San Diego Union*: "one of the best buys for the money in today's convertible market." *Popular Mechanics*: "The TR7 is now the car it always should have been."

The TR7 convertible finally arrived in July, priced at $7,995. Limited to five paint colors, two interior colors, and black top only, it was greeted with enthusiasm by the dealers.

Mike Dale explains the TR7 convertible to Jim McCraw of Motor Trend, to his left, during the sneak preview in February 1979. A spy photo of the activities appeared in the *Birmingham Telegraph* the following day. *Plain English Archive*

This is a 1979 Spitfire 1500, early version. It still has the chrome bumpers and relatively small bumper guards first installed in 1975. *Plain English Archive*

We announced that convertible sales were expected to be plus business for Triumph, not taking away from TR7 coupe and Spitfire sales. Throughout the summer, the Triumph advertising campaign featured more "wedge" images—Whistler's *Mother* in a triangular frame, a three-cornered doghouse, and a Goodyear blimp shaped like a doorstop. The headline was now "Get Into the Shape," and the first convertible ad said "Triumph Invites You to a New Opening." While we were selling TR7s hard, the TR8 was always in the news, as John Buffum and Doug Shepherd scored more rally successes and the Group 44

IMSA car was winning in both SCCA Trans-Am and IMSA GTO.

The Ranks Begin to Thin

John Dugdale retired at the end of 1979. A group of us held a farewell luncheon for him at the Stony Hill Inn in Hackensack, a longtime favorite restaurant. After remarks by Graham Whitehead and Mike Dale, John's own brief speech was a model of wit and humor with, typically, a message about what he thought the future of the company could be. His departure left a big gap. Like club secretary Fred Horner, who had retired in 1977, John had been in the

This Spitfire was introduced midyear in 1979. New impact standards were met by the addition of grossly oversized bumper guards, and a new black grille/bumper extended forward with a spoiler below. *Plain English Archive*

car industry in the Americas since the 1940s, starting with Rootes Motors in 1949 in Argentina and moving to New York a year later.

John retained his ties to the company as editor of *Jaguar Journal*, the *TSOA Newsletter*, and *MG Magazine*, which he had founded in 1979. The company retained control of the Triumph and Jaguar magazines but signed the rights to *MG Magazine* over to John, who ran it as a commercial enterprise for several years. He died May 10, 2000, at the age of 86.

On to the 1980s

British Leyland decided to close the Triumph factory at Canley. TR7 and TR8 production would go to the new Rover plant at Solihull, outside Birmingham. Only a few years old, this plant was built for Rover 3500 production and had a capacity of 50,000 cars per year. With all the latest equipment and a skilled workforce, it was expected to produce very high quality cars, which proved to be true. This time, unlike the Speke to Coventry move, there would be no waiting period or shortage of cars.

Road & Track track-tested three TR8s at the end of 1980. John Buffum stands with his SCCA Champion TR8. Bob Tullius is with the Group 44 IMSA racer than won five events in 1980. In the foreground is the 1980 TR8 convertible. *Plain English Archive*

The factory closing that drew headlines did not belong to Triumph, but to its long-time rival. At the same party on the factory grounds at Abingdon where the company held its Golden Jubilee 50th anniversary party, Michael Edwardes announced the company's decision to close the factory and end MG production. The factory was outdated, as were the cars themselves, and there was no money in the budget to rebuild from the ground up.

Along with the startling factory closures and the canceling of MG, Sir Michael had reshuffled the executive players at BL so that Pratt Thompson was now chairman of BL International, and Percy Plant, an unknown name, headed JRT. Ray Horrocks, who had been chairman of Austin-Morris, took the title of managing director, cars, based in London and reporting to Edwardes. He was responsible for all car operations, BL Components, and Land Rover. All export sales and marketing activities were centralized again in a subsidiary with the unfortunate acronym "BLEO" (BL Europe and Overseas Operations). Graham Whitehead joined the BLEO board. As a finale to 1979, Edwardes announced that the British government had advanced a further $330 million to support the future programs of BL Ltd., which was now showing a small profit.

At the beginning of 1980, Bob Burden resigned to take a senior job at Doyle Dane Bernbach, the advertising agency, on the Volkswagen account. Even in hard times, at BL/JRT we always had fun and stuck together. When it stopped being fun, people started to leave on their own. Bob had a good opportunity and took it. Bob's replacement, Allen Taylor, had worked for the MG agency, Bozell & Jacobs, for 18 years.

John Dugdale was replaced as product publicity manager by another ad man, this time from Romano, Berger and Wollman, Triumph's agency. Glenn Howell was a journalist, photographer, and associate editor of *AutoWeek* before joining the agency. Glenn did his job well but left us later in the year to join Isuzu in his native California.

The 1980 Spitfire received major coverage in the January-February *TSOA Newsletter*. Author Dick Langworth went through the history of the car, beginning in 1963, and the many modifications, improvements, and successes in 17 years. Unchanged from 1979, the 1980 model was priced at a whopping $7,365, more than three times the price of the original 1963 model and over $1,500 more than the 1979. All of the praise could not mask the real message: The factory was closing and, while TR7/8 production would go to the Rover plant at Solihull, Spitfires

would stop. The pressure of time on the design had finished it—the 1980 model could not even be sold in California.

The Shadow of Jaguar

Lyman Gaylord and I were running hard toward the March introduction of the TR8 and Rover 3500. News releases, press kits, early road tests for the long-lead magazines . . . all of the usual procedures. But it hardly seemed to matter to management. Certain that Triumph production would go the way of MGB and lacking confidence in the Rover, our marketing people were concentrating on Jaguar. Dealer confidence was extremely low. Mike Dale and Mike Jackling were already involved in what would be a year-long odyssey around the country, working endlessly to persuade Jaguar dealers to stick with the company, despite the loss of other BL franchises and poor product delivery by Jaguar. Without a dealer organization, the company could not survive, however good the products coming from Coventry might become.

Under the shadow of these Jaguar concerns, we welcomed the automotive press to the Hotel del Coronado in cool March weather. Most of the journalists were there to see our new cars, but the magazine writers and some who wrote on business were asking probing questions about the state of the company, how we could survive without MG, and why our prices were well ahead of our competitors. The answers were necessarily vague but always carried the message that the company would stay in business. How tough were things? We decided we could not afford to have an official photographer. Lyman and I, usually snapping away, were too busy, so the event went completely unrecorded.

We had a fine engineering story to tell on both the TR8 and the Rover. Engineers from both companies told the story of power and handling and we showed a short film of the cars in American scenes. Grasping their press kits, handed out in white shopping bags with the product logos on either side, the journalists paired off and went out on the road. We waited expectantly for their lunchtime return and were not disappointed. They loved the TR8 and most were favorably impressed by the Rover.

The TR8 offered a high-performance drivetrain; an adequate chassis; a roomy, comfortable (if cheaply finished) interior; most modern options, like automatic, air conditioning, and power steering; and styling-you-could-get-used-to. It weighed 2,588 pounds and had 133 horsepower at 5,000 rpm, enough to get you to 60 from rest in 8.5 seconds. The quickest time was

The 1980 TR7 30th Anniversary Edition had stripes, fog lights, special steering wheel, and other trim at no extra cost. The package was a promotional tool to help clear overstock of the cars at dealerships. *Plain English Archive*

turned by California cars, which had fuel injection, but the twin-carburetor 49-state cars felt equally good. Overall, it was quite reliable. The chassis had been well developed, having been used on the five-speed TR7 since 1977. With Solihull quality, it was the best car ever offered by Triumph in the American market.

There were no negative road tests. *Road & Track* tested street, race, and rally versions of the TR8 for a cover story, calling the performance of all three "impressive." *Car and Driver* said the TR8 was "nothing less than the reinvention of the sports car." *Motor Trend* named it "That rarest of things: a modern sports car." *Road Test* named it "Best New Sports Car of 1980." And Wade Hoyt, writing for *Penthouse*, urged us to try the TR8 and "Return to those thrilling days of yesteryear when the air was clean, sex was dirty, and cars had balls!" We had a winner, but the factory would

only be sending us a little over 2,000 cars. Would that be enough? At $11,900 list price, perhaps so.

30th Anniversary Edition

Nineteen-eighty was not a good year for the car business and especially not for us. The British pound was at around $2.45, so our prices were high. The TR7 convertible now listed for $9,235, over $1,000 higher than the 1979. The TR7 had gone on sale in January and by April, we had already started a special promotion, the 30th Anniversary Edition. Celebrating "Three Decades of Triumph Roadsters," the special edition had side stripes, chrome wheel trims, luggage rack, three-spoke alloy steering wheel, coco floor mats, a special dash plaque, and an AM/FM stereo. The 30-year concept was based on the bulbous Triumph TRX prototype show car of 1950.

All black with brilliant red metallic 3M striping, the TR7 Spider is the only real "collectible" in the TR7 lineup. Made only for a short time in 1980, the Spider used the alloy wheels from the TR8 and a special interior package. *Plain English Archive*

Any excuse will do in the car business to promote sales, but the 30th Anniversary Edition was not highly regarded in the company and was not even covered in the *TSOA Newsletter*. It did help boost sales a bit but not enough. High list prices were scaring the customers away. In June we had to resort to rebates of $1,000 on TR7s and $500 on Spitfires. Sales boomed in July and August, and when the bloom was off the Anniversary Edition, there was a very much more exciting model ready to take over, the TR7 Spider.

I asked Bruce McWilliams if the Spider was his inspiration but he gave complete credit to Alan Edis, who was director of product development at JRT in England. Edis took a TR7 to Turin and worked up the Spider concept in Giovanni Michelotti's studio. Bruce supported it wholeheartedly and praised Edis for unfailingly valid judgment on products.

The Spider had the kind of finish that should have been applied to all TR7s and 8s. All were built at Solihull, and the quality of the black paint was excellent. Setting off the exterior were 3M® reflective stripes, lettering, and badges in sparkling red, including the Triumph laurel wreath on the front panel. TR8 alloy wheels completed the exterior package. The rich-looking interior had special upholstery in black and gray and high-quality pewter gray carpeting. It used the three-spoke alloy steering wheel. It was a 1980 model being introduced in September 1980, but it still looked wonderful. Priced at $10,585 on the East Coast and $11,010 in California with required fuel injection, it was over $1,000 more expensive than a regular TR7, but sold out anyway. Around 2,000 were built, and they are virtually the only TR7s that draw real collector interest.

The 30th Anniversary Edition and the Spider were for the U.S. market only and are not usually mentioned in UK Triumph books. Because of their brief existence, for only a few

The attractive Spider interior had seats upholstered in two-tone gray with black stripes, special plush carpeting, and a three-spoke wheel. *Plain English Archive*

Winner at Sebring! The Group 44 TR8 won its class and placed sixth overall in the 12-hour Sebring endurance classic in 1980. Crewmen swarm around the car at a pit stop. It appears that Bill Adam is getting out of the car to make a driver change with Bob Tullius, who stands ready to assist. *Plain English Archive*

months in one model year, they are relatively unknown here as well.

Trophies Still Pile Up

Racing and rally competition was still the main source of publicity for us. Having three established racing teams with a huge existing investment in cars, parts, and development made it sensible to continue racing as long as we could. The cost of the operations was actually less than we would have to spend on a major national advertising campaign, and the publicity results were excellent. There weren't many magazine ads for the TR8, but there were lots of headlines in the sports pages and the automotive magazines as the car won event after event.

John Buffum and Doug Shepherd were SCCA pro rally champions again, Buffum for the fourth time in a row! The team also won the North American Rally Cup but not without trouble. A nasty crash in the historic Press On Regardless rally in Michigan wrecked the TR8 and injured Buffum's foot. In a virtual tie with Mazda driver Rod Millen, John and Doug badly needed a new vehicle and there was no time to build one. They finished the season in a UK Rally Team TR8 that was flown over for the last two events.

Nineteen-eighty was the second season for Group 44 with the TR8 in IMSA racing, running two cars, one for Bob Tullius and the other for Bill Adam. Starting the season with a class victory and sixth overall at Sebring, the pair went on to a total of five wins, five seconds and two thirds out of 15 events. Bob came second in IMSA season points.

More Territory, Fewer People

At the beginning of May we announced that, after a year of planning, the company was taking over direct distribution of cars nationwide. It would not renew the contracts of the remaining four independent distributors, Royston Distributors, Inc., Devon, Pennsylvania; Continental Cars, based in St. Louis; Overseas Motors of Fort Worth; and British Motor Car Distributors of Compton, California. These distributor territories covered 23 states, which were now incorporated into the Northeast, Southern, Central, and Western Zones. In addition to giving a year's notice, JRT bought back parts and cars in stock, and guaranteed each distributor a percentage of U.S. sales for three years, based on the volume of cars the distributor might have sold.

With full control of vehicle distribution, JRT was now able to offer all dealers a computerized parts ordering and financial control system. The system gave all dealers access to all parts warehouses in the country and included car search capability. Any dealer could locate a car of a particular color and specification anywhere in the country. We now had standard dealer sales agreements and a consolidated parts and car distribution network covering the entire country. This was a much more efficient and profitable way of doing business, and something that our management had been striving to attain for years.

Few employees from the distributors joined JRT. One who made the move was James Groth, the long-time advertising and public relations manager for BMCD. James became West Coast ad and PR manager. His broad marketing knowledge proved very useful in the PR function, as the company became Jaguar-only and again, years later, when he joined the Hornburg Jaguar dealership in Los Angeles.

As sales plunged over the 1980–1981 period, the company workforce was cut nearly in half. Over 200 were let go. There were "Black Fridays" and "Blue Mondays" when groups of 8 or 10 people would get their termination notices. Some had long service and were ready to retire. Others had been with the company for only a year or two, but all of these forced separations were difficult and they cut across all levels of responsibility. Those of us who stayed were not always sure whether we were loyal to the company, confident that things would work out, or just lucky to have jobs in a difficult time.

The Central Zone office in Mt. Clemens, Michigan, was closed at the end of October, affecting 70 people. Some of them stayed on as district managers and a very few came to Leonia,

but most were terminated. Within a year, both the Southeast Zone in Jacksonville, Florida, and the Northeast Zone in Carlstadt, New Jersey, would be shuttered and their functions moved into Leonia. The district sales and service managers who had operated out of zone facilities now had to work from home and car, investing in their own computers, fax machines, etc. Only the Western Zone office and warehouse in Brisbane, California, south of San Francisco, remained open and still functions for Jaguar 20 years later.

The Change to Jaguar

By the fall of 1980, all of us knew that there would be no more Triumph sports cars. No public statement had yet been made, but the expensive new Rover factory at Solihull was not producing enough cars to pay the electric bill and would soon have to go the way of Canley, where Spitfire and TR7 production had stopped at the end of the summer. It was the end of a long run. The original Canley factory had become a Standard Cars assembly plant immediately after World War 1, 62 years before.

At the National Dealer Advisory Council meeting in November, Graham Whitehead assured the dealers that all financial obligations would be met by the company, even in the unlikely event that JRT would go out of business in North America. He said that 1981 TR7 and TR8 production at Solihull would begin in January and that economic pressure would force the prices even higher. The 1981 TR7 suggested retail would go to $10,500. Sales forecasts were down to no more than 5,000 units for the TR7. Later in the meeting, Mike Dale told the dealers than there were no plans to replace the TR7/8 in the future.

Graham responded to several questions about Jaguar, saying that "Jaguar would clearly be the mainstay of JRT's effort in the United States in the near term." He then said that Jaguar's chairman, John Egan, would attend dealer meetings scheduled for December and would go over basics like quality, supply, and warranty at that time.

We were all leading double lives in 1980. One part of my desk and my attention was occupied with the tasks of promoting the new Triumphs, scheduling the press fleet, sending out press kits, and acting as though we were still in the sports car business. The other part, steadily growing in importance, was talking up Jaguar to anyone who would listen. As it happened, 1980 was the worst sales year for Jaguar since the 1960s, with only 3,009 units retailed.

In 1979 we had sold the Series II sedan for most of the year and received the new 1979 Series III very late. The 1980 Series IIIs did not arrive until spring and the majority were in white, Taxicab Yellow, and bright red. No wonder the dealers were suspicious. However, in April, Sir Michael Edwardes had persuaded John Egan to leave a very good job at Massey-Ferguson in Canada to come back to Britain and run Jaguar. The brief was simple: "Fix it or close it!" Egan, having changed jobs and moved, was not about to close it but it wasn't going to be easy. On his first day at work he had to muscle his way through a crowd of pickets to get to his office. He had seen it all before. His job prior to Massey-Ferguson had been with British Leyland, setting up Unipart.

Other than settling the strike, Egan worked inside, evaluating his executives, looking at production problems, feeling his way. He stayed away from the United States. He knew that every dealer he met would ask him the same awkward questions. By the time the December dealer meetings came around, he was confident that he had enough answers. On his trip around the country, he faced the JRT management as well as the dealers, saying first that the U.S. market was fundamental to the success of Jaguar.

Egan said his goals were to achieve quality and durability comparable to the competition; to control production timing to suit the U.S. model year (the dealers cheered!); and to control the economics of productivity, component supply, and future product development. He said that 1981 models were late but would arrive in January. They did. He said that the 1982 models would arrive in time for October. They did. Such was the turnaround in supply and confidence that sales went up 50 percent in 1981 to 4,500 units and would go up a similar amount in 1982.

Egan's confidence was catching. After hearing him, we were sure the company could keep going with Jaguar. But we still had 1980 model Triumphs to sell.

An MG7? A TRB?

One of Bruce McWilliams' last budget-restyling efforts came during 1980, when half the world seemed to be engaged in trying to find ways to "save MG." There were serious discussions about making an MG version of the TR7! In the corporation's financially strapped condition, there was no question of altering body shape so it would have to be done with tape and badges, like the TR 250. For further distinction, such a car might have been powered by the Austin-Morris O series 2-liter, OHC engine, giving power equivalent to the Triumph slant four.

Without any enthusiasm for the project, Bruce and his minions worked long hours and produced a car that was, at the very least, an interesting exercise. It was reviewed in Leonia and sent to England for a look-see by the BL superchiefs. Among them only Sir Michael Edwardes seemed to think it was really a viable project, and it did not come to pass.

This last-ditch styling experiment grafted an MG grille onto a Triumph which was never intended to have one. The Porsche pop-up headlights looked quite good but the overall appearance was very strange. *Mike Cook*

The back of Bruce McWilliams' "MGTR" was much more attractive than the front with Rover 3500 taillights and a sturdy chrome luggage rack. The MG badge looks quite at home Special alloy wheels were fitted. *Mike Cook*

The 1981 TR7 convertible for the U.S. market had special chromed plastic wheel covers, new luxurious cloth upholstery, and the new, metal-framed Triumph world badge. *Plain English Archive*

Hard Decisions

The January-February 1981 *TSOA Newsletter* headlined: "$1,000 Rebates for Triumph Spitfire Sports Cars!" Next to the story, which said the rebates applied to 1980 models, was a short piece about the end of Spitfire production at Canley. It was a lugubrious start to the year. Making it even more solemn was an article inside by Bruce McWilliams paying tribute to Giovanni Michelotti. The source of so much Triumph styling, beginning with the TR4 in 1962 and running to the mid-1970s, Michelotti had died during 1980.

In his tribute, Bruce noted that Michelotti had worked for Ghia and Vignale before starting his own studio and was credited with

designing the egg-crate grille for Ferrari that has become its trademark. "Micho" worked closely with Triumph Chief Engineer Harry Webster, first on the Herald and then in creating the first Spitfire prototype. Later he was involved in updating and restyling virtually every car in the Triumph line.

Bruce McWilliams left the company at the beginning of January to take up an appointment with DeLorean Cars, which at that time still seemed to be a viable proposition. Having worked so many years in product development for Triumph and other cars, Bruce could see that most of this work would be done, in future, at Jaguar in England. It was time for him to move on. He was a man who could plan on paper but

Ken Slagle drove the last factory-sponsored Triumph in SCCA competition, winning the 1981 C Production championship in his brilliant yellow TR8 ahead of a horde of Z-cars. *Plain English Archive*

loved to get in a studio with a car and experiment until he achieved a break-through new appearance for it. We missed his cheerful presence and forthright opinions.

In June, the 1981 TR7 and TR8 went on sale. The TR7 specifications were exciting because now all North American cars had fuel injection. The steering wheels were changed, the interiors were done in attractive, high-quality pleated cloth and there were new inside handles. Six new colors were offered with color-keyed tan or dark blue convertible tops. A handsome metal-backed gold and BRG laurel wreath emblem adorned the

front panel. The price was $10,995. With similar changes, the 1981 TR8 was priced at $12,995. By the time you ordered air conditioning and a radio, the price came close to $14,000! The 1981s were all convertibles, and they were all lame ducks.

Sir Michael Edwardes had not wanted to announce more factory closings until he had to. On April 18, an article in the *Financial Times* stated: "BL has warned union leaders that production of the TR7 sports car might be suspended indefinitely from September." The same article said that the company was notifying suppliers that the uncertain market for TR sports cars prevented the company forecasting orders beyond the end of August. It was too much of a leak to deny. By May the word was out officially.

The factory at Solihull would close. Rover 3500 production would move to the Austin-Morris factory at Cowley, outside Oxford. Triumph sports car production would end. Since the Spitfire and the Dolomite sedan range had ceased production when Canley closed, the only Triumph car in the company's future was the Acclaim, basically a Honda Civic built under license as part of a development agreement BL made with Honda at the close of 1979. Projected for release in summer 1981, BL would sell the car in England and Europe and Honda would do so in Japan.

Solihull was one of the newest factories in the corporation but it could not make money with two of its three production lines operating at half speed. BL needed to reduce head count, and closing this factory would eliminate several thousand jobs, including some at the body plant. The company had to cut back in order to qualify for further government financing. Finally, Triumph export sales had dropped drastically, and the company was losing money on every car sold.

It was almost funny to read an article just below the closing announcement that said TR sales in the United States were up over the previous year. The article credited the $1,000 rebates that applied to TR7 and TR8, as well as Spitfire. Management did not want stocks of leftover cars hanging around at dealerships. If we were going to Jaguar exclusively, better to sell off the MGs and Triumphs and conclude the difficult business of cutting the dealer group down to manageable size. There were still over 400 dealers and the desired number of Jaguar outlets was half of that.

Chris Andrews died of cancer on September 9 at just 64. He had made a big contribution to the stability of the company during the last tough years.

Racing Goes On

After finishing one-two at Daytona in the IMSA 1980 season finale, Group 44 ran both TR8s at Sebring in 1981, Bob Tullius finishing fourth in class. Jaguar racing then took priority and the Group built and campaigned an all-new, tube-framed XJS in the Trans-Am series. Despite having been away from Jaguar for two years while running the TR8, they brought the XJS into second place at the end of the season.

Ken Slagle, who had been in contention for the SCCA CP championship in 1980 until eliminated in a crash, came back strong and won in 1981, the brilliant yellow TR topping a crowd of

Joe Huffaker has built race cars out of everything from Bugeye Sprites to V-12 Jaguars. Here he is with the 1980 Huffaker Engineering TR8s. Lee Mueller drove Number 8, and Number 11 was for Bruce Qvale. *Plain English Archive*

In 1980 the TR8 was a perfect magazine cover subject. *Car and Driver* posed a metallic green convertible at a glider school and wrote a very positive road test, which was reprinted by JRT as one of the few pieces of literature produced about the car. *Plain English Archive*

TRIUMPH TR8 A little performance with your fresh air?

Datsun Z-cars.

John Buffum again divided his time between North America and the UK, driving his last event in a TR8 contesting the RAC Rally in England. Huffaker Engineering's contract was not renewed for 1981, due to lack of budget, so Lee Mueller did not compete in CP with the black TR8. However, the TR8 was officially raced in SCCA for a year after it was discontinued. Sponsored by JRT, Ken Slagle, defending his 1981 championship, crashed again in 1982, knocked off the Road Atlanta's pit straight by another competitor.

The Group 44 GTO TR8s went into storage and now appear in vintage events. The last Huffaker Engineering car resides in the Pacific Northwest with photographer/racer Bob Dunsmore. Slagle's car is now resurrected in the collection of Vintage Triumph Register member Vern Brannon and will appear in some vintage events.

Reflections on the TR8

The TR8 was the best sports car ever built by Triumph. With the TR8, Triumph put all the right pieces together and made a sports car capable of doing everything right.

When it was all over, only 2,815 TR8s, coupes, and convertibles had been built. Of these, all but 20 were export models, virtually all of which came to North America. There are a surprising number of them still around, frequently on sale in enthusiast publications for very low dollars. It is hard to believe that this well-equipped, fast, modern sports car can still be bought in good condition for under $10,000. Where are all the enthusiast collectors?

The TR8 should not have ended an era—it should have begun a new one. But, the car was delayed for so long that when it was introduced, Triumph and its parent, BL Ltd., were sinking too fast to be saved by one successful new model. With V-8 power and modern design and appointments, it met American expectations of sports car performance and could have been as strong a contender in the marketplace as it was on the track. Sadly, BL's financial troubles were too deep by the time the car started production, making the TR8 nothing more than a brilliant swan song.

Triumph Finishes Where It Started— With the Real Enthusiasts

October-December 1981 was the final issue of the *TSOA Newsletter*. The company was severing ties with the Triumph, MG, and Austin-Healey clubs, keeping only the administration of the Jaguar Clubs of North America. The Vintage Triumph Register, now with 2,000 members and growing steadily, was more than capable of carrying on the tradition and would incorporate the *TSOA Newsletter* in the *English Channel*, VTR's own newsletter. All TSOA memberships and records were transferred to VTR.

The final *Newsletter* displayed the cover of my first issue from October 1958. John Dugdale and I wrote valedictory messages about history, and enthusiasm and thinking ahead to the time when a new Triumph sports car might emerge. John praised VTR and the Triumph Register of America for their efforts, and hoped they would help bring about "the rebirth of Triumph in America one day." I said: "Drive your Triumph. Take care of it. Enjoy! I certainly have!"

VTR President Steve Rossi came to Leonia for the handover. He shook hands with me, John, and Graham Whitehead, and that was it.

Triumph Fades Away

The assembly line at Solihull shut down after building a few hundred 1981 TR7s and TR8s. Now, Triumph hopes were tied to the blunt little Acclaim sedan to be built in the BL factory at Cowley, Oxford. It looked so much like its Honda Civic sibling that the success of the project was dubious. The interior was much better finished than the Civic and the suspension had been tuned, but it was a loser. It survived only through 1984, after which a later version was badged a Rover. BL became the Rover Group, making only Rover, Land Rover, and MG. This company retained the rights to other historic names from Britain's automotive past— Austin, Austin-Healey, Morris, Riley, Wolseley, and, of course, Triumph.

Ahead of the curve for once, Rover Group saw the start of the SUV craze and opened a new Range-Rover/Land Rover importing company in the United States. Growth was slow but steady, although the importation of the Sterling sedan, a poor-quality Accura clone, was a flop. The company was firmly reestablished in North America, but in the home market Rover and MG sales could not support the corporation, and in 1993 it was purchased by BMW. BMW executives talked about reviving some of the historic marques, mentioning Wolseley, Riley, and Austin-Healey, but not Triumph.

To the surprise of the industry, under a succession of managers and with some well-designed products, BMW could not make Rover work, losing billions trying to fix the infrastructure, repair relations with the work force, and convince the public that the cars were reliable. The financial drain and negative effect on the corporate image caused the resignation of BMW's chairman, Berndt Pisetschreider, and his deputy, Wolfgang Reitzle. Things were so bad that BMW gave up! During 2000, the Rover/MG car business was virtually given away to a consortium of British investors, and the Land Rover division was sold to Ford. For reasons not revealed, BMW retained the rights to the other historic British marque names, including Triumph.

In 1982, Jaguar Rover Triumph in the United States became Jaguar Cars Inc. The story of marketing Triumph cars in America had come to a sad end, but the Triumph was not finished. In driveways and garages across America, in England and other countries, all of the Triumph cars that beat the competition over the years still survive. At some future date the name may be revived and a new saga will begin. Until then, the Triumph marque will be kept alive and on the road by the people who love the cars for both their past glories and for the driving enjoyment they give today, and promise for the future.

Appendices

Triumph Sales In
The United States

The figures below are primarily from company records. Some totals are approximate. The information available did not allow showing sales by model for individual years.

Certain models overlap due to sales of "leftovers." For example, the TR250, which was only a 1968 model, went on sale in November 1967 and new leftovers were sold through 1969. Leftover figures beyond 1981 were not available.

Estimates are given for Spitfire Mk IV and GT-6 Mk 3 because the British Leyland statisticians did not break out figures for those models.

Model	Years	Sales Total
Pre-TR2	1948–1951	252
TR2	1952–1955	3,000
TR3	1955–1957	6,481
TR3A	1957–1962	49,673
TR3B	1962–1963	3,263
TR4	1961–1966	26,669
TR4A	1965–1968	16,311
TR250	1967–1969	6,913
TR6	1969–1977	63,027
TR7	1975–1981	(Est.) 65,030
TR8	1980–1981	(Est.) 2,797
Sports Six	1962–1964	679
Spitfire	1963–1965	19,431
Spitfire Mk II	1965–1968	16,168
Spitfire Mk III	1967–1973	(Est.) 23,292
Spitfire Mk IV	1971–1973	(Est.) 17,911
Spitfire 1500	1973–1981	62,917
2000 Sedan	1965–1969	1,805
TR10 Sedan	1957–1959	9,378
TR10 Wagon	1957–1960	6,872
Herald Sedan	1960–1962	3,612
Herald Coupe	1960–1961	1,049
Herald Convertible (948 cc)	1960–1962	2,822
Herald 1200 Sedan	1961–1967	4,609
Herald 1200 Convertible	1961–1968	11,654
GT-6	1967–1969	7,006
GT-6+	1968–1970	(Est.) 9,539
GT-6 Mk 3	1971–1974	(Est.) 8,036
Stag	1971–1973	2,993

Triumph Clubs

There has been a tendency for car enthusiasts to form themselves into little groups with a very narrow focus, rather than into simple marque clubs, and Triumph people are no different. It is suggested that if you are a neophyte Triumph enthusiast that you go for the general club first, learn from that, and go on to seek more specialized information.

The Vintage Triumph Register
Bimonthly newsletter, quarterly magazine
PO Box 655
Howell, MI 48844
www.vtr.org
Covers all years and models

Triumph Register of America
c/o Ron Hartley
28342 Lake Logan Rd.
Logan, OH 43138
Specializes in TR2 through TR4

Club Triumph
Membership Secretary
Freepost (SWB 20389)
Christchurch BH23 4ZZ
United Kingdom
club.triumph.org.uk
For all Triumphs

TR Register
1B Hawksworth
Southmead Industrial Park
Didcot, Oxon OX11 7HR
England
011 44 1235 818 866 Fax 818 867
For TR enthusiasts

Index

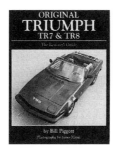
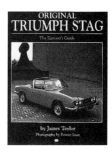
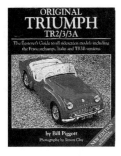
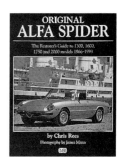
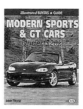